PENGUIN BOOKS

THE FILTHY LIE

Hellmut Karle was born in Germany and was brought to England
in 1939 when his parents fled from Nazi persecution. Educated at
Torbay Grammar School and the University of Reading, he gradu-
ated in psychology and took postgraduate training in clinical and
educational psychology in Durham and North Wales. After four
years in Wales, he worked as educational psychologist in East Sussex for ten years and in 1972 took up a part-time post as clinical
psychologist at Guy's Hospital, London, where he remained until
1991, having become Acting Head of Child Psychological Services.
From 1981 to 1986 he was Director of the Linbury Research project, a countrywide investigation of specific learning disabilities or
'dyslexia'. During that period and since, he has been in private
practice in Sussex. He has published two previous books, *Thorson's
Guide to Hypnotherapy* and *Hypnotherapy: A Practical Handbook* (with
J. H. Boys) and numerous papers on psychotherapy, hypnosis and
dyslexia.

Janet Radcliffe Richards is Lecturer in Philosophy at the Open University and author of *The Sceptical Feminist*, published by Penguin.
She has also written various texts and articles on moral and political philosophy, medical ethics, practical reason and philosophy of
science.

HELLMUT KARLE

THE FILTHY LIE

DISCOVERING AND RECOVERING FROM CHILDHOOD ABUSE

PENGUIN BOOKS

PENGUIN BOOKS

Published by the Penguin Group
Penguin Books Ltd, 27 Wrights Lane, London W8 5TZ, England
Penguin Books USA Inc., 375 Hudson Street, New York, New York 10014, USA
Penguin Books Australia Ltd, Ringwood, Victoria, Australia
Penguin Books Canada Ltd, 10 Alcorn Avenue, Toronto, Ontario, Canada M4V 3B2
Penguin Books (NZ) Ltd, 182–190 Wairau Road, Auckland 10, New Zealand

Penguin Books Ltd, Registered Offices: Harmondsworth, Middlesex, England

First published by Hamish Hamilton Ltd 1992
Published in Penguin Books 1993
1 3 5 7 9 10 8 6 4 2

Printed in England by Clays Ltd, St Ives plc

Contents

Acknowledgements

To Jennie Boys Karle for her unfailing professional support and encouragement in my work with Mrs Collins. Also for her endless patience and indefatigable work in assembling the material, reading and editing one version after another of this book.

To Kate and Margaret, editors at Hamish Hamilton and Penguin Books, for their invaluable help in making this book publishable – and most of all for their enthusiasm.

To the Department of Psychiatry, Guy's Hospital, for permission to refer to the case notes.

But most of all to Meggie Collins herself, for her courage in allowing her story to be revealed, first to me, then to herself, and finally to the world.

Foreword

By their frankness and self-revelation in this book, 'Meggie Collins' and Hellmut Karle have placed the reader in the most privileged position in psychiatry: that of the supervisor of psychotherapy, who hears not only the intimate disclosures of the patient or client, but also the emotional reactions of the therapist to these disclosures, his doubts, mistakes, failures, triumphs, and his own personal predicament in the work. In fact, this book goes one better than that, for the reader hears the client's story in her own words, which is more rare in supervision. The reader is thus able to participate in the unfolding drama of the therapy process, and if he has a heart at all, become quite deeply emotionally involved himself.

For the drama of the therapy grows from the deeper and more universal drama of Mrs Collins's life. Anyone can learn profound human truths from this book. There is no jargon in it, only simple poignant human experience. It is almost incidental that it is also an education for the general reader in one form of state-of-the-art psychotherapy, and in some of the facts of human psychology, which although shared by all of us in some form, when carried to an extreme seem almost unbelievable to the onlooker. Seen from the inside as experienced by the individual, such phenomena as so-called 'multiple personality' become more understandable. One learns what it actually feels like to be a child who was never secure enough

The Filthy Lie

to grow up in one piece. The miracle is that so much can be done for such a person so late, when there is every reason to think it might be *too* late.

The reader may well feel that Mrs Collins's story cries out a need for social action in greater investment in both prevention and treatment. Her story vividly illustrates this need. How that need is to be met – that is another question. Meeting it, by whatever means we can devise, would reduce unimaginable human suffering, and at the same time reduce the demands on the overstretched resources of the Health Service.

Dr D. Macdiarmid
Consultant Psychotherapist, Guy's Hospital
Senior Lecturer in Psychotherapy, United Medical Schools

Introduction

This book is an engrossing read of a most unusual kind. It tells the remarkable story of an adult woman's coming to recollect and understand the sexual abuse she suffered as a child, and of her beginning to put together the pieces of her damaged life, through psychotherapy.

Now some people who are concerned about sexual abuse of children, and who would otherwise expect to be interested in this book, may find their hackles rising at the mere mention of psychotherapy. The context is one in which professionals with 'psych' at the front of their titles[1] can easily seem the greatest villains of all. Although when Freud first heard stories of childhood abuse from his women patients he took them at face value, it is well known that he later changed his mind and came to regard them as fantasies arising from the women's own childhood sexual desires for their fathers. And, following him, generations of therapists of various sorts were trained automatically to regard reports of abuse as reflections of fantasy.[2]

What to say about Freud and his successors, now that this

[1] For the distinction between the various 'psychs' see the Appendix, page 272.

[2] Not all abusers are men, and by no means all abused children are girls. Nevertheless, the fantasy theory was applied generally to reports of sexual abuse.

theory has turned out so resoundingly to be false, is not a simple matter. Seriously mistaken theories are rarely the stupidities or iniquities so easily presumed by critics made wise by hindsight, and are often quite reasonable interpretations of the facts available at the time. On the other hand, this particular theory – which twisted fathers' sexual desires for their daughters into their daughters' for them, and the fathers' actual abuse into rather disreputable fantasies of the daughters – seems particularly sinister: a case of blaming the victim if there ever was one. And it is argued by some recent critics that Freud was certainly in a position to know what the truth was, and had reasons of his own for suppressing it.[3]

But whatever the origins of this looking-glass travesty, what can be in no doubt is the harm it must have done. The victims had already suffered violation and intimidation by adults in positions of trust, were typically oppressed with feelings of guilt and self-loathing, and had feared or actually encountered accusations of lying if they tried to find help. And if, after all this, they fell into the hands of therapists, what they found was much the same again. Professionals purporting to be on their side told them that their only hope lay in recognizing that their own desires had led them into fantasy; or, in other words, that any guilt was indeed theirs, and that they were, if not actually lying, then at least deluded. If the therapists had actually conspired with the abusers to drive the victims to madness and despair it is hard to see how they could have done better.

Fortunately, however, by the time the therapy described in this book began, all this had changed. Meggie Collins, the

[3] Masson, J. M. (1984).

heroine (as Hellmut Karle clearly regards her) of the story told here, had endured all the typical sufferings of an abused child. But although Mr Karle had, like all his generation, been trained in the fantasy theory, he and many others had repudiated it by the time Mrs Collins was sent to him for help. A passing mention of interference by her father, in the course of therapy apparently sought only for obesity, was therefore taken by him with complete seriousness – not in being accepted without question, but certainly as a matter for thorough investigation.

The relationship that resulted from this beginning is the subject of this many-layered book.

At the simplest level, this is the story of Mrs Collins herself: of the neglect and abuse she suffered as a child, of the problems it caused her as an adult, and – by way of consolation to the reader preparing to endure at second hand the dreadful blackness of her early life – the start of something like a happy ending. But it is not simply the story of a life, because it appears here in the order not of its occurrence, but of her later rediscovery of it, begun in therapy and increasingly confirmed by outside sources. And there is yet another aspect. Probably because of the hypnotic techniques used to elicit lost memories, there is at several points the extraordinary impression that her early life is being not merely remembered, but rather re-lived, and seen through the eyes of a child.

Second, the book is a therapist's record of therapy from his own point of view. And here we find not only what we might expect – his theories, his diagnoses and assessments, his plans for procedure – but also an unexpected account of the therapy's developing a life of its own, and persistently going off the official rails. For all the seriousness of the subject, there is something very entertaining about Mr Karle's description of the way in which he kept finding himself tripped up by his own motives and his client's manœuvrings, and breaking half the rules of his profession as fast as he laid them out. (Which of course – since the therapy seems to have been so successful – raises the question of whether the rules need to be reconsidered.)

And then, third, there are all the theoretical problems. Constraints of space have allowed rather little discussion of the extraordinary goings-on that developed during the therapy: the apparent regression under hypnosis into former states of mind, and the development of a multiple personality whose different elements might appear at any time. Enough is said, however, to reassure the sceptical reader (or at least this sceptical reader) that the author is not simply taking these at face value, and is well aware that they might have to be understood differently – perhaps as devices through which Mrs Collins expressed what was too difficult to say directly. Since much of the theoretical material is in the Appendix, incidentally, readers with special interests in that area, or with special scepticism about psychotherapy, might well be advised to start there.

Whatever their special interests, however, nearly all readers are likely to find that this book significantly changes their perceptions of child abuse. We all know, in a general way, that it is widespread and that it ruins lives, and we are sincere when we say how dreadful it all is. But that is a very different matter from being shown one such life from the point of view of the victim, as happens here. It is difficult to bear such suffering even at second hand; and when the book and the therapy end – leaving us as alarmed as Mrs Collins to find that it is really over – we are left acutely aware that out there, somewhere, there is a still real Mrs Collins, still having to cope with a life only partly healed. And, through her, we are left with a heightened sense of the other damaged adults whom no one has yet begun to help, and of the children still enduring the violation and fear that ruined her childhood.

The book does not deal with the problem of how to stop the abuse; it is a study of victims, rather than abusers, and its main concern is with the treatment of people who have already suffered. To the extent that it has a purpose beyond showing what child abuse is really like, it is to argue that analytic psychotherapy (though of a rather unorthodox kind) offers a far better hope of mitigating its effects than the drugs and other medical treatments Mrs Collins endured for nearly three decades. It also claims that this would be overwhelmingly cheaper for the health service.

All this will, presumably, be controversial. It is by no means obviously true that understanding the cause of a problem gives any indication of how to cure (as opposed to prevent) it: you cannot unburn a cake by understanding how it was burnt in the first place. If it is true that psychotherapy is the most effective treatment for damage of this kind, that needs to be established by long experiment and observation, and by systematic comparison with other methods.

Nevertheless, it would be hard to deny that this story presents – to say the very least – a strong case on the author's side. And, meanwhile, if there are going to be experiments with different therapies, my own guess is that virtually all patients would prefer to try this one first. To have the unhappiness that underlies their often difficult, attention-seeking personalities recognized and tackled directly, rather than numbed or suppressed with drugs, must be a consolation in its own right, and as such well worth trying.

And that raises one final aspect of the book: one that is not explicit, but must be apparent to any perceptive reader. Mrs Collins (who remains 'Mrs Collins' during a two-year therapy: no 'Mr Karle'/'Meggie' asymmetry of status) is treated throughout not only with compassion, but with respect. All too often sufferers of various kinds who find themselves in the toils of the caring professions will find that although caring may indeed be offered in abundance, it comes only on the unspoken (and no doubt usually unrecognized) condition that the patients will pay for this by submitting to being treated as children or as objects of well-intentioned study. Unless they are to be rejected as uncooperative, or even mentally unbalanced, they may have to endure anything from routine baby-talk ('Just pop on the scales for me, dear') to the frightfulness of the 'ward round' encountered by Mrs Collins on page 55 of this book. I once saw one of these: a poor, confused schizophrenic was brought in her nightdress and dressing gown to face a kindly but patronizing public inquisition by a roomful of caring professionals, and then dismissed so that the discussion could continue behind her back. It was hard to believe that they could even have wondered what it must feel like to be in her position. Mrs Collins was fortunate enough to fall, eventually, into a situation where her dignity was kept intact and increasing, and boundaries drawn that left her, at last, inviolate in her own domain. And if that had nothing to do with the manifest improvement of her life, I'll eat her (now happily redundant) extra-outsize coat and hat.

In one way the authors of this book have already had their success; but now, in making their story public, they raise the possibility of its extending far beyond themselves. Between them they have shown not only what can be done for damaged adults, but also, perhaps *more* clearly then ever before, what child abuse really is. If as a result even one unhappy adult is restored to equanimity, or even one apathetic mother stirred into saving her child from what Mrs Collins endured, the effort and courage that have gone into the writing of this book will have been fully rewarded. It is a reward the authors deserve; I hope it is one they are given a thousand times over.

Janet Radcliffe Richards
Department of Philosophy, the Open University
January 1992

Note

All names in this book, except that of the author, have been changed, as have all place names and personal details, family details etc., by which the central character – 'Meggie Collins' – could be identified.

The story, however, remains one of fact; it has not been in any way 'fictionalized' or dramatized, and the psychological dynamics, although incomplete in those respects that could lead to the identification of 'Mrs Collins' or members of her family, are true to the facts.

In order to avoid awkward circumlocutions, the pronoun 'he' has been used throughout for 'the therapist' and 'she' for 'the client'. This is not to be seen as implying that this gender allocation is considered usual, desirable, or anything else. It so happened that the therapist in this story is a man, the client a woman. It is hoped that the reader will accept this usage without reading into it any ulterior or covert meaning.

'Tout psychologue est obligé de faire l'aveu même de ses faiblesses s'il croit par là jeter du jour sur quelque problème obscur.'

'Any psychologist must be prepared to expose his own weaknesses or errors if that could help to clarify what otherwise might remain obscure.'

J. R. L. Delboef, *Le Sommeil et les Rêves*, Paris, 1885, quoted by Sigmund Freud, *The Interpretation of Dreams*, Leipzig and Vienna, 1899

*

'If someone had listened to me in the past and helped me, I would not have led the kind of life I have, and felt that terrible shame and guilt about myself and everyone else, and may have had a healthier Life, and would have been able to cope with Life's problems better than I have.'

Meggie Collins

1

December–February, Year One

'I think I've been depressed all my life. You see, when I was a little girl, my father interfered with me.'

I had the impression that silence fell over the whole ward. The woman by whose bed I was sitting was weeping gently, as she had done since we had begun to talk. This visit had not been intended to disclose such a dramatic and sensitive topic – it was little more than a social call. An open surgical ward with a dozen or so beds was not the place in which I would either expect or choose to discuss something like this.

Margaret – or 'Meggie', as she was generally known – Collins had been referred to me by a chest physician. Although the post I held in the hospital was in the Department of Child and Adolescent Psychiatry, adult patients were referred to me from time to time because of particular specialties for which I was known, and one of these was the use of hypnosis. At that time it seemed I was the only person in the hospital to use such methods, and this was the reason I had been asked to see Mrs Collins.

She had been referred for help with over-eating and over-weight. She was so overweight – double her proper weight – that the strain on her heart was becoming serious and the chest physician was insistent that she must lose weight: fifty-seven kilograms or so (about nine stone). All ordinary efforts had proved unsuccessful, so he had thought of using hypnosis, and therefore asked me to see Mrs Collins.

This seemed to me a golden opportunity. Hypnosis had been unfashionable for many years in Britain, commonly considered to be fraudulent, and not taken seriously by the majority of health professions. As I had used hypnotic methods for many years with some success for treating a wide range of disorders, I was trying to spread the use of such methods in all areas of medicine and clinical psychology. Now and again, usually when all else had failed, I would be invited to try hypnotic techniques on patients. If this worked with Mrs Collins, then hypnosis might gain a better reputation in the Department of Medicine, and so benefit other patients in the future.

Mrs Collins certainly looked overweight – almost as wide as she was tall. At that first interview, we had to wait a few minutes before beginning while she caught her breath after the effort of climbing the stairs.

Fresh-faced and lively, she chatted about her over-eating problem very cheerfully, seeming not to be especially concerned over it but apparently willing to try and reduce her weight, since the doctor had insisted. She was obviously intelligent, with a quick mind and a lovely sense of humour. She told me she was very used to hospitals, as she had had several operations at different times in her life, and was currently attending several clinics at this hospital.

We spent the first half of the hour I allot to such interviews just getting to know each other. Mrs Collins told me she had been recently widowed. She had four children: a son, Lee, who was now grown up and living with his girlfriend; a daughter of fourteen, Sharon; a son of twelve, Dean; and another daughter, Michelle, who was nearly six. She had been married before and divorced and had then married a man rather older than herself, who was the father of the three younger children.

Mrs Collins told me that she tended to get a bit depressed at times, and she thought that this was partly why she sometimes ate too much. She would eat more when 'down', especially when watching television in the evenings. It sounded like the very common pattern of 'comfort eating', and as though it ought to be pretty straightforward to treat.

However, eating disorders of any kind are rarely simple, and one should always be on the look-out for underlying anxieties, depression of mood, and stresses of all kinds in addition to those to which the over- or under-eater admits readily. However, Mrs Collins was herself so straightforward in manner that I accepted the assurance, implicit in the fact that the consultant who had referred her had not mentioned any, that there had been no previous problems.

The perfect vision provided by hindsight shows, of course, that this was an error, a serious omission, and one which was soon exposed.

Mrs Collins was happy to try hypnosis as a means of coping with her over-eating, and a trial run showed that she had a very good aptitude for this technique. I then described how she should carry out a self-hypnosis exercise every day, and additionally whenever she found herself wanting to eat between meals. I described how she could take herself into the hypnotic state, become fully relaxed and at peace in mind and body, and then picture herself in various situations which would link feelings of relaxation and ease with *not* eating such things as sandwiches and biscuits, her greatest downfalls. She promised to use the exercise as I suggested, and we arranged a follow-up appointment for a week later. It all seemed very hopeful, and I felt confident that the programme would work satisfactorily, probably with little further attention from me. I looked forward complacently to writing back to the specialist who had referred Mrs Collins to tell him of the successful completion of the task he had set me.

At her second interview, a week later, she reported having been able to use the self-hypnosis exercise successfully and pleasurably, and felt that as a result she had resorted less to comfort eating. She was obviously keen to please me, making much of my skill and helpfulness towards her. I repeated the hypnotic induction and added a little to the images and suggestions she was to use in her practice at home, and all seemed to go well.

The following session did not seem successful. When we repeated the hypnotic exercise, Mrs Collins did not respond well. When we had completed the exercise, and there was still a little time left before the end of the session, the reason for this became clear. She told me that she had become rather depressed during the week and was having difficulties in getting to sleep. In addition, she was not able to carry out the self-hypnosis exercise as well as she had done at first: it really was not working at all well.

This, it must be said, is a common experience when using hypnotic techniques: however much you explain to clients that they *treat themselves*, that persistence and application in using self-hypnosis is what will help them resolve the problems from which they suffer, many people find it difficult to give the time and attention that is needed.

I asked Mrs Collins to tell me what she felt the difficulty was. She told me that she had often been badly depressed over the years, that she felt there was something in her past that was troubling her, but that she could not think what it might be. I said that we had really run out of time at this point, but that we should talk about all this on another occasion and see if we could find out what the problem was and whether we could do anything to help change the effect 'it' seemed to be having on her life. However, this would now have to wait until after the imminent Christmas break. In the meantime, I would make her a tape-recording: one side of the tape would contain a re-play of the eating-control programme, while the other side would be designed to help her go to sleep more easily.

This last interview took place immediately before Christmas. That evening, I recorded the tape that we had agreed she should have and sent it to her. When I returned to the hospital after the break, I received a telephone call from a social worker, Heather Worthington, from the borough where Mrs Collins lived. Miss Worthington told me that Mrs Collins had just been admitted to the local hospital, and had asked her to tell me that she would very much like to see me. She added that on New Year's Day Mrs Collins had become very upset, and had rubbed corrosive paint-stripper into her legs, injuring herself so badly that she had required skin grafts. This was not the first time that Mrs Collins had done this, and in fact she had a long history of self-mutilation and suicide attempts.

This background was news to me: when the consultant had asked me to see Mrs Collins, he had not mentioned any of this, and her hospital file – which no doubt recorded this history – had not been sent to me.

Next day, I went down to the hospital where Mrs Collins had been admitted. She was in bed, her legs protected from the bedclothes by a rack. A woman and a young boy were sitting beside the bed. As I approached and Mrs Collins greeted me, these two made hurried farewells and left.

In reply to my asking what had happened, she told me that on New Year's Day her eldest child, Lee, had become so awkward, demanding, and violent towards Sharon, that she had 'thrown him out of the house'. By the end of the day she had become so depressed and had felt so guilty that she had felt an intense need to punish herself for her 'wickedness' towards Lee, and so had resorted to the self-mutilation that she had used before for similar reasons.

'... When I was a little girl, my father interfered with me.'

Very conscious of the ears I believed to be pricking up around the ward, I suggested that we leave further discussion until she had been discharged and could come and see me in the privacy of my own office. I went on to explain that I felt this was something that should be talked about properly and in detail. Uncharacteristically, I offered to see her regularly to try and help her, without any of the normal or usual preliminaries. We talked more generally for a short while, and arranged a date for her to come and see me the following week.

Mrs Collins had asked for more than just help with her overweight and comfort eating, but in a disguised way, when she had spoken of being depressed, and had come nearer still to articulating her deeper needs when I went to see her after her skin grafts. In the event, I had simply offered to help her with her unhappiness and its sources, without pausing to think through, let alone negotiate with her, the implications of all this, an omission discussed in more detail in the Appendix (see page 274).

Her unexpected and unprompted exposure of an obviously profound distress demanded my sympathy, concern and professional interest, and I reacted spontaneously to her appeal for help. I *wanted* to help her, and this need inside me had overridden my normal caution and bypassed the diagnostic procedures which I consider, and teach, to be mandatory. Long after the event, I began to recognize that I had already developed a 'counter-transference' – that I was reacting as much on the basis of my own needs, wishes, and fantasies as on a foundation of a professional judgement (see page 285 in the Appendix for a discussion of 'transference' and 'counter-transference'). The penalties for my failure to stop and think became evident only much later.

One *never* offers therapy without first knowing at least an outline of the client's history, evaluating their mental and emotional state, and their suitability for whatever form of therapy one practises. Yet on the flimsiest contact with and knowledge of Mrs Collins, I had offered her therapy. At that moment, I was *aware* of only one reservation: the possibility of further self-mutilation, and (since they commonly go together) suicide or suicidal gestures. I therefore insisted, following a practice which I apply whenever a client speaks of, or acts out, self-damaging behaviour, that if she were ever to do anything of this kind again, I would discharge her at once. (This is discussed in detail in the Appendix: see page 278.)

As one of the results of my spontaneous and un-thought-out offer of therapy, I did not lay down any other rules, guidelines, or conditions for therapy, and gave her no explanation of what we would embark upon and what it might involve for her, all vital ingredients of a safe and manageable contract. But none of that was in my mind then. I had been seduced by her plea for help and her evident needs. (See Appendix, page 274.)

We met a week later, back in my own office. Mrs Collins had obviously already developed a degree of trust and confidence in me during those preliminary sessions before Christmas, when we had been overtly concerned solely with weight control. The disclosure of her childhood experience had made that plain, as well as the way she had spoken just before Christmas.

I began this interview by asking her to tell me generally about herself, giving her no direction or lead. She began by telling me about her childhood.

I think, well, the best way is to start by explaining that my father had been married before, and my mother was already pregnant with my eldest sister, Julie, when they married.

I don't remember the first house we lived in, because when I was still small, we moved into a big town house with a market in the front of the house and a railway at the back. It was in south London.

I was about eighteen months old when I had measles very bad and was shut in this room so I would not give it to anyone else. They thought the measles affected my ears, and I became deaf. I remember being in a cot in this room, all alone and frightened.

The next thing I remember is the day I started my first school, the Infants, when I was five, standing outside the school gate half excited, half frightened. I was wearing a hearing aid and all my top clothes had to have pockets to put these big batteries in, and wires went up inside my vest to which a microphone was attached. Then another wire led up to my ears.

My father was nearly always drunk when he came home from work because he always went to the pub before he came home. A couple of times a week he would come home first, then he and my mother would go out.

8

The Filthy Lie

We were all afraid of my Dad as he was very strict and would belt us if we did not behave or we spoke at the meal table. We dare not disobey him, or my mother. My father wore a thick leather belt which he would use if we did disobey. My father would often hit my mother when they argued. Sometimes he cut her head open or hurt her and she would cry. We would cringe in fear when he started.

By the time I actually started Infant School there was six children in the family. There was Jack and Mary, from Dad's first marriage, my own elder sister Julie, myself, my younger sister Lizzy, and baby brother Barry. My Mum was pregnant again.

When I was about six I got a doll and a pram for Christmas, but not long after it got pinched when me and my friend went up the market. My mum got very angry with me and started shouting at me saying I would never get another one as I had not looked after this one, and she hit me and I was sent to bed. I never did get another one. But I felt very hurt by being punished, as I thought it was not my fault but I was told it was. It took a bit of time to realize it was my fault for leaving the doll in the first place, even with my friend.

Sometimes we would take shopping bags and climb the fence at the bottom of the garden and get down on to the railway after a coal train had passed, and walk along the line picking up pieces of coal for Mum, and sometimes we'd run across the lines in 'Dares'.

Mum used to send us on Mondays to the pawnshop with Dad's suit and get it out again on Fridays. Dad was a builder and Mum did jobs like cleaning in shops and another time worked in the warehouse round the corner from our house.

One day in Junior School, I put my hand up to be excused to the toilet and my teacher said no, I had to wait until playtime. But I couldn't wait, so I sat there on my seat and wet myself. All the kids

9

were laughing at me and calling me names in the playground. I was so embarrassed.

One day, I just couldn't stand it any more, so I put some clothes in a bag and went to my aunt's in Clapham and told her Mum had sent me over as I hadn't been well and needed a rest.

I loved living with my Aunt Kate. She was good and kind, and treated me the same as her own daughters – and I didn't have to worry about my Dad or anything. I went to school over there.

My Nan was angry with me living with my aunt, especially as Mum was still drawing Family Allowance for me and not paying my aunt for keeping me. I felt guilty about this and it hurt to think Mum couldn't even let my aunt have the Family Allowance to help keep me. I think that was mainly the reason my Nan told my aunt to send me home. But it's surprising how much it hurt me to think I was not worth eight shillings a week to my Mum for my keep.

My brothers and sisters were always calling me names like Deafy and Smelly and making fun of me and telling everyone I wet the bed. I felt terribly ashamed of myself. I tried to stay awake at nights so I would not wet but I would always fall asleep in the end and still wake up wet.

I got to be more and more trouble to my Mum – wetting beds, being cheeky, back-answering, refusing to do as I was told. I had become very withdrawn and would be cheeky and disobedient. I was bad-tempered, slamming things about. I was beaten frequently for my behaviour, but I did not really care any more when Dad beat me.

When she seemed to come to the end of what she wanted to tell me, I asked her to tell me more about her feelings of depression. She repeated what she had told me in hospital: that she had felt guilty for having thrown Lee out of the house at the New Year, and that this showed her to be a 'bad mother'. She spoke of herself in various ways indicating that she felt herself generally to be of little value, and her self-esteem was obviously very low, as was very clearly demonstrated by the horrendous injuries she had inflicted upon herself with paint-stripper.

Such self-condemnatory feelings characterize depressive states. When depression of mood is accompanied by self-mutilatory behaviour such as she had repeatedly shown, one should expect and search for angry, aggressive, violent and hostile feelings which have become detached from their original target. This is generally someone who was important to the client in childhood, usually a parent, who was experienced by the client as depriving, disappointing or otherwise unfulfilling. These feelings are so disturbing and overwhelming that they are impossible to express and are therefore turned inwards against the sufferer himself. There was much in what she had said so far about the violence of her father and the picture she had presented of her mother as rather uncaring and insensitive, but there was, as I already knew, more to it.

At last, I reminded her of what she had said when I visited her in hospital: 'My father interfered with me.' She looked startled.

'Did I say that? I don't remember telling you that.'

'What happened?'

'I don't remember saying anything like that, not about him. I didn't, did I?'

'Oh yes, that is what you said, and I told you that I would try and help you because you told me that you had been depressed and unhappy ever since.'

'No, I couldn't have said that.'

11

'Tell me about it.'

For a time, Mrs Collins continued to insist that she could not have said anything of the sort, while I equally persistently pressed her to say more. I could not accept that she should have 'forgotten' within ten days or so telling me something so powerful in itself, especially as it was precisely that disclosure that had led to her being there talking to me. It is not uncommon for people to regret being frank about highly personal and emotionally charged memories or other material, but uncommon for them to forget. On the contrary, clients often 'remember' more than actually passed between them and the therapist, including material which they would have liked the therapist to know but which they feared to state openly.

After a few minutes of something like 'You did ...', 'I couldn't have ...', she said: 'Well, I'm sure I didn't tell you, but since you seem to know about it, yes, my father interfered with me when I was quite little.'

'Tell me about it.'

'Well, that's it, really. He interfered with me.'

I pressed her further. Understandably, she was reluctant to speak about this event, and even when she began to talk more, I had to prompt her from time to time.

One day when I was about seven years old, there was a party of some sort going on in the downstairs living-room. It might have been Christmas, well, it was like that, because the stallholders would come in for a drink then.

I think I was just running out of the living-room, my Dad called me to him from the kitchen. So I went to him.

He pushed the kitchen door closed and picked me up and put me

12

on his knee and started telling me what a pretty little girl I was. I started to get frightened, I don't know why, but it was not like my Dad to make a fuss of us or sit us on his knee or have any time for us, drunk or sober, so it was scary to be sitting on his knee and him saying I was pretty. I wanted to get down but he had his arm round my waist.

And then he, well, he interfered with me.

Here she stopped. That, she insisted, was the whole story. I asked her what she felt about this.

'He shouldn't have done that.'

No matter how I put the question, Mrs Collins denied either that she had any feelings about it or that it had been wrong. I was sure there was more.

'What happened then?'

Well, I suppose I started to struggle and cry but he held me tighter. He put his hand on my private parts. He was talking to me but I was not listening as I was frightened and confused as I did not like what he was doing.

I managed to struggle free and run out of the kitchen. He called after me but I ran up the stairs hoping to find my mother so she would make everything all right and comfort me and explain to me what my Dad was doing and tell me everything was all right. But I was wrong.

When I found her and tried to tell her about it, she got very angry and said: 'Daddies don't do things like that,' and I was to be ashamed of myself for telling such lies and filth. I was sent to my room and told to stay there until I learned not to say such things again.

Mrs Collins related this horrifying story of abuse and betrayal with no feeling at all in her voice. The sexual molestation by her father was described with hardly any distress; she seemed to be puzzled by her mother's denial of what she had told her, but that was all. This lack of emotion became the focus for several subsequent sessions, and was a recurring theme throughout the following months.

The calm, almost detached way in which Mrs Collins described this experience contrasted sharply with my own feelings as I listened to the story. Her father's behaviour was not anything unfamiliar to me professionally, but familiarity had not dulled my reaction of anger and indignation at such abuse of a trusting child. It was her mother's behaviour which aroused my even greater anger. Mrs Collins's story had perhaps the greater impact for the cool way in which it was related. I had responded to her story and could feel inside myself the shock at the betrayal she as a child must have felt. I could also feel myself becoming angry with Mrs Collins herself for relating this horror so quietly and matter-of-factly. Those were my reactions as a man.

As Mrs Collins's therapist, I had to hide those feelings, although taking note of them. I was already sure that a great deal of Mrs Collins's behaviour and personal state was the result of repressed feelings of anger – violent anger – and the story she had just related gave a very good indication why that should be so.

The bare facts that Mrs Collins so blandly related were horrifying: sexual molestation by her father, followed by her mother's denial of her story and her accusation that Mrs Collins was lying. This betrayal of the child's trust *must* have generated strong feelings in her, but these had, apparently, been completely repressed. There *was* no emotion in the way she spoke

14

of it. This marked dissociation from all feeling, taken together with Mrs Collins's unemotional way in general of speaking about her parents, made it seem likely that the search for the powerful feelings she was expressing through her self-damaging behaviour – and through her depression – should focus on her parents.

When Mrs Collins arrived for her next session, early in February, I asked her to talk more about how she felt about the story she had told me. She had little to say. Her father, she thought, was wrong to do what he had done, but when I asked how she felt about her mother's denial of what had happened and her mother's condemnation of herself, she became defensive. The more I asked how she *felt* about her mother's response, the more anxious and defensive she became. Once again, I had to suppress the anger I could feel rising inside as she attempted to justify her mother, a woman whom I was beginning to regard as a monster.

It is not uncommon in psychotherapy, especially with clients who dissociate their feelings – that is, split the feelings off from their causes and repress or divert them into quite different channels – for the therapist to experience the dissociated feelings as though they were his own: for the therapist himself to feel the emotional response to an experience that the client felt at that time, but now no longer can feel and so relates the story with *no* feeling.

When the therapist *experiences* feelings which actually belong to the client, this can be a very valuable guide to what is happening *in the client*, and it is vital that the therapist recognizes that these feelings do not belong to him but are projected. The use of this process in therapy – 'projective identification' – is brilliantly described by Patrick Casement in

15

his invaluable book *On Learning from the Patient*.

I pressed Mrs Collins more and more about how she felt about what had been done to her. But it seemed she had *no* feelings, either about her father or about her mother's failure to take any protective or comforting action.

I tried reversing the situation.

'If your daughter were to tell you she had been interfered with, you would listen and take it seriously, then?'

'Oh yes I would! I'd take a knife to him, I wouldn't care what they did to me, I'd see to him.'

'How d'you feel then about *your* mother not listening to you or taking you seriously?'

'Well, that's different. How was she to know I wasn't just telling lies?'

She went on to speak with very strong and deep feelings of her outrage and fury at reading in newspapers of children being molested by adults, and especially at what she felt to be the altogether inadequate punishment meted out to the offenders by the courts.

A child's mother is the primary care-taker, the sole source of food, love, protection, warmth – all that the young child needs most. Just because she *is* so essential to the child, she is likely to be the immediate object of any feelings aroused in her child if there is any deprivation or denial of the child's basic needs. Mrs Collins's account so far of her early life made it clear that of her parents, her mother had been the more constant presence, and Mrs Collins had of course been totally dependent on her. Her defensive manner when talking about her mother, and what sounded like an excessively vehement denial of any hostile feelings towards her, strengthened the case. I continued to press her about her mother.

The more I pressed, the more distressed Mrs Collins became. Indeed, the more explicitly I pointed out her mother's negligence, the more Mrs Collins became angry with *me*, albeit hesitantly and evidently with considerable ambivalence. It was patent that a struggle was going on inside her: I was 'her doctor', I was listening to her, taking her seriously, I seemed to care – but I was pressing her to be, at the least, critical of her mother, and that she *could not* do.

In infancy and early childhood, Mother is God: she is the source of life, the sole source of everything good, the protector against a potentially hostile world, she is perfect. One of the painful experiences of adolescence is the discovery that Mother – and Father – are *not* perfect: God proves to have clay feet of inadequacies of all kinds.

Mrs Collins did not seem to have made that transition. Mother was still, in her eyes, perfect. She seemed to be unable to see any flaw or fault in her mother. All criticism, anger, disappointment – any and all negative feelings had been denied, repressed, made unconscious. That is the common foundation of depression – and especially of self-damage, mutilation, and suicide attempts – because the negative feelings which are rejected, denied, and made unconscious, are then turned in on the self.

Mrs Collins could feel *consciously* only admiration, respect, and love for her mother.

The rage she expressed openly concerning other abused children was equally patent. She could recognize the discontinuity and contradiction between those two sets of feelings: those concerning the perpetrators of abuse and the mothers who failed to protect their children on the one hand, and her own protective attitudes to *her* mother on the other. From

17

what, I asked myself, was she protecting her mother?

I noted this as an area that was likely to prove crucial in the beginnings of her depression, but I did not wish to jump to conclusions, to miss important facts, or to alienate or frighten Mrs Collins by being too insistent at this early stage, and seeming uninterested in anything else.

The fact that, however uncomfortably and hesitantly, Mrs Collins became angry at me as we talked about her mother was encouraging. The central aspect of psychotherapy is the 'transference': the client reacts to the therapist with the feelings and reactions which were aroused by and belong to the significant people in childhood, parents especially, and it seemed that the anger she was feeling at this point probably 'belonged' to her mother. When that, and other feelings that had become repressed and were now beginning to be displaced on to me, were fully exposed and understood, Mrs Collins would no longer turn them in on herself: she would be on the way out of her depression. (See Appendix, page 285, for a fuller discussion of the 'transference' and its importance in therapy.)

2

February–May, Year One

Mrs Collins had agreed at the last session that she should be weighed periodically when she came to see me. When she arrived for the next appointment, this was done before I collected her from the waiting-room, by the Sister in the Day Unit at the clinic. She had lost four kilograms – more than half a stone.

I asked Mrs Collins to tell me more about her life. She began by saying she had gone into care when she was eleven, and then spent some years in a boarding school in Kent, before returning home when she reached school-leaving age. Shortly after that, she had tried to protect her mother from being 'beaten up' by her father, and had been beaten up herself. She had then taken her father to court, when an injunction was made against him. He had never beaten her again.

She went on to say that she had married a soldier, Mick, when she was eighteen, but he had beaten her regularly and 'gone with' prostitutes, she said, so she had divorced him. At some time, about which she was vague, she had had a miscarriage, and then become pregnant again, this time by Chas, a friend of one of her brothers. Her elder son, Lee, was the product of that encounter. She had later married again. This second husband – Bert – was a man considerably older than she, by whom she had had the three younger children.

The story as she related it was again flat, and without

19

emphasis, feeling, or any sense of continuity or causality. She seemed to regard her life as a series of events without rhyme or reason – everything 'just happened' – without any choice, will, or power on her part. Apart from the childhood things she had told me before, the only events she seemed to recall in detail and with some vividness were the facts of her medical history: the various operations she had undergone, from several kidney operations to an experimental surgical procedure in her twenties, which had given her reasonable hearing for the first time in her life. As a result of these operations, she now no longer had to wear hearing aids as she had done throughout her childhood and adolescence.

'Tell me more about your childhood.'

'Well, when I was about eight, I suppose, I was raped by a neighbour.'

I was astonished, taken aback: there had been no hint at all that other such major traumata were to be revealed, but to be sure, it made sense. Having been abused by her father and denied belief and support by her mother, she was vulnerable. None the less, this revelation was every bit as unexpected as the initial one. Hiding my surprise, even shock, as best I could, I replied: 'What happened?'

'Well, I didn't tell no one, because I knew no one would believe me.'

'Why did you think that no one would believe you?'

'I was afraid, and anyway, my mother had told me that Daddies didn't do things like that, so I knew she would just think I was telling filthy lies again.'

She went on to tell me that this man had continued to 'interfere' with her for some time, until she had run away from home, as she had told me before, and had gone to her Aunt

Kate for a time. When she was sent home, she had become so upset then that she had jumped off Waterloo Bridge, but had been rescued from the river. That was when she had been taken into care.

It was obvious that the abuse by the neighbour had been as damaging as the episode with her father, and, as she said herself, that episode had made it impossible for her to go to her mother for comfort and protection. I asked her to tell me more about what had happened.

'Well, I went to call at my friend's but she was out and her father answered the door. He was Mr Baker. He said I was to wait till my friend came back, so I went in. Then he raped me.'

That was all she would say for a while. Once again, it was said with no evident feeling other than one of puzzlement and an odd kind of resignation. It felt almost that pressing her for more detail was more like voyeurism than proper inquiry, yet the vagueness and lack of detail could not be accepted, since they themselves were a way of distancing herself from this experience, thus leaving the dissociated and buried, repressed, or denied feelings still untouched. I asked her to go on.

'Well, that's all really.'

Asking her how she felt was a dead end. 'I was frightened,' was about as far as we could get.

'And you didn't tell anyone?'

'Well I couldn't tell my Mum. Mr Baker was my friend's Daddy, and Mum had said Daddies don't do things like that, so it would be no good telling her.'

I continued to press her. Bit by bit, she related how Mr Baker had taken off her knickers, threatening to kill her if she were ever to tell anyone, and had then manipulated her genitals. He had then lain down on top of her, and she had felt something

21

hurting her 'somewhere below'. She said she thought she must have fainted or blacked out, and when she had come round, she had found that he was wiping her with his handkerchief before replacing her knickers and sending her home, with further threats if ever she were to tell anyone. Now she had started, she went on without further prompting.

I went home then, but there wasn't anybody there. I stripped and washed meself over and over again, but still felt no cleaner, and I was hurting. I found some stains on my knickers, and so I put them in the fire, thinking, I s'pose, that I'd wet myself. Then I tried to kill myself with a knife, but I stopped because it hurt, so instead I fetched a pillow, put it in the oven, and turned on the gas.

Well, the next thing I remember was of being picked up and taken to the garden, and someone slapping my face.

I asked what had been said to her about this. She told me no one had ever asked her anything about it or made any comment. This story was told with *some* emotion, unlike her earlier relation of the initial abuse by her parents: she looked and sounded a little sad. However, no matter how hard I pressed her, she insisted that there was no question of telling anyone about this event, least of all her mother. Her mother would have been angry again and punished her for her 'filthy lies'. She had been frightened, not only by what had been done to her, but also by the threats uttered by the man, her own total helplessness, and was vividly aware of the feeling of defilement and dirtiness that resulted from the experience. The feeling of utter helplessness because of the lack of any protection against her abuser from her parents, her mother especially, was very clear.

Some feeling certainly was present in her account, but the

main coloration was an air of hopelessness and helplessness, which seemed a direct representation of how she had felt at the time. Another feeling seemed to be one of inevitability: that in some way she should expect to be abused in this way. It was, she seemed to feel, even appropriate – deserved.

She said that Mr Baker had continued to molest her for the next two years or so. He had a shop in the vicinity which was much used by her parents. One of the regular tasks she and her siblings were given was to collect the groceries their mother had ordered. This task often fell to her lot, and on most such occasions Mr Baker would deal with any other customers, close the shop, and then abuse her sexually, although never again attempting intercourse.

Somehow the outrage I experienced as she told the story seemed to pass her by completely, although I knew, from her own reactions to reports of abuse of other children, that she was not immune to such feelings: such feelings, once again, did not seem to apply to herself.

Indeed, Mrs Collins showed massive resistance to all I did to get her to explore deeper and different feelings. Asked once more how she felt when she heard of other children being abused in similar ways, she again expressed real anger and a violent wish for revenge or retribution, but she was quite unable to relate these to herself, or to Mr Baker. Towards him, she felt nothing now but resignation, puzzlement as to how he could have felt any pleasure or satisfaction in what he had done, and a kind of passive, almost wistful, desire that he should have desisted from inflicting such distress and pain on herself. Nor was there any hint of what she must have felt *then*.

Her resistance was even stronger when I probed for the way

she felt about not being able to tell her mother, or indeed anyone else. She again said she was sure that she would not have been believed, and would have been punished for lying. At the same time she felt – as is the case almost universally among abused children – that somehow she was, and would have been considered, entirely and exclusively to blame for what had occurred.

Mr Baker continued to molest her each time that she had to go to his shop for her parents, although he had not raped her again, and 'only' interfered with her. She had eventually become so desperate she had run away from home and made her way to her aunt's house, as she had told me before, explaining to her aunt that her mother had sent her there for a rest because she had become so troublesome. She repeated that this period had been one of the happiest in her life, until her Nan had insisted that she must return home. Shortly after her return, she had again been sent to Mr Baker's shop, and had once again run away rather than face what would happen there. This time, she had caught a bus at random. When the bus crossed the river, she had realized that here was a way out. She had got off the bus and jumped off the bridge, wishing, hoping, and expecting to die. She was eleven years old.

The story so far, and all attempts to get at the underlying and hidden feelings, had occupied five one-hour interviews. Mrs Collins had cancelled one at the end of February, but otherwise arrived, not just on time, but generally well before the time of her appointment. She was always smartly turned out, well coiffed and with none of the self-neglect one so often sees in severely depressed people. Her leg was healing, and she seemed generally well. Her manner outside my office was cheerful and relaxed, while in the sessions she showed little emotion of any kind. *And* she was losing weight. She had lost around five kilograms since our first contact, although, since just before Christmas, we had not even mentioned her weight other than when we agreed that she should be weighed period-ically.

The story about Mr Baker – the initial rape, the long period of repeated molestation by him, and her first two suicide attempts – emerged shortly before a three-week break around Easter.

Mrs Collins showed considerable anxiety about the inter-ruption; she complained in the preceding weeks about increased difficulty in sleeping. We had met no more than eight times by now; the first three sessions, held before Christmas, were those in which we had tried to help with her over-eating through hypnosis, but even during those early sessions, Mrs Collins had already begun to form a very deep and powerful attachment to me.

Breaks in therapy are always disturbing. Anxiety, fear of being abandoned, anger at the therapist, and many other feelings reflecting the client's childhood experiences of being neglected, abandoned, or otherwise rejected, emerge in more or less disguised ways, and are especially powerful and distressing because they stem from a time when the client was small and helpless, and the feelings are correspondingly overwhelming and frightening.

Mrs Collins's renewed difficulty in sleeping seemed to me to be directly due to her anxiety about the impending separation from me.

To help her with this, I recorded a tape for her to use at home. I did not remember that she already *had* such a tape, one I had made for her for just this purpose before Christmas, and that the request for this help had more to do with her need to be *given* something by me – and not a little, perhaps, with *my* need to give her something good – than any new difficulty over sleeping.

With hindsight, I could see that I had begun to represent to her the 'ideal parent' whom she had never experienced in real life. Much later in therapy I came to realize that her need to feel looked after by me, which she was quite unable to articulate directly, had induced me to make the tape, the effect of which was that she could keep something of me during the break – like a child cuddling her teddy-bear during mother's absence.

The fact that I had not recognized the underlying motive of Mrs Collins's request for help with her sleeping opened the door to further and increasingly demanding expectations later. I failed to perceive and articulate what was happening: I was *reacting*, and not *acting*; I was not fully in control, and some control was now being exerted by both Mrs Collins's unconscious wishes and needs, and my own.

Mrs Collins's first appointment after Easter was cancelled by her by telephone. She gave no reason. I felt, however, that she was expressing her anger towards me for leaving her, and punishing me for putting my holiday before what *she* so desperately wanted and needed from me. Mrs Collins herself, if challenged, would have totally denied any such wish or feeling, and would do so truthfully. The feelings were all *unconscious*, but her increasing need was for me to be the 'good mother' she had never had. The fact that I could never *be* that mother did not in any way diminish the intensity of her unconscious need.

She did attend the following week, expressing great relief at being able to see me again. She had found the interval, so she said, very stressful, and had been very depressed. The session consisted of little more than re-establishing contact: we talked very generally about what she had done during the interval, everyday events – feeling our way back to the relationship that had paused.

I had a number of commitments at this point that made it impossible for a time to see Mrs Collins weekly. This lack of continuity and the unpredictability of appointments produced an undermining uncertainty and general sense of my unreliability for her, which were to characterize the whole course of therapy. Again with hindsight, I realized that my actual unreliability and inconsistency in this respect, unintentional though they were, were a re-enactment for Mrs Collins of her childhood experiences.

Even at the time, however, I felt guiltily that my willingness to accept irregularity in appointments stemmed at least in part from some self-protective urge on my part: a belated endeavour to take control and to impose boundaries. Much later, another and rather more sinister theme became apparent: the seduction into abuse which one sees over and over in many different forms in work with people whose experience in life is of abuse. In all sorts of subtle ways, often perceptible only with difficulty, people who were abused as children seem to attract negative behaviour from even the best-intentioned helpers later in life.

The effect on Mrs Collins of the irregularity of our planned sessions was obvious: her feelings of worthlessness and unimportance made it inevitable that she should experience the irregularity of the appointments I offered her as confirming her view of herself as unimportant and of no worth. She experienced it as evidence of my lack of concern. Quite obviously, it seemed to her, I should consider the other calls on my time to be more important than her. None of these feelings were expressed except through their opposite: a submissive and admiring acceptance of the fact that I was so busy.

The whole thing was made even less satisfactory by stresses in my personal life and consequent ill-health. I was not aware of this at the time in any form other than feeling somewhat more readily tired than in the past. Clients, however, once engaged in the therapeutic relationship, are extremely perceptive of the slightest signs of malaise, fatigue, anxiety or other stress reactions, real or imaginary, on the part of the therapist, and will inevitably assume that it is they themselves who are responsible. This commonly shows in intensification of depression of mood, increased agitation, withdrawal and/or self-punitive or self-injuring actions – all representing a desperate attempt to regain control of repressed and unconscious but nevertheless terrifying aggression.

At last, we were able to resume regular weekly appointments. I had by now a clear idea of at least one of the major factors in her depression, her poor self-image and her vulnerability: the unacknowledged feelings about her mother. I made no attempt, however, to press her further at this stage towards uncovering the feelings of betrayal, grief and rage that I was sure were somewhere present, beneath the respect for, dependence on, and adulation of her mother. It was very obvious from the distress and discomfort Mrs Collins showed whenever I asked too insistently about how she felt at her mother's refusal to believe what she had told her, that she could not yet trust me enough to go further. She had learned in very early childhood to inhibit any feelings of grief, anger, or aggression – and indeed any awareness of these feelings – by dissociating and repressing them. That is, they had been separated off and blocked from consciousness: they had become *un*conscious. Consciously, she kept an idealized image of a good mother. It is better, it seems, to feel oneself to be bad, and Mother to be good, than the reverse: it feels safer. Mrs Collins did not yet feel safe enough with me to let go of the mother she had.

3

May–August, Year One

At the next interview – the ninth since therapy proper began – Mrs Collins brought with her a note from the Sister: she had lost a further three kilograms – about half a stone – over the preceding two months. I congratulated her on this continuing success.

Mrs Collins then told me again about the time she had jumped into the Thames at the age of eleven or so, and how she had been rescued and taken to a children's home. In due course, she had appeared before the Juvenile Court, where the magistrates had asked her if she wished to return to her home or remain in care. She had told them firmly that she did not want to go home, and a care order was made. Before long, the local authority placed her in a special school in Kent, where she spent what she recalled as the happiest years of her life. However, even here she had felt different from the other children, not only because of her deafness but because of her now ingrained feeling of being dirty, defiled, and bad. She had always loved animals and she was comforted here by the animals that were kept at the school, especially a pig called Sally, to whom she confided her thoughts and feelings.

She then switched to an earlier time, when she had once owned a rabbit, the only living thing to whom she had been able to tell what was being done to her by Mr Baker.

I once had a rabbit called Fluffy. She meant a lot to me. One day I came home from school and went to see her to clean and feed her and she was gone. The hutch was empty. I panicked, thinking she had got out on her own, so I was looking round the garden. When I couldn't find her I went running indoors, crying. My sisters were there and I told them I couldn't find Fluffy and they said with grins on their faces that Mum sold her to the Chandlers two doors away.

I ran back into the garden and climbed the fence and looked over at the gardens. I didn't have to look very hard as her skin or fur was hanging on the line. I screamed and cried and swore and cursed and went absolutely mad.

I was deeply hurt and swore at everyone and Dad gave me the belt for swearing. I knew I could not take much more. I thought about killing myself but didn't know how to, and for days I tried to decide what to do but couldn't think.

This memory seemed to involve more consciously negative feeling towards her mother than any Mrs Collins had yet disclosed, but I decided not to pursue this further yet. A still deeper relationship with me, which would require a longer period of sessions to develop, would be needed to make her feel safe enough to recover the feelings which she must have experienced at the time and then buried; still present but totally blocked from her consciousness and turned in on herself. I had planned a brief holiday which would involve a further gap in our sessions, and I felt it would be unwise to press further in this direction with that gap approaching. Instead, I steered Mrs Collins into telling me more of her history.

When she had left school at the age of fifteen, she had worked for nearly a year in Hastings, living in a hostel.

It wasn't really too bad there, but apart from going to work I didn't really see much of the place. I'd go down to the beach now and then for a swim. I didn't really make any friends in the hostel; I mean I spoke to some people sometimes but not as friends, just to be polite more than anything. I never went out with any of them. I was very lonely there and I didn't even have my animals. I didn't know how – or even want – to make friends.

I left school in the July so it was light then in the evenings but later the dark nights came, and one night it was dark as I came home from work. As I walked up the hill, this man tried to trap me with his bike against the wall but I managed to get away. It scared the hell out of me and I decided I couldn't stand it on my own, not in the dark nights, so I went home to Bermondsey. I had nowhere else I could go.

I hated it there, I hated my family. They would go on and on at me about my running away and not going home and how I'd hurt and worried Mum. As far as they were concerned I'd caused a lot of trouble and was weak and couldn't take the life there. They were right, I couldn't. I'd taken so much I couldn't take any more. I couldn't stand Dad and I didn't exactly like Mum too much and it hurt because I didn't know why I felt like it.

Life carried on as before, Dad still getting drunk and Mum going out with him sometimes. One Saturday night Dad came home very drunk and started arguing with Mum. I think he was angry because Mum hadn't gone out for a drink as she usually did. Dad started smashing the lights and pulled the plug out of the TV and yelled at the younger ones to go to bed. Mum argued with him and he started hitting her and I lost my temper and jumped on Dad's back and pulled him off Mum and fought with him. The younger children started screaming and the house was in darkness except for the glow of the fire and the street lamp outside.

Suddenly someone shone a torch around the room. It was a

The Filthy Lie

policeman, a local beat bobby who makes regular checks on the shops. He had heard my brothers and sisters screaming and came into the house. He chased my Dad up the stairs to his bedroom but Dad locked the door. The policeman said to Mum and I that he didn't think Dad would start up again but if he did he would be up the corner.

Lizzy, my next sister down to me, and I got the younger ones to bed then went back to the best room to Mum. Mum and Lizzy sat down by the table and I stood by the fireplace. We started to talk and suddenly the door flung open and Dad walked in. He didn't say a word. He strolled over to me and put his fist in my face so hard I saw stars and went flying. I don't know exactly what happened the next few minutes but the screaming started again and the policeman came running back and run up after Dad again but Dad had locked the door again. I was staggering about with a broken jaw.

I had to go to hospital, and decided to take Dad to court, partly because I couldn't stand him any more but also I thought what would happen to Mum if I left home. I thought at the time I was doing the right thing and tried to be strong about it even when Mum asked me not to go through with it. Even on the day we were going to court on the bus, Mum kept saying, 'Don't go through with it Meggie, I think he's learned his lesson,' but I was determined, right until I saw Dad in the waiting-room in the court. He looked sad and I broke down and cried to the policeman who had come to the house that night and said I couldn't go through with it but he said I must, it was too late to back down now and it was the right thing to do for everyone's sake. The Judge asked Dad why he did it and Dad said he wasn't well. The Judge said if that's what drink does to you, you should leave it alone and fined Dad and bound him over.

33

Dad never spoke to me again for nearly eight years.

This last fact appeared to have hurt her considerably, although there was a benefit: 'He never touched me again.' Her recollection was that he totally ignored her existence until, when she was in her twenties, she went into hospital for a major operation. When she came round from the anaesthetic, he was sitting at her bedside, and the silence was over. It was striking that his ostracism had been so important to her. Despite the fact that she dated the onset of her difficulties to being sexually molested by him, she did not appear to *blame* him at all.

The break in our sessions planned to allow me a brief holiday was lengthened by my falling ill, and I was away unexpectedly for three weeks. Once again, Mrs Collins failed the next appointment, this time without telephoning first to cancel. I sent her an appointment for the following week, which she then cancelled. She kept the next appointment. The gap had been seven weeks long. We then had three sessions in successive weeks before she again cancelled an appointment.

This irregular pattern – almost 'catch-as-catch-can' characterized the first eight months of therapy. The dynamics of this irregularity, the feelings and the motives that influenced both Mrs Collins and myself, were complex, and by no means clear.

Periodically, Mrs Collins would spontaneously recover fragments of memories which she felt to be important but which were often incomplete. At this point, I suggested using hypnosis, although in a very different way to that in which we had employed it when we first met. Now we were to use hypnotic techniques to recover the missing portions of memory, and at the same time try to uncover some of the emotions that were missing, or that were so heavily disguised or changed that they usually appeared only as anxiety, fear or self-blame. In addition, I thought that hypnotic techniques could be used to make these memories more tolerable for her, and to change the impact they had on her.

The memories of experiences which were severely frightening to a child can become separated off from the central memory of the adult, but persist within the mind rather like an embedded foreign body – a septic splinter in your psychic finger. That memory then remains encapsulated, and is unmodified by subsequent experience. It is as though – and may feel exactly and literally as if – the awareness, feelings, and beliefs of the child at that moment continue to exist, locked in a moment of terror, as a separate entity held within the person.

A student of mine had worked with a lady who had a terror of closed doors, which gradually expanded until she could not bear, for instance, to be in her kitchen unless all the doors, including those of the cupboards and the fridge, were open. This state was traced back in therapy, using hypnosis, to an incident the client recalled from early in childhood, when she had found herself unable to open the door of her room, and had gone into a panic. While in hypnosis, this lady was asked to move forwards in time, until the original and isolated memory of being apparently locked into her room was reconnected with the memory of her mother later opening the door and comforting her. Thus the separated-off memory, isolated, and stored intact and unmodified by subsequent events, became part once again of the continuum of her memory and so lost its disruptive potency. The client, having achieved this integration, lost her fear of closed doors.

Techniques of this kind could, I felt, be helpful in aiding Mrs Collins to clarify what had actually happened to her at various times. It might enable her to recognize the external reality of these events and therefore to see herself as a severely abused child rather than as a wicked one: that she was not responsible for them. I also hoped that the immediate and vivid way in which the feelings associated with such memories can be experienced when explored in hypnosis might break through her overwhelming self-blame, her belief in her personal worthlessness, and her conviction that she was (in her mother's voice), 'filthy'.

Hypnosis has an additional virtue for some clients: it allows the possibility that the memories that the client fears might make the therapist reject or condemn him or her can emerge without the client having to accept full responsibility for them. It can therefore be a device which gives permission for a memory to be recalled and reported when otherwise the client is too anxious, guilty or ashamed about it to speak out.

Mrs Collins agreed to this, as indeed she agreed to virtually anything I suggested. I decided that we should tackle the initial episode of sexual abuse, and in particular the devastating effect of her mother's betrayal. We had already, of course, retrieved a detailed memory of that experience, but had made no attempt to change the resultant feelings, or to clarify the destructive contradiction within it: that she *had* experienced the abuse at the hands of her father, but her infallible mother had declared this to be false.

I prepared the ground for this by asking Mrs Collins to tell me what would have made this experience less distressing and less damaging.

'Well, I wanted her to comfort me and tell me it was all right.'

'What would you have liked her to do to comfort you?'

'I don't know.'

'What would you do if your daughter had come running to you in such a distressed state?'

'Oh, I'd comfort her of course!'

'How would you do that?'

'Well, I'd pick her up and give her a kiss and a cuddle.'

'What would you tell her?'

'That it was all right and she didn't need to be upset now.'

'Might you tell her that what had happened was not her fault?'

'Well, yes, of course.'

'If your mother *had* told you it was not your fault and that something wrong and bad had been done to you, how would you have felt about it?'

'Oh, that would have made me feel quite different. It would have been all right then.'

She thought that my suggestion of imagining her 'adult self' comforting the 'child self' as she would comfort another child was more than a little fanciful, and could not see how this device could possibly have any effect, but, with a laugh, said 'You're the doctor, you should know!'

I used the same induction of hypnosis which had been congenial to Mrs Collins when she first came to see me, and she spent some time 'in her Private Place' – a mental picture of the happy place she could recall: a field by a church she could see from her bedroom at the boarding school, with a flock of sheep and lambs – to allow herself to become relaxed in body and mind, enjoying a sense of freedom from all that troubled her. I then asked her to picture herself going backwards through time, going back to the day of that party in their downstairs living-room, and to the point when she heard her father call to her from the kitchen. She was about seven years old, I reminded her, so she was going back to being seven years old again, and would be able to see, hear and feel all that happened on that occasion.

Mrs Collins seemed to shrink visibly and to adopt a quite childlike posture in her chair. She *looked* seven years old, despite her size and shape. When she spoke, it was in the voice of a small child: anyone listening from outside the room would have had no doubt that I was interviewing a distressed seven-year-old.

Mrs Collins seemed to be re-living an experience of many years ago with complete conviction and subjective reality. In reply to prompting, she related what was happening. Her account followed closely the way she had described the event originally, but in the voice and vocabulary of a little child, and with strong and clearly visible feelings.

At the point when her mother had berated her and she was running up the stairs to her bedroom, I told her that the adult Mrs Collins should now appear on the stairs, stop Little Meggie as she ran up, pick her up and comfort her. Mrs Collins moved uneasily in her chair, pushing an invisible something away from her with increasing violence, and then slowly subsided again and snuggled against the side of the chair. I asked if she had succeeded in comforting Little Meggie, and Mrs Collins nodded, after an interval saying that the child had not wanted to be picked up and had struggled but was now feeling a little better.

I then asked her to explain to Little Meggie that what her

father had done to her had been wrong; perhaps it had to do with his being drunk, but it was wrong and she, Little Meggie, was entirely blameless. After an interval, Mrs Collins said that she had been able to persuade the child of this. I then asked her to explain also that Little Meggie's *mother* had been wrong in what she had said. Perhaps she had been mistaken, or had not properly understood, but for her mother to tell Little Meggie that she was telling filthy lies was simply wrong and she, Mrs Collins, knew Little Meggie was telling the truth because she had seen what had happened herself.

Expressions of various emotions came and went on her face for some time after this instruction; at times she looked frightened, angry, distressed. Tears came and gradually subsided again. After some ten or more minutes, the tension in her face and body subsided, and she looked at peace. For a moment, it seemed as though she were about to put her thumb in her mouth. I asked if Little Meggie was now comforted, and Mrs Collins agreed she was. I suggested that Mrs Collins should now return to the present day and to normal wakefulness.

Mrs Collins found this a shattering experience. She had, so she felt, not simply re-played the episode in memory, but *relived* it, it had been so vivid and realistic. She had *felt* herself to be seven years old, had *recognized* the dress she wore, had *felt* herself sitting on her father's lap, had *felt* his hand on her body, had *seen* her mother on the stairs, had *heard* her voice scolding her. Above all the seven-year-old had reacted strongly to the unknown woman who had met her on the stairs, first trying to escape her and then gradually accepting the comfort the woman had offered her.

At the same time, her adult self had *seen* the distressed and weeping child running up the stairs towards her, had felt the

39

child's vigorous, almost violent resistance to being picked up and held, had felt the child's distress and resistance gradually subside: the whole episode had, despite its unreasonable nature, been wholly realistic. Like anyone experiencing such a dual state of awareness, and occupying two centres of consciousness simultaneously but separately, she wondered at the experience, but could not do other than accept it as real. She *had* experienced it, and nothing could change that.

I had noted the expressions of distress and anger on Mrs Collins's/Little Meggie's face when I suggested that her mother had been wrong, and I now pursued this. Mrs Collins calmly and objectively described how she had felt the child reacting with anger and distress at this point. It was clear to her that Little Meggie could not accept that her mother was wrong, until she realized that perhaps her mother had made a mistake. That, it seemed, *was* acceptable, but that her mother should have been *wrong* was not.

Mrs Collins herself seemed quite unaware of the incongruity of this. By treating her child self as though she were another person entirely, and therefore that the child's mother was not her own mother, she could say, think and believe that the child's mother had been wrong in what she had done. She was as yet nowhere near able to recognize the wrongness of and betrayal by her *own* mother. This clearly would need further work.

4

Throughout this period, we met weekly, without interruptions. Mrs Collins continued to lose weight steadily, and at the beginning of September had lost eleven kilograms (twenty-four pounds) altogether.

Mrs Collins continued to tell me more about her history. When she had been placed in a children's home after her attempt to kill herself by jumping off Waterloo Bridge, she had run away on a number of occasions, trying to get back to the aunt with whom she had spent six happy months. At that time she was twelve years old. This led her on to tell me that she had been given no information at all about menstruation. Her first period occurred while she was in hospital recovering from an appendectomy. Her alarm at finding blood in her bed had been reduced by the explanation given her by a nurse, but she retained a marked disgust for the process, and always suffered considerable pain.

She wondered why her mother had not prepared her for menstruation, going round and round the fact that her mother had been unable to accept or cope with anything related to sexual matters. She was vaguely aware of a connection between this prudish reticence and her mother's denial of the sexual abuse by her father, but was confused by the fact that her mother had clearly been sexually active. Not only had she borne children, but after her first husband's death she had

41

re-married, so that however inhibited she seemed to be about sexuality, she was by no means asexual. This seemed to Mrs Collins to be contradictory and incomprehensible.

The following week, Mrs Collins told me what had happened after her father had been bound over by the court. At this time, she was about seventeen, and was living at home again.

I had a breakdown and spent ten months in hospital. I was advised not to go home – but I did, thinking things would have calmed down. But no, they were still bitter against me and I couldn't cope, so I decided to try and kill myself.

I went to Waterloo Bridge again. I decided not to jump in case someone saw me, so I went down the stairs by the bridge and sat crying at the water's edge for a while. Then I slid into the water, but somebody must have been watching me, as I had no sooner slid into the water when someone grabbed hold of me and pulled me out.

I was taken to some hospital for treatment, then the police took me to another place. They said it was another hospital, but they didn't say what kind. It was dark out and I didn't pay much attention to anything on the way there. When we got there, there was a big door and I heard bolts being pulled open and I got scared. I tried to run but the police grabbed me and with the help of the nurses they picked me up and carried me screaming and struggling. It took four of them to carry me as I was struggling so much, but they got me into a room which was a padded cell, and two more nurses came when the police went. They were holding me down on a mattress on the floor pulling my clothes off until I was naked. They even took my sanitary belt and towel. Then they shut the door and left me there naked, screaming and banging about.

I was terrified. I couldn't understand why they were doing this to me. I wasn't mad, or insane, or a criminal – so why?

Mrs Collins recalled being interviewed by a doctor who had taken her into a side room, sat down and waited for her to talk, looking out of the window the while and picking his nose. She could find nothing to say, and the 'interviews' were of no help. Mrs Collins was forcibly detained in this hospital for a month and given medication. She was then discharged, recalling no treatment other than admission and medication.

When they let me go, I had nowhere to go so I slept on Waterloo station for a few nights. I couldn't go home, I couldn't face that again. So I found a room to share with a girl called Della. She seemed a nice girl. She got me a job at the factory where she worked and we became friends and started going out to cinemas and dancing and ice-skating. Her boyfriend was away in the army.

I was eighteen in the spring, and Della's boyfriend wrote to say he was coming home on leave and she was to meet him. Della made me go with her. We met her boyfriend and was having coffee in a café when her boyfriend saw a man he knew and called him over to sit with us. This man's name was Mick Lawrence. We all went to the pictures in town and for a meal. Mick asked me if he could see me again. I said yes so we arranged to meet the next day. He was a very handsome man and I liked him a lot. The next day we went for a meal, and then went to Trafalgar Square and paddled in the fountain.

He asked me to marry him. I was a bit taken aback by this but I liked him very much and I said I would have to think about it as we had only known each other just over one day. He said he'd keep asking me until I said yes. I guess I thought I loved him because when he asked me next day I said yes. He wanted to get married straight away so we went to see my mother to get her consent. She signed the papers and forged Dad's signature as him and me still

43

were not talking. Mum didn't like Mick and he didn't like her but she said she would come to the wedding.

We couldn't afford anything nice as neither of us had any money saved and all we could afford was the licence and a half-crown ring from Woolworths. So we got married six days after meeting. Mum treated us to sausage and chips in a nearby café for a wedding meal.

Mrs Collins told me that she had found intercourse painful as well as distasteful, that her husband became angry at her reluctance, and before long he had become violent towards her.

Mick was not a romantic person. I was, but not sexually. I liked to snuggle up to him, but he didn't like it. One day I went to sit on his lap, but he didn't want me to so he got up and stood behind the armchair. I went behind him and put my arms around his waist. He got angry and took one of my arms and twisted it around my back and pushed it up. I told him he was hurting me, but he kept pushing my arm until I thought he was breaking it. I begged him to stop, but he didn't, so I swore at him and he went berserk. He hit me and punched me and told me to go into our room. No one tried to help me.

Mick was sent to Germany, and I left for a job as a nanny in Hertford. I loved it. I loved the children and wanted some of my own.

Mick wrote often saying he was trying to find a place for us. The man of the house started to give me the impression he was after me, though I may have been wrong, so I panicked and left and went back to Mum's.

Eventually, she went to join Mick in Germany. After much to-ing and fro-ing, they were allotted married quarters there.

Our sex life was almost non-existent. About once in about one to two months, Mick would suddenly turn over in bed and get on top of me with no kissing or caressing, or any trouble to get me in the mood. Whether I wanted sex or not didn't matter to him. There was no love play and I never even got time to get aroused, let alone anything else. A majority of the time he couldn't get satisfaction and would curse me, so it became less and less. Sometimes I felt I wanted him to make love to me but was afraid to make any move, partly because I didn't know how and partly because Mick didn't believe a woman should start the first move and partly because I was afraid of failing him again.

On our first wedding anniversary, Mick took me out for a meal to a Chinese restaurant. He wanted me to eat Chinese, but I didn't want to. I said I wanted steak and chips and he got angry with me again and when we got home I got another good hiding for going against his wishes.

Things got worse. I spent all my time going to work at my cleaning job and coming home, working till I was exhausted. Mick went out alone now. Friends began telling me Mick was going out with another woman, but I wouldn't believe them. I didn't want to believe them.

The story went on. At one point, Mick had suggested that she should stay with her mother for a weekend. Since he had never allowed her to go anywhere, she became suspicious, and instead of catching a train, went to a cinema until late and then went home. Late that evening, Mick also arrived – accompanied by a woman. That earned her another beating.

I decided I couldn't take any more. The beating, yes, but women, no. Then I decided quite calmly what to do. He wouldn't be back till next morning, so I would be all right to do what I wanted. So very calmly I had a bath and took an overdose of sleeping pills and laid a clean towel in the bottom of the bath and a pillow for my head. I got one of Mick's razor-blades and got in the bath and cut my wrists. I didn't feel a thing, no pain. I was numb. Blood started pouring out and I became unconscious.

Next thing I remember was coming round in hospital. Mick was there and I said something like, 'What are you doing here? Why aren't you with your fancy bit?' and he turned and walked out. I didn't see him again until I discharged myself. I was very disappointed I hadn't succeeded in killing myself and felt like trying again. I saw a psychiatrist and he put me under hypnosis, just the once, and made me feel much calmer and relaxed. That was my one and only time I had that done. But somehow I went home and faced Mick. He told me I owed him the money for the razor-blade I used.

One night I decided to go to the pub for a drink, and I got drunk deliberately. I met some soldiers who knew Mick and said they didn't want me to walk home alone in the dark, that they would see me home. There was three of them. So they walked me home. When we got there, they insisted they saw me up to my room, but when we got to my door, they pushed me into the room. I fell over. I was too scared to cry out, so they picked me up and threw me on the bed and took it in turns to have intercourse with me. Then they left. I cried all night and knew it was my own fault. I shouldn't have got drunk again, or allowed them to walk me home and I felt very ashamed of myself and dirty. I was afraid they might come back again, so I left next morning.

I was beginning to feel overloaded with horrors. It seemed as though Mrs Collins had yet another dreadful experience to recount at every interview, and I wondered at times whether these stories had actually happened. I wondered also whether my accepting and supportive response to what she had already told me might be encouraging her to manufacture further horrors in order to engage my continuing interest. This would not, of course, be in any way a conscious process, and Mrs Collins was in no doubt about the historicity of the memories she reported. My doubtfulness may also well have been a self-protective device, a way of shielding myself from the horrors she had experienced and was now exposing to me.

The effects of the bleak and affectionless childhood that Mrs Collins had described meant that her only experience of physical contact with adult males had come to be either violent or sexual, or, more usually, both. She had known no other meaningful interaction with men. It was possible, therefore, that the content of the last few interviews expressed a feeling, at some profoundly unconscious level, that the only way my interest and attention could be maintained was by feeding me sexual tit-bits.

For some weeks, Mrs Collins had become progressively more distressed and was by now in a state of continual, unremitting and intense inner turmoil. Despite the agonizing nature of all she had so far told me, she felt that there was very much more that she could not remember, and she had become determined to unearth all the memories that had been blocked or buried. She wanted desperately, *needed*, to understand how she had acted with such passivity, had failed to 'stand up for herself', and had simply accepted whatever anyone wanted to do to her.

Her courage was impressive. The work we had already done had imposed enormous stresses on her, but seemed to have stimulated in her the birth of a new attitude: that there might be reasons other than her presumed weakness, intrinsic worthlessness and badness. She repeated frequently that she was a coward, not normal, and this was why she had been treated in the way she had, but beneath this assumption there was nevertheless a feeling that perhaps there *was* something else. Above all, so she now declared, she wanted to recover *all* the lost events of her own life and history and make them her own again.

However, she was finding it very difficult indeed to cope with running a household, looking after her children and generally managing her life, at the same time as experiencing the increasing stress of her therapy, and especially that of the discoveries she was making about her own life. It seemed to me that there was an increasing risk that Mrs Collins might damage or try to kill herself because of her continuously high level of mental torment at the discoveries she was making almost daily.

I also considered it likely that we would make much more satisfactory progress if I were able to see her more frequently, and thereby step up both the pressure required and the support needed for her to work her way through all the material that was now surging back into consciousness.

I felt that three interviews a week (the maximum number of days I attended the hospital), to get Mrs Collins through what seemed to me to be a particularly difficult and potentially dangerous phase of her therapy, stood a far better chance of success than weekly interviews. Increasing her sessions, however, also meant increasing the pressure on her, and really required her to be relieved of her daily responsibilities and to be looked after. I thought too that she would feel a great deal safer in continuing therapy (as we, of course, had to) if she were in the protected environment of a ward, and I suggested that I should arrange this with the consultant.

A preliminary visit to the ward was arranged, when a psychiatric examination would be carried out as well as general assessment for admission. Mrs Collins came to see me directly after this visit. She had found it a tremendous ordeal: she had been interviewed in front of all the ward staff and had been intensely embarrassed. The worst part, however, was the examination (psychiatric and physical) which followed. She told me that this had been intolerable for her, because the doctor had been Indian.

In reply to my asking why this was so important to her, she told me that when she was in her early twenties, she had rented a room in the house of a friend, whose husband – whom she referred to only as 'the landlord' or as 'Lil's husband' – had raped her. He had been Indian or Pakistani and the doctor had reminded her of this man and of what he had done to her.

As she was speaking of this, she appeared not only distressed, agitated and generally disturbed, but somehow vague. She slumped in her chair, unlike her usual alert self, and her speech was slurred. Her responses to the questions and comments I offered became more and more *distrait* and vague until a silence intervened. At length she said: 'I s'pose I'll have to tell you. I took all me tablets while I was in the waiting-room, and I'm feeling pretty rotten now.'

I was furious. If I held to the terms of the contract between us, I would have to terminate treatment then and there, leaving Mrs Collins in a far worse state than before we had begun therapy, even though there was the safeguard of admission to hospital and the certainty that her care would be taken over by one or other of the psychiatrists in the unit, if only because she had overdosed. It would also mean that the progress we had made would be effectively undone. In addition, I have to admit that – being by no means immune to pride and vanity – I did not want to give up.

However, if I did not adhere to the contract, but continued with her therapy, I would almost certainly be making a rod for my own back: the contract would lose all validity and credibility, and whenever the going got rough again, Mrs Collins would feel perfectly safe, however unconsciously, in producing further behaviour of this kind to obstruct or halt the treatment, or otherwise control both me and the therapy.

While internally reflecting on this question, I did what had to be done: I asked to see the bottles from which she had taken the pills and identified tranquillizers and sleeping tablets among them, before taking her to the Emergency Department. By the time we got there, Mrs Collins was leaning heavily on my arm and seemed almost comatose. Leaving her for a moment to lean against the wall, I looked for a wheelchair. The moment my back was turned she ran off, and was half-way across the yard outside before I saw her. I retrieved her, not without difficulty as she did not want to return, and with considerable relief I handed her over to a nurse.

In the course of all this brouhaha, I decided that I would continue treatment with Mrs Collins, albeit with a further warning that treatment would stop if she should again try to injure herself. She was by this time very contrite and apprehensive. Before leaving her, I told her I would see her at her usual time next week, but that any more behaviour like this overdose, and it would be the end, with no appeal and no third chance. Wanly, aware now of the imminence of a stomach pump – a familiar and wholly unpleasant experience to her – she apologized.

I had no doubt that the explanation Mrs Collins gave me for

her overdose was perfectly true, and equally sure that it was not the whole truth. To take an overdose on the hospital premises, and in my own clinic at that, obviously could not be intended as a real attempt at self-destruction. It was, however, equally obviously a very aggressive and punitive gesture in my direction: 'Look what you have made me do!' was the message I read behind her action, like a child's cry. I also sensed another message: 'And *now* do you still care?' My handling of the situation seemed to me to carry the appropriate messages: yes, I did care about her and would not reject or abandon her, but equally I was not going to – nor could – put everything right for her, and she had to face the real-life consequences of her actions.

Mrs Collins was kept in the hospital overnight, but was not then admitted to the psychiatric unit, and went home the following day. She kept her appointment with me the next week. It was not at all clear to me what had really precipitated the 'overdose': the resemblance of the Registrar to the Indian landlord who had raped her, and the intense anxiety and agitation this had aroused in her, did not seem the whole story.

It struck me how strangely circumstances and coincidences seemed to militate against allowing the Mrs Collinses of this world to experience anything good. Admission had, after all, been intended to be a positive experience. Somehow, even the best intentions turned into repetitions of the abuse which had become so integral a part of her life.

She said she could, in fact, remember very little of the details of the rape by her landlord, but now she desperately wanted to regain full consciousness of that experience despite the distress that she anticipated it would cause her. I felt distinctly uneasy about Mrs Collins recovering the memory of what had so obviously been an intensely disturbing experience, when she was already so agitated. However, it seemed likely that she would remain at least as agitated and distressed as she already was if we did *not* make an attempt to seek out this hidden memory. In addition, she would feel that I was unwilling to hear the story, that I would be disgusted and repelled when I did, and that I would therefore reject her, if it was as revolting as she expected it to be.

On balance, therefore, I thought we should pursue this lost memory. If things got too difficult for her, I could suggest, while she was in hypnosis, that any intolerable memory should become unconscious again for the time being. If that were unsuccessful and she remained intolerably aware of this memory after the session, we had a safeguard, in that she had already been accepted for admission on to the psychiatric ward and so could be protected and cared for if it proved to be really necessary.

On the other hand, if we were successful in recovering the memory and could deal properly with the emotions it aroused, it would almost certainly reduce the pressure on her of the repressed memories struggling to reach awareness, and so would improve her current state. In the meantime, she was admitted.

Her first week as an in-patient was very stressful. She spent much of the time weeping in her room during the day, refusing to speak to anyone, and often wandering around at night, unable to sleep. On those night-time occasions, however, she did speak to the nursing staff about what was troubling her, and indeed told them a great deal of what she had already told me, although she continued to insist to me that she was completely unable to tell anyone but me about the things that had happened to her.

It was now a year since we had first met, and Christmas was nearing again. I had myself been offered admission for an operation a week before the holiday, and I was told that I would need two to three weeks' convalescence. I felt considerable relief that Mrs Collins would be cared for during my absence, since otherwise I would have been extremely anxious for her welfare, and indeed her safety. I anticipated that she would once again be angry at my desertion of her and that she would have fantasies about having damaged me, fantasies which would stimulate enormous guilt and were highly likely to stimulate more self-damaging behaviour.

She had by now become intensely dependent on me. In addition, aggressive and hostile feelings which fundamentally related to her parents had been displaced on to me: her overdose was an example of this. It meant that an illness, or anything untoward in my life, would inevitably arouse her feelings of responsibility for the event.

I attended a ward round – a meeting of all the staff, the consultant psychiatrist, his junior doctors, the nurses, occupational therapists, about twenty people in all – at which she was discussed in detail. The case was presented by the Registrar, who said that he had found her difficult to examine. She had been very cagey with him and told him very little of significance, saying, 'Mr Karle knows all about me and I don't want to repeat all that again.' The ward staff said she was continuously agitated, that she wept frequently, usually refused to talk about what was troubling her, and then would suddenly pour out intimate and detailed accounts of abuse that she had experienced. I was then asked to give my impression

53

and understanding of her difficulties. I took a deep breath.

In preparing to offer my views of Mrs Collins at the ward round, I had carefully reviewed all I knew of her. The readiness with which she was able to recover the actual identity of herself as a small child, the subjective reality of that experience, and the outward signs in terms of her appearance, voice, language, and manner, of *becoming* a child again in hypnosis, taken together with the numerous and large gaps in her memory, had begun to suggest to me the possibility that she might be a case of Multiple Personality Syndrome.

Perhaps some explanation of this is necessary. Multiple Personality Syndrome is not the same as schizophrenia. Schizophrenia is often – mistakenly – called 'split personality', but is quite different. In MPS, two or more separate personalities seem to inhabit the same body; the person seems to have periods of time, which may last minutes, hours, days, or even weeks, for which they later have no memory at all, and during which time they behave in ways that are totally different from their normal ways. During these episodes, they call themselves by a different name, live a quite different life, and altogether appear to be a different *person*.

At that time, there was not much literature on this condition. According to those books I had read, the 'secondary personality' is generally aware of the 'primary' – knows about that person, knows what they know, and so on – but the 'primary' does not know anything at all about the 'secondary', not even that it exists. In cases of more than one 'secondary', the 'primary' knows nothing of the 'secondaries', while the latter may or may not know about each other.

The existence or reality of such a state is generally dismissed in Britain, in contrast with the United States, where it is much more generally accepted as a real condition. I had actually met and recognized several cases of this kind before, and in one instance the diagnosis that I had suggested had been accepted formally by the DHSS. I had already tentatively mentioned the possibility that Mrs Collins was a case of Multiple Personality Syndrome to a few colleagues, who had been completely disbelieving, and I was consequently apprehensive of the reception this suggestion would meet from the consultant and his colleagues.

The team listened politely, but with patent disbelief when I now said that I thought that Mrs Collins was a case of Multiple Personality Syndrome. They made it clear, quite tactfully, that in their view Mrs Collins was play-acting, and that she had taken me in. Their view echoed the opinions of my immediate colleagues that Mrs Collins had developed this charade to maintain my interest, and that it had no reality.

Mrs Collins was then brought into the room and interviewed briefly by the consultant psychiatrist. She visibly found this very upsetting, and told me later that she had been shaken to be interviewed in front of a crowd like that. She also had been shocked and angered to find that I was party to this ordeal, and found it impossible to accept that such a procedure should be considered right and appropriate. Privately, I shared her views, but made the point that she needed the care that the ward and its staff provided, and that neither she nor I could make the rules to suit ourselves. Her resistance to and anger at this indignity, even though it was expressed openly only to me, seemed to me an advance on her past submissiveness and compulsive compliance.

We had one further interview following this meeting before I was due to go into hospital myself. Mrs Collins told me that she would spend Christmas at home with her three younger children, and said she was looking forward to this. She made no mention of Lee, or of what had happened at the same season last year. She admitted that she would miss our regular sessions, and I suggested that she should write her thoughts down to give me in due course as a way of going on talking to me, and so lessening the sense of separation. With light-hearted warnings to me about her poor writing and spelling, Mrs Collins agreed.

5

January, Year Two

I returned from convalescence in the middle of January. Mrs
Collins was weighed when she arrived at the clinic: she was
now down to 80·5 kilograms (twelve stone nine pounds). We
spoke briefly about our mutual satisfaction at this progress
before catching up on what had happened during the break.

Mrs Collins had followed my suggestion of writing to me
during the break in our sessions, and now she gave me what
she had written. The greater part of this was about the most
important people and episodes in her life, and not, as I had
suggested, her present thoughts and feelings. Most of her
writing proved to be in the form of repeats or re-working of
things she had already told me, but with more detail added.

She was utterly preoccupied with retrieving her personal
history. She made no mention of her suicidal gesture nor of
any other self-destructive or self-damaging behaviour.

Early in this session, Mrs Collins told me she had 'found
herself' in a chemist's shop in the adjoining High Street, buying
razor-blades, Panadol, aspirin, and the like. On several
occasions in the interviews that followed, she 'discovered' such
things in her handbag while taking out a handkerchief, or
extracting her latest piece of writing to give to me. She was
fully aware of how desperate she herself felt during this period.
She knew that she had somehow obtained the means of killing
herself, but at the same time insisted that she had no intention

57

of harming herself, and simply could not see this contradiction. The dissociation or 'split' between Mrs Collins's central self and the 'secondary' who evidently was bent on suicide was patent, deep, and profoundly disconcerting to me each time it appeared.

Without belittling the suffering she was experiencing, I emphasized that we needed to explore the underlying causes of her difficulties and disturbance. Mrs Collins, however, insistently focused on her relationships with her children, the complaints she had about the way she was being treated on the ward, her difficulties in sleeping, her continuous weeping, and other present-day difficulties. It was by no means clear whether her earlier eagerness to unearth the traumata that were responsible for her sufferings was a genuine drive towards and wish for health – or compliance with my suggestions. In the end, however, she agreed.

We had already worked through the original abuse by her father, but I was concerned that the aftermath – the protection of her idealized mother – remained largely untouched. Her fierce preservation of her mother's innocence, even at the cost of her own, so that she forfeited all sense of value or goodness in herself, remained. Her experience of being totally unprotected as a child remained equally untouched: to her it simply existed as a fact, and was a direct result, she believed, of her personal weakness, cowardice and inadequacy. Her ability to hold equally firmly in her mind two patently incompatible and mutually contradictory ideas reflected her startling capacity to dissociate, not just between separate personalities, but even within one single consciousness.

In discussing what we were going to do, Mrs Collins identified the rape by Mr Baker as a crucial episode. She could see intellectually that she would not consider any other child to be culpable, but the feelings of self-blame she felt in herself were far too deeply rooted to be changed by discussion. She was quite able to *state* her innocence, and equally unable to *feel* it.

We arranged three appointments for the following week, on successive days. My plan was that we should use hypnotic techniques in the first two sessions in order to recover buried memories, and work with them in order to modify the effect they had had on her thinking, feeling and behaviour. In the third, we would work through the material disclosed in these first two sessions, without using hypnosis. Since there would be a four-day gap after each third consecutive session, I also felt it would be wise to use the third session of each such three-day period as a 'de-briefing' session rather than for further exploration and uncovering.

Mrs Collins had experienced the first exploration under hypnosis – of the first incident with her father – very vividly and powerfully. She had, as far as she was concerned, *been* seven years old again. The rape by Mr Baker would, in all probability, be just as vivid, real, and 'immediate', and it seemed to me that this would be very disturbing indeed for her. Some sort of 'distancing' technique, which would not at the same time diminish the reality of the event, would be helpful. It would also be useful to find some image that would enable Mrs Collins to deal with the memory and the feelings involved in a constructive way. When we had returned to the first episode with her father, we had used the image of her adult self as a source of comfort, and this had been quite effective in reducing her distress.

Once Mrs Collins was in hypnosis and she seemed relaxed,

I suggested she should picture herself sitting before a television set connected to a video recorder. She was familiar with this equipment since she possessed it herself. I asked her to imagine that beside the recorder were a number of video tapes which contained a complete record of her life. She was to select the tape covering the years between seven and nine, insert it in the recorder and switch on. At first, I said, she would find that the screen showed only random patterns of black and white, but gradually a picture would form which showed her entering Mr Baker's house.

In her previous report of this event, Mrs Collins had shown very little feeling at all, but now she quickly began to show increasing distress in her voice, bodily movements and facial expression. To all intents, she was witnessing the episode being 'replayed' in front of her. All the feelings originally associated with this event appeared to be now present. In response to my questions, she described what was happening on the television screen.

He's taking me indoors. He's telling me to sit down, and I'm sitting on the top step. He's pushing me backwards, and I'm crying. Now he's pulling my knickers off, and he's lying down on top of me.

I suggested at this point that she should now see her adult self appear, take the child in her arms and cuddle and comfort her while the scene of Mr Baker's house faded away.

It took her a long time to reach the point where she could report that her child self now had ceased to struggle and had accepted the proffered comfort. I suggested that she should now switch off the recorder, take the tape out and withdraw from the cassette the length of tape on which this scene was recorded, cut it off and then re-join the cut ends of the tape.

The now separate portion of tape which contained this episode she was to roll up and place in a steel box which she should lock. The memory of the event was not to be destroyed, but kept safely until such a time as it was no longer of importance to her and her life, and could be 'thrown away'. When Mrs Collins reported that she had 'done' this, I suggested she return to my room and to normal consciousness. She said, as we discussed the episode, that she felt a sense of considerable relief.

The following day, however, with unusual directness and confidence, she pointed out the gross error I had made in this session. I had suggested that her adult self should intervene before the rape. But as the rape *had*, after all, taken place in reality, nothing, no amount of imagination, could undo that.

My carelessness shocked me. What had motivated me, I wondered, to use the same dissociative mechanism as had occurred spontaneously in Mrs Collins and was represented by her losing this memory in the first place? I had, like any ordinary person, been horrified at her experiences and moved to intense sympathy and pity for her. Perhaps I had been endeavouring to protect myself as well as her by 'burying' the memory and its horrors. I had, it seemed, been identifying with her to a far greater extent than I had been aware. Mrs Collins, however, had been better aware of her needs than I.

The session and its contents had not been entirely negative or unhelpful, however. The remainder of the day had been filled, she said, with a sense of great relief, but she had slept little during the following night, and during those wakeful hours, had recovered many more memories. She felt that we needed to re-work the episode I had bungled, and this we did. We agreed that she should intervene with comfort and protection at the very end of the episode – when Little Meggie left the house.

Mrs Collins again reported what she observed. She described once again how Mr Baker had invited her into the house and had made her sit on the top step, before pushing her prone and removing her knickers. With obvious effort to master her distress even at the remove of the 'TV' device, she described how Mr Baker lay on top of the child and pushed himself down on her until finally rising, wiping the child between her legs with his handkerchief, putting her knickers on again and, with many threats that he would kill her if she spoke to anyone of what had happened, sent her out of the house. It was at this point that I asked Mrs Collins to appear in the scene and comfort her child self.

This re-play of the event appeared to affect her as deeply as the first time, and she described great difficulty in holding the child, who was struggling to get away and refusing for a long time to accept any comfort or reassurance. The episode over, Mrs Collins expressed great satisfaction: she felt that something inside her had indeed changed, although in some ways it seemed to have created many more questions than it resolved. That evening, she wrote about this session.

Today we went back to when I was about eight years old, to the day Mr Baker raped me. It was very hard, and awful to go through it again, but again worth it to learn the truth of what happened and to learn that it wasn't my fault. Thank god for Mr Karle for putting me there again to help Little Meggie. It was a great comfort to Little Meggie.

But although I felt good in a way, I didn't feel as good as I had yesterday. I guess I expected to, but I didn't as there were so many unanswered questions. I feel sad that I couldn't tell Mum, but she might have said the same as she did with Dad, and not believe me and say I was dirty, and I felt dirty enough as it was.

I need to know, but it takes time and one can only do so much at a time and I was anxious to know the answers. So many questions kept coming into my head as I walked back to the ward. I got annoyed at myself and angry for not being able to know the answers.

Her ambivalence about the whole process, how I would react to the memories she recalled, whether I could really be trusted not to respond in the way so many others had in the past, was clear:

How Mr Karle puts up with me I don't know. I must make him feel embarrassed with some of the things I have to ask, but I'm sure he understands how I feel and that I need to know the answers – and I'm sure he wouldn't mind how I put it, because he's sincere, dedicated and truthful and I still have so much faith in him.

I don't care what experiences, however bad, I have to go through to learn the truth about myself and to face them and be free of the burden I've felt for so many years. To be able to live a normal life and be a woman, I mean a proper woman, both sexually and other ways, and I'm sure that my faith and belief in Mr Karle will help me to answer all these questions and learn all my past, good or bad. It's important to me to know everything. With Mr Karle's help I'll get there one day and be really free from the weight I carry at the back of my head, as well as my real weight.

The idealization of me, almost adulation, that Mrs Collins put on paper, emerged quite clearly, if less explicitly, in our interviews. In person she was more controlled, circumspect, and discreet, and hid the loving – and also erotic – quality of the feelings which were so patent in her writing. I debated at length with myself whether this was the time at which we should bring these feelings into the open. She felt herself to be 'in love' with me, and to be so as an adult, but at some time she would have to recognize that her yearning for care and affection from me was the displaced longing for her father and mother.

Mrs Collins *felt* her attachment and need, and her longings, to be directed to me. Exploring the origin, and recognizing the original objects of these feelings, is always a delicate and difficult process. The fact that the therapist regards these tender feelings as topics to be examined in the same way as all the other things which emerge in the course of therapy is almost inevitably experienced as a direct and highly personal rejection, and this is especially so for people whose life experiences have all been of rejection and lack of love.

I debated with myself whether this was the right time to explore and talk about her feelings for me, and decided that there was other work – disclosure and exploration of earlier experiences – which should be done first. Cowardice on my part may have played some part in this decision, legitimate though the rationalizations I used may have been.

I've still got a lot of weight to lose before I can really get more confidence as whether any man would look at me twice. I'd be the happiest person in the world if I thought I could have a chance with a man I like very much but I guess I know he doesn't want to know me, not in the way I would like to know him. Even if I lost weight, he still wouldn't. You can't force anyone to like you. Rather, they like you or they don't. So I'll have to live with that never-knowing feeling which I hate but can't do anything about. He doesn't even

*know I exist as a woman, let alone anything else. He'd run a mile
if he knew, that much I do know for sure. He must never know,
that's why I can't tell anyone, not even Mr Karle.*

This patent self-deception appeared to be unrecognized by Mrs
Collins herself. It seemed to me that the 'man I like very much'
could be no one but me, and by drawing attention to 'not being
able to tell' me, she actually underlined the disclosure.

The following day, Mrs Collins was more composed and
lively than I had seen her for a long time. The re-working of
the episode with Mr Baker had achieved something, although
how deeply the change had been effected or how long it would
last was uncertain. Her appetite for understanding had been
sharply increased, and she was full of questions, some of which
she had written down on a paper she gave me immediately.
This included a curiously disjointed passage.

Why did I always just let him until that last time?
Knife and Gas
Wetting bed
Wetting during day
Need to talk and get it off my chest about the last time
Why didn't he actually rape me again
*What was so special about that last time to any other time to make
me want to cry*

A question she had not written but asked herself and me
insistently and repeatedly, almost obsessively, was whether Mr
Baker had actually achieved vaginal penetration. She could
not be sure whether he had done any more than press his
penis against her. Over and over she asked whether she had
been a virgin when she married or not. I could get no indication

of why this question should be so important to her: to her it simply was vital to have it answered.

With even more affect, she asked why she was not crying when finally released by Mr Baker after this first episode, and why she had not told her mother. I offered no answers, letting her talk her way through this morass of questions, until she herself focused firmly on the one that she considered to be the most important part still missing from her memory. There had been an episode in Mr Baker's shop which was clearly different from all the previous occasions – this much she knew, but the rest was blank. She knew it was especially important since the event had caused her not only to run away, but had made her jump into the river with the firm intention of drowning.

We used hypnosis again. Mrs Collins showed the same strange regression in appearance and voice that occurred each time we used this technique to go back to an earlier time in her life, and soon showed intense distress again. She reported that Mr Baker had not followed his usual practice of masturbating her at the back of the shop, but had instead placed her on a table. At this point she ceased to reply to my asking her what was happening and began to moan, writhing in the chair and showing still greater distress, but saying nothing. After a little while she said: 'Please stop it, please stop it.' The voice she used was her normal adult voice, not the childish tone that marked her speech during episodes of regression, and I realized she was addressing me rather than Mr Baker. We closed the episode, letting the scene fade from her mind, and I reassured and calmed her before asking her to return to normal consciousness.

The following day, she told me that she had felt very disturbed after the session and throughout the rest of the day,

66

wanting to talk to the nurses about what she was feeling but unable to say anything. The night had been disturbed by nightmares. She had written:

Today I saw Mr Karle. I knew that something had happened on my last visit to Mr Baker's shop but didn't know what, so Mr Karle took me back under hypnosis. When I started to see what was happening to me, I could also feel it actually happening. It was the most terrible thing I had to see and feel. I tried I guess to fight away from it and couldn't really put it into words. I was disgusted by what had happened in that shop and I tried to fight against it even under hypnosis. It was a shock to learn what I did, and when I came out of the trance I still found it difficult to talk. I didn't know how to. I felt so ashamed and angry with myself that I could have forgotten such a horrible thing like that. Mr Karle always makes me feel calm and relaxed normally, and I thought I was when I left but I couldn't stop thinking about it. I needed to talk about it, but didn't know how.

I got very upset back on the ward and cried on my bed. I was feeling angry with everyone, including Mr Karle, and myself, and my mother. But not with the one person I should be angry with –
Mr Baker. I don't understand this. It doesn't make sense. I guess this is why I felt angry with Mr Karle, because he hadn't made me talk about it. I felt angry and ashamed of being unable to talk.

I had gone to art classes when I came back to the ward and was drawing, when I looked down and saw this picture which I realized was Mr Baker's shop, with a table in it and Mr Baker. I got upset by this, grabbed the picture, ran out down the stairs and into the toilet and was sick.

The picture had been of Mr Baker's shop, with a man in it. The most prominent feature of the picture had been a table. I asked why this was important. Mrs Collins showed intense embarrassment and instead of addressing my question began to talk of her feeling that part of her wanted to tell me what had happened and another part refused.

'Can't you help me? D'you know what it was about?'

'I can only guess. I don't know what happened until you tell me.'

Mrs Collins pressed me to disclose my guess. She resisted all my attempts to prompt her into telling me what she obviously needed to talk about, or to address this reluctance itself, and in the end, I offered my interpretation: that the episode had involved oral sex.

'Yes, you're right, but he did it to me first.'

That was said with great emphasis. Eventually, I managed to ask her to tell me more about the table in the picture.

I had to go to shop again at Mr Baker's. There was a lady in the shop at the time and I was told to wait. I knew why, and what was going to happen, because it always did. After she went, he took the basket and list and put them down. He locked the door and turned the sign, pulling the blind. He took me up the back of the shop again, only this time instead of standing me by the shelf, he lifted me up and put me on the big table at the back of the shop.

Fear hit me harder as I realized he was not doing what he normally did and I did not know what he was going to do. Then I thought he was going to do to me what he had done to me at his house when I was eight years old, raped as I know now, I think. He laid me on the table and pushed my skirt up to my chest and pulled my knickers down and took them off. I didn't know what to do or expect and was too terrified to move. I started to cry and he told me to shut up and keep still or he would hurt me. I wanted to get away but was too frightened to move, so I laid there naked from the waist down except for my shoes and socks. He stood there looking down at me for a while, then he lifted my legs, pulled me towards the end of the table and pushed my legs back so my knees bent and my legs were wide apart and I was fully exposed below.

I lifted my head a bit to see what he was going to do and he was standing there holding my legs apart, looking at me all funny like. His eyes were staring at me below. He looked at me again and told me to keep still and not make a sound. Then he knelt on the floor so his face was almost level with me. He moved his hands down my thighs and pulled my vagina open with his hands or fingers. I couldn't see him now, only his hair. I tried to reach it and grab it but I couldn't reach. I tried to cry out but not much sound came. I could feel his eyes on me and feel his fingers moving me about. Then I felt a strange thing touch me, poking and licking and sucking at me and I realized his head was pushed down to my vagina and his tongue was licking and sucking at me and pushing harder into me.

I was petrified, embarrassed, ashamed. I felt dirty, the panic was building up more and more but I didn't have the guts to move, and after what seemed it would never end, I wanted to die. I wished he'd kill me. I so wanted to die. Then he got up and came round to the side of the table to where my head was and looked at my face. Then he undid his trousers and lifted his huge gigantic penis out. It was standing out on its own. He put his hand on my face round my mouth squeezing it until my mouth opened, then he tried pushing his penis into my mouth. I raised my hands to try and push him away, and he lifted his other hand and hit me across the head and stomach. This stunned me for a moment but it was long enough for him to push his penis into my mouth. It was vile and I was choking and couldn't get my breath. I prayed for death to come, but it didn't.

I couldn't stand it any more so I managed to bite him somehow, I don't know how, but he yelled and stepped back, and I rolled off the table and ran. I didn't even think about my knickers until later, I just ran off crying, as fast as I could. I ran until I couldn't run any more and found an alley to hide in and curled up like a ball in a corner, too frightened to move or make a sound. I bit my lip so's not to make a sound in case he had come after me.

I stayed there a long time until I dozed off to sleep. It was dark and late but I don't know how late. I realized I had no knickers on and I was cold. I crept out of the alley looking all round and ran home. Most of the house was dark. I got in through the coal hole to sneak up to my room as I didn't know what to do. I got black from the coal and when I crept in my Mum and Dad were waiting for me.

They started shouting where had I been and accusing me of being thoughtless at staying out so late worrying them and my Dad gave me a good strapping with his belt, but I didn't feel a thing. I was numb with shock. Then they asked me where the shopping was. I couldn't answer. They accused me of losing the things I was supposed to have got by playing and said I would have to go back to the shop for them. I was told to wash as I was covered in coal, and get to bed, where I decided to run away next morning after the others went to school. I had to think where I could go and decided to go to my aunt's.

I could never tell anyone as they would not believe me. Mum had said Daddies didn't do things to little girls and Mr Baker was a Daddy, so they wouldn't believe me. I felt ashamed and dirty. Next morning I washed and scrubbed but could not feel clean, then I put some clothes in a bag and went to my aunt's in Clapham and told her Mum had sent me over as I hadn't been well and needed a rest. She accepted this for a week until she found out Mum didn't know

*where I was and that I had run away from home. Mum and my
aunt talked and decided I could stay with my aunt.*

*She never asked why I'd run away or anything. She should have
asked at least.*

As she spoke of feeling that her mother *must* have seen her
child's distress and yet never said anything, never asked what
was wrong, she sounded and looked almost angry with her
mother – and I nearly held my breath. But she broke away
from that theme immediately. The breakthrough – if that it
really was – had been short-lived, but progress had been made
towards disclosing and 'owning' the rage and grief of the
appalling betrayal she had suffered.

6

The following week, I tried to get Mrs Collins to continue where she had stopped just before the end of the last session, when she had become almost explicitly angry with her mother. The intense conflict between her conscious respect, dependence, and submission to her mother on the one hand, and her essentially unconscious, denied and displaced rage at her mother's failure and betrayal of her as a child on the other, were central in the aetiology of Mrs Collins's adult psychological state. She told me that when her mother died, she had thought a great deal about what a hard time she had given her mother through her bad behaviour, her frequent running away, and so on, and had felt very guilty that she had never actually said 'sorry' to her. This guilt had been much enhanced when she had been told by her mother's doctor that her death had been due to an injury done many years earlier, and she had felt dreadfully ashamed of having been such a bad daughter: she had in fact felt that *she* had killed her mother.

At the same time, she could not understand why her mother had never tried to find out what was wrong, or to seek help for her. Mrs Collins contrasted her mother's lack of care of and interest in her with her own actions when Lee had developed problems of different kinds, including enuresis, but all she could feel was a sort of puzzlement at her mother's behaviour.

We talked about the recovered memory of the last visit to

Mr Baker. Relating the episode had made a change: my guess as to the content, together with my continued acceptance of her, despite Mrs Collins's anticipation that I would share her feelings of disgust at herself – the reaction she expected to this account – seemed to have represented to her a new and different way of coping with it. In particular, the emphasis on Mr Baker as the *agent* of this brutality, and herself as the *victim*, seemed to have dented her previous picture of herself as exclusively responsible, thus liberating also the very first glimpse of anger. She now said she was very pleased that another piece of the jigsaw of her life had emerged and been fitted in: more now made sense, especially her flight to her aunt and the suicide attempt six months later. The feeling of *understanding* visibly elated her.

The following day she looked angry. I was delighted – but that was premature. She spoke with real feeling about her anger at one of the doctors on the ward who had arranged to talk with her and had failed to turn up on each occasion he had promised. When tackled about this at accidental encounters with her, he had made further dates, and again had failed to keep them. She had been able to bring this up at the Community Meeting and to express openly her anger at his unreliability. It seemed to me that this doctor's unreliability gave her a hook on which to hang anger that belonged elsewhere.

But she went on to express more anger: she was angry with everybody – and at last said she was angry with me. I had failed her by not resolving the problem of whether her virginity had been taken by Mr Baker: that I was being 'vague' about this. Then quite suddenly the atmosphere changed; she began talking of her fear that I would be disgusted with her.

The time for the end of our interview arrived, and she was in full flood, exploring her feelings in relation to me in a more open and insightful way than she had ever been able to achieve before. She was moving forward in her self-awareness so powerfully that, as my next appointment had been cancelled, I let her go on until she came to the end of what she wanted to say. I was delighted with her discovery of anger, even though she clearly had a long way to go before she could allow herself to identify and acknowledge the true targets of her rage.

By running over our allotted time, I was aware that I was playing into her greediness for care, attention, and comfort, but I failed to tackle it. Two things held me back. At a fully conscious level, I wanted, and thought it appropriate, to give her the opportunity that fortuitously was available, to go through what she had started, rather than interrupt it. I felt there would be a risk that she would be disappointed, that she would feel rejected by me if I had interrupted her, that she would imagine that I was not able or willing to accept what she was saying. I was afraid too of other reactions which would either set her back substantially or might even block this particular line for some time to come. At a rather less conscious level, which I perceived only long after the event, I believe I was actually *afraid* of the accusation of rejection and condemnation that she would level at me, however politely or disguisedly, if I were to stop her.

From the beginning, my conviction had been that the proper target for the work we were doing was Mrs Collins's rage at the inadequacy of the care she had received as a little girl, and her consequent rage – and grief – at the betrayal this represented, that Mrs Collins had repressed so effectively for so many years. However, the way into these feelings was through

74

encouraging her to talk about her frustration and anger at me. My inability, and what I had to admit was also some reluctance, to help her to bring this out into the open in the sessions actively obstructed her in this process. I was colluding with her fear of what destruction her anger would wreak: by *not* addressing it, I was colluding with her avoidance of the anger. Without doubt, my fearfulness prolonged therapy although I did not recognize that at the time.

Mrs Collins now talked about how she felt that she was beginning to come out of the morass of despair that was the aftermath of her childhood experiences, and she felt a strong desire to do something that would help others who had under-gone similar experiences and who, like herself, had been unable to find anyone who could recognize this distress or provide the help they needed. Her anger at those who had failed to help her in one way or another throughout her life re-surfaced. She wanted to tell the professionals that they had failed her and to educate them to recognize and respect people like herself. I was not sure whether she was conscious of a further motive: a vengeful desire to repay the neglect she had suffered.

What could she do? After all, she said, she had no education and no training, and therefore could not work in one of the helping professions, but she nevertheless felt strongly that she had something to contribute that would be of value.

I felt like cheering. She really was one of the most astounding and impressive people I could recall meeting. Even allowing for the neurotic displacement of her anger from her parents on to professionals – justified though some of that actually was – her desire for recognition, retribution and amends, her strength, her resilience and her courage were astonishing Given the background she had described and her life to date, it seemed wellnigh impossible that she could have retained the inner resources not just to survive, but to work towards a resolution of what her life had done to her. And then to arrive, as she seemed to be doing, at a feeling of personal worth after the many years of abuse and self-damage – this was amazing. My joy in what was happening was not unmixed with pride that I was responsible for the progress she was making in restructuring her life – and for succeeding in doing what so many others had failed to do in the past. She had indeed engaged my attention! And, of course, the approval for which she yearned from me was fully hers.

At the same time, there were decidedly less encouraging aspects to her desire to help others. Part of the motivation was her need to please me, to idealize, emulate, and model her future life on me and thereby, it seemed, create a place for herself in my life. None the less, that she could ask this question, and especially make the declaration that she had something of value to offer the world, was cause for immense satisfaction.

I had been deeply impressed with what she had been writing in the previous few weeks. On the train home, I had found myself barely able to suppress tears from time to time – and sometimes, for example in her descriptions of some childhood events, laughter – when reading her story, moved powerfully by the directness and dignity with which she wrote.

Before I had realized the full import of what this proposal represented, I had yielded to her and suggested that we should write a book together, using her writing and my account of her therapy. I found myself almost pursuing her now, almost indeed courting her. Yet again, an old pattern was re-playing itself: she possessed something that a man – I – wanted.

At first, Mrs Collins did not believe I was serious. She could not write good English and her spelling was dreadful, she said, but the suggestion made an obvious impact. She did not believe that her poor English would not be a hindrance, or that her writing could be a real, unique and valuable contribution. Eventually, with many reservations but a visible pleasure, she agreed to collaborate in this undertaking.

At the time, I felt a vague sense of unease underlying my interest in what I had suggested. This gradually crystallized into an understanding of what had occurred and of what I had been seduced into doing – or seduced her into doing – only after the interview was over and I had time to reflect. In the meantime, the interview continued.

For the first time now, she expressed positive feelings about her future life, only to dash them to the ground again in the next sentence by insisting that all the things that had been done to her had irredeemably soiled her, made her rotten; no man could ever look at her or want her, knowing what she had been through. I told her a story, one which came from my own life and fitted Mrs Collins, in its metaphorical meaning, as though designed for her.

'I know a very old house, probably about five hundred years old. It's not built out of bricks or stone, but has a wooden frame, filled in with panels of plaster. The owner wanted to build more rooms on to the end, but the authorities insisted that the extension had to be built exactly like the original house. So he found some beams from a very old barn that had been pulled down. When they were delivered to his house, he nearly gave up the idea on the spot, because they were all rotten and dirty; they looked useless, as though they would never hold up. But when he got to work on them with a saw and an axe, he found that under the rottenness and muck on the outside, there was hard, solid, good timber. He had to cut away a lot of dirt and rotten wood, but they turned out to be solid and strong underneath, and eventually they formed part of a fine house of which he was proud.'

She seemed to accept the metaphor and what it conveyed, and used it in her own writing – showing her identification with and attempted incorporation of me.

Mr Karle says it takes time to get used to being a new person and that we had worked hard and learnt a lot and it takes time to build a bit more confidence in myself. After talking to Mr Karle, I knew he was right. It will take time to get used to my new feelings. I am handling things much better and dealing with any problems all right. A few months ago, I couldn't manage any problems. I am handling things better and I am still losing weight. I lost 6 lbs this week and I was pleased at that as well. I am bound to have a few down days – after all everybody else does.

It's taken me nearly two days to understand and make sense of what Mr Karle said about if a person thinks they can't do something, then they won't – unless they at least try first.

And about the wooden beams that seemed dirty and rotten on top with the appearance that they were rotten right through, but when cleaned up and the rottenness removed, there was good healthy wood underneath. Good, clean, healthy and useful wood, that could be used to build up on as long as you take your time, bit at a time. After all it's taken about 35 years for someone to remove my rotten feelings about myself and for me to understand and be a different, good, healthy person. It'll take time to get used to it. But he said take one step at a time and I'd get there. Don't try to rush it.

The following week, I saw Mrs Collins again. She had visited her home for a weekend since the last session, and the ward team had asked her to set a date herself for when she should be discharged. She asked for my views and advice. I took the same line: it was for her to decide whether she still needed the protection that the ward provided and the respite from her domestic responsibilities, or whether she felt ready to take these up again. She decided to go home.

The task we had agreed upon for this session was to find out if Mr Baker had actually achieved full vaginal penetration on that first occasion. She was still obsessed with the question of whether she had been actually physically virgin at the time of her first marriage, although she was unable to give any explanation of the importance this question had for her.

Once again, she 'went back' to the event in hypnosis, so that she could observe exactly what had happened, but from outside the scene, and in her adult self. I made strong suggestions that she should remain detached and calm, able to observe what happened but without being directly involved.

When she indicated that the episode was complete and that she was satisfied, I asked her to let herself return to the present day but remain in hypnosis.

Mrs Collins had said on several occasions that she thought that there were yet other gaps in her memory which she wished to identify and perhaps fill, so at that point I asked her to imagine that she was looking at an immense and complicated jigsaw representing her life. She should then scan it thoroughly and establish whether there were any really significant pieces missing or whether it was relatively complete. After a while, during which she appeared literally to be surveying and checking a picture before her, she told me that there were a number of gaps in the picture she was scanning.

Once out of hypnosis again, she told me that she now had

the information she wanted. That evening she wrote about this episode.

I could see Mr Baker from behind and the sight of him made me realize he was not wholly inside the girl who seemed asleep but that his penis was only about half inside her. Although I felt calm watching him move faster and faster, I did feel the jerk of his body as he ejected. I felt the sudden jerk of him, but it didn't really bother me as it just answered other questions as to whether he had penetrated me and whether he had entered the front or not, and also how it was I got wet. So my question answered made me feel better, and I felt quite well, though maybe a little uncomfortable below.

She went on a little later to talk about the 'jigsaw' image.

The jigsaw was a bit different as I expected all the pieces to fit now. But they didn't. There was a few pieces missing but I didn't know what pieces. It looked like two pieces, but what they were I didn't know. It seemed to be between Dad and Mr Baker. My mind also thought of my landlord who'd raped me. I couldn't place those missing pieces and could only think of Dad, Mr Baker and the landlord. I felt a little confused later, thinking about it after. What are the missing pieces? I kept thinking and trying to picture the jigsaw again.

Then I realized there was three pieces missing, one on the second line and two other pieces together were missing. I hadn't taken it in at first because they was side by side. I started getting flashes in my mind of Dad coming down the stairs in his shirt only with his hand between his legs covering himself, which he often did if he was in bed and wanted to go to the toilet. He never bothered to put his trousers on if he wanted to go to the loo, so it was not unusual to see him this way, but I felt bothered by this picture and I don't know why really.

The other picture I keep getting is Mr Baker's upstairs hall but I don't know why. I don't remember ever going up there so how could I picture it if I don't know it? But both these pictures make me feel tearful. Why? I had felt calmer until I tried to figure the puzzle and saw these pictures in my mind. What is the missing pieces?

I began to doubt whether I really want to know, but finally decided I have to know if possible. Whether it's good or bad, I have to complete the puzzle, otherwise I won't feel right. I must know and I hope it's good for a change – but I want to feel completely free in my mind.

I know I've got a bit more to deal with but I know I'm going to be all right now. My faith and trust in the human race is almost restored and will be complete very soon. I'm getting more confidence in myself and will carry on to lose all the weight I need to lose and do a lot of things I've always wanted to do and make my children happy and proud I am their Mum, and deal or cope with life as it comes. The past will be the past and the future happy and hopeful and loving.

This euphoric paragraph seemed to be a very thinly veiled plea: 'Now I am all right, please will you love me?'

We agreed that we would use the next session to identify at least one of the missing jigsaw pieces and discover what it contained.

Once again, we used the device of a video recorder and television screen, with a cassette representing her memory store. When it was over, she told me what she had learned.

I saw Dad coming down the stairs in his shirt. Then I saw myself coming out of the toilet and making my way up the short flight of stairs to the first floor landing where my room was. I was in my knickers and vest as I was off sick from school. I was surprised to see Dad coming down the stairs from his room to go to the toilet. I felt uneasy knowing he was in the house with me alone, so I quickly ran into my room and shut the door and got back into bed and tried to relax. I thought to myself if I had known he wasn't at work I would have gone to school no matter how ill I felt. No one told me he was there. Mum was in hospital and the rest were at school and nursery.

Then Dad came into my room. He walked over to the bed and lifted the bedclothes up and got in beside me. He lifted my head and put his arm round my shoulders and kissed my forehead. He was talking but I couldn't hear him as I wasn't wearing my hearing aid. I didn't normally wear it in bed. I didn't like this, I was scared. Then he turned slightly towards me and kissed my forehead again and put his other hand on my arm and stroked my arm a couple of times. Then he put his hand on my chest and started rubbing my chest – I did not have any breasts to rub – but he rubbed my chest all over and down to my stomach, then over my hip and down the outside of my leg, then up the inside of my leg until he reached my knickers. Then he rubbed his hand over my knickers over my private. Then he put some fingers inside the leg of my knickers and had a feel about. I was crying out to him 'Please Daddy, please don't', but he wasn't taking any notice of me. I wanted to scream, but no one was around to hear me and Mum was ill in hospital.

He took his hand out of the leg of my knickers and put it down inside them forcing my legs further apart to get his hand further at me. His whole hand was rubbing over the outside of my private, then his fingers went inside a bit, running up and down from my back passage to the front. He put a finger, one I think, up inside my *vagina and was rubbing very hard and hurting me. I kept sobbing and pleading for him to stop. He was still gripping my arm at the top so I couldn't get away although I don't think I tried too hard as I was too frightened. He took his hand out and got hold of my hand and pulled me over to him and put my hand on his private parts. His hand was over mine pressing my hand down over his penis and on to his testicles. He put my hand on his penis and was making my hand rub up and down over it until my hand got all wet and slimy. All the time I kept crying, begging and pleading for him to stop.*

Then suddenly he did, and got up and went out of the room. He must have been saying something because his lips were moving. He must have forgot I was deaf or hadn't noticed I had no hearing aid on, I don't know which. I hid under the bedclothes and sobbed my heart out thinking how horrible he is and so wicked. I hated him with all my heart. I wished he was dead, I couldn't help it. I wished he was dead. Although Mum was in hospital I felt angry with her as well. I felt so dirty and horrible, and bruised and sore down below. I never did tell Mum or anyone about this time.

Mrs Collins was able to put this previously quite forgotten event into perspective. It had taken place just after her father had thrown her mother downstairs when she was pregnant. She had haemorrhaged and miscarried, the baby dying. After her mother's death many years later, there had been an inquest. Now she recalled that she had been questioned long and hard by the Coroner about this pregnancy and miscarriage. She now realized that her mother had actually been killed by her husband, even though her death came many years after the relevant assault. The guilt she had felt, believing that the trouble she had caused her mother for so many years had contributed to her mother's death, was now gone.

You know, it's surprising that once you re-live a thing, once you start to see what's happening, how it all comes pouring back as though you are actually going through it. But the pain is not there like it really was. I can hear myself and see myself and feel myself, but it doesn't feel the actual terror or anxiety so it's not so terrifying or painful as it was at the real time. I asked myself: Why me? Why did he pick on me, what was so special about me? But I can't answer them.

I can't understand how any man can do things to children, even more so to your own child. I feel hurt to know what he did, but I accept it now as the past and have no feeling about it. There is no excuse for what he did, but I can't change it, it's like crying over spilt milk. Now I know why I always hated to touch any man's private parts, including my husband's, and why I felt dirty and always wanted to bath after intercourse – more so if a man's sperm touched me in any way – and I always washed the sheets afterwards.

Learning all these past events explains quite a lot of things to me and I see things in a different way. It explains why I became a naughty child and played my mother up and why I ran away. Why I didn't want to live at home, why I always felt uneasy and scared of my Dad, why I got a fear of men, why I felt dirty and ashamed of myself, why I couldn't tell anyone about the rape or assaults, why I felt dirty about sex, why I always felt guilty about anyone who died, and many, many more things. Now I know the answers to my childhood, the answers to all my questions, and it explains everything, so I don't have to carry the guilt, shame and dirty feelings about myself, and I can feel peace of mind and body. I can hope to be able to lead a normal healthy life and help my children to do the same, and teach them that they can always come to me and I would listen. I've always wanted to give my children a better life than I had, but I think I over-did it a bit at times and spoilt them a bit too much. They have to learn that they can't always have everything in life they want. So I have to change my ways of giving them and doing everything for them. It's not easy for the kids either to have to do more for themselves, but we'll get there.

My treatment is almost over now but my life is not. I have a lot to look forward to now.

7

February, Year Two

After Mrs Collins's discharge we were back to weekly sessions. Difficulties mounted rapidly, as a result, I was quite sure, of Mrs Collins's anger and resentment about the reduction of our sessions. I tried without success to help her acknowledge these feelings, and the next interview was relatively empty. She spoke at first only about current or everyday problems with her family, exhibiting a vague helplessness, and then went on to talk about her eldest child, Lee, describing how difficult and uncomfortable that pregnancy had been, and their intense and mutually destructive relationship.

She then spoke at length of her loathing of and refusal to accept any behaviour from her husband which she interpreted as potentially violent, even when she was aware that it was not intended as such. Then Mrs Collins took up another theme, now even more clearly relating to her feelings about me and the reduction in her sessions.

Another thing I was keen on, and still am, is time, and trust, and people's word. I won't say I trusted people, but I hoped they wouldn't let me down on things, like if someone said they would ring me at a certain time, day or week and didn't, I would feel let down.

Time was important to me, so was people's word. I believed what people said. Then I began to disbelieve anyone and everyone. If someone said they'd ring, I'd wait, but didn't believe they would.

Or appointments, I would never believe I would be seen at that time, even though I would still get there on time, just hoping I would.

Then I started thinking it was me. They had something against me or they didn't really want to see or know me, or didn't have time for me. I didn't believe or trust myself. I lost faith in people and myself.

In this disguised way, Mrs Collins was making her feelings about my treatment of her very clear indeed. She was patently using writing as a way of passing information and feelings over to me without having to face me. She felt that she *had* told me – by handing me her writing – but in consequence we sometimes lost the opportunity of addressing directly the very important material she was bringing to the sessions. It was only by strenuous efforts on my part that she would actually tell me any of what she had written, so making it directly available in the session.

She had telephoned only very occasionally in the past, but now began more and more frequently to leave messages with my secretary asking me to ring her, and she seemed to ignore completely what I told her about limiting contact to the sessions themselves. Ostensibly she would be very understanding that I was very busy, or did not always receive the messages within minutes of her calling. Her voice and manner when I returned calls on occasion, however, showed very clearly a vivid resentment that I was not willing to be as accessible to her as she needed me to be. She would tell me at length how impossible it was for her to tolerate her distress, and then wait.

Her capacity for 'splitting' also meant that, despite what she wrote, she never once made the slightest open complaint about the occasions when I kept her waiting. The more I persisted in trying to bring into the open that she was as angry as her written account expressed on these occasions, the more blank she became, with assurances that she understood how busy I must be. In fact, she always arrived at the clinic an hour or more before the time of her appointment and arranged her transport home for an hour or more after the planned end of the appointment, thus ensuring at least three times as much time in the clinic as was required for her session. Her anger about *my* time-keeping was so expressed that she could deny its application to me, thus disarming the anticipated possible anger of my response.

Mrs Collins had remarked on my occasional glances at the clock on the wall of my office, and said how much she disliked noticing me do so.

If I see a doctor and he gives the impression he's not listening to me or seems anxious, I'd take it he wasn't interested in my case and wanted to get rid of me. So I would leave or couldn't talk to them as I felt they didn't want to know. Or if I saw someone I was talking to looking at their watch or clock, they couldn't wait to get rid of me. It sounds terrible, I know, but that was how I felt about things.

Shortly after she wrote this passage, she presented me with a small alarm clock to put on my desk, so that I could glance at it without this being apparent to her. I tried repeatedly and hard to get Mrs Collins to give her voice to what she said in writing, but with no success at all.

She was now giving me great quantities of writing at every session, composed partly of the re-working of memories she had previously written and spoken about, more of her history, and her ruminations on therapy itself. Often I found myself chuckling at the delightful images she painted, while at other times, the continuing sexual provocation in much of what she wrote was patent.

I remember the first time I began to grow marrows. I didn't have any success in getting marrows until Mum was over one day and told me why I wasn't getting any marrows. I didn't believe her at first when she told me what to do and showed me the difference in the flowers: the male and the female flowers, and how to pollinate them. I thought she was pulling my leg. It was so funny, I just couldn't believe it. I just laughed. But she was right, as I found out it worked. The male flower had a point like a man's penis, and the female flower a sort of entrance like a woman's vagina, and you had to pick off the male point and put it into the female hole to pollinate them to get marrows. I'd always thought plants pollinated themselves, or the bees pollinated them, although I didn't know how. I haven't grown any veg or really done any gardening for two years now except to cut the grass. But I might try this year.

Now another piece of the jigsaw was about to be put in place. From time to time, she had referred to a friend called Mavis, with whom she had spent much of her childhood. Mavis and her parents had been a second – and apparently happier – family for her. Now she turned back to this topic.

When I was a kid, I had a friend called Mavis. She was a bit older than me. She suffered with epileptic fits. She was a nice girl in her own way, but people used to say she was a bit funny in the head. To me she wasn't. We used to spend a lot of time together when we could, like best friends. I used to stay at her house a lot at weekends and holidays, when I was allowed. I think my mother was glad to get rid of me for a few days because I used to play her up so much.

Mavis's mum and dad I called Aunty Rene and Uncle Tom. They had a stall in the market not far from our house. It was a vegetable stall. Mavis was an only child.

Mavis and I used to go to her church when I stayed over there some weekends and school holidays. She was a catholic and went to confession Saturday evenings and Mass on Sundays and procession once a month I think. I would always go with her if I was staying there but I was Church of England so I didn't do confession or Mass in her church but I'd sit in the church and wait for her.

I loved her parents. I used to wish they were my parents as they were nice people. They didn't drink or fight like my parents and they treated me nice, I didn't get beaten or sworn at or punished if I made a mistake or wet the bed. Mavis had her own room and I shared with her when I stayed there.

Suddenly I stopped going there or being friends. I don't know why because we used to have a lot of fun. Maybe we had a row, or maybe Mum thought I was enjoying myself and stopped me, but anyway I stopped going. For some reason, Uncle Tom acted peculiar after that. Maybe Mum told him how naughty I was at home – who knows – but he was never the same to me after. And when he died suddenly of a heart attack, I should have been upset. I wasn't, I was glad, a sense of relief I suppose. But I don't know why, or understand, because we used to have such fun. It doesn't make sense, but why it doesn't make sense, I don't know. I'm sure I used to love them and wish they were my parents – then suddenly I didn't. Why? I haven't thought about them for years, and now thinking about them makes me feel uneasy. Maybe it's just because I don't remember what went wrong, and why I couldn't go there any more. Why was I glad when he died? Why do I feel bothered even now after all these years? Why am I feeling angry now?

She was caught in a dilemma: she wanted to drop the whole topic and forget Mavis and her family because she was becoming so disturbed by the memory of them, and at the same time she simply could not stop talking about them. The same topic preoccupied her between sessions. In her writing, and more subtly during the sessions, the subject seemed to be somehow interwoven with her feelings about me. I sensed that these had changed, that some new theme had entered into the attitudes, expectations and feelings from childhood, relating to the major figures in her life then which were projected on to me – the 'transference'. It was not clear however, what this change was. Once again, I did not immediately recognize the obvious. A new *source* of transferential material had emerged: Uncle Tom.

While we were approaching this new area of distress – slowly and with much back-tracking – I recognized only a part of what was going on: that Mrs Collins was struggling with her increasingly strong positive feelings towards me. I felt that there was a very seductive quality in the mixture of her expressions of distress – which I read as an invitation to explore further – and her intense and very thinly disguised appeals for me to respond to her sexually: the only sort of intimacy she knew. People who suffered sexual abuse in childhood commonly experience great difficulty and confusion over affectionate contact and relationships. The only way in which they can relate in such a way is sexually: affection is replaced by sex.

It seemed to me that Mrs Collins might also be using what she had by now learned would keep my interest alive – at least until I made the longed-for response. And at the same time, the distress and the longing for release were also there, and true.

91

I want to forget this part of my life, it makes me feel angry for some reason. I do go on, don't I. Blast it [violent scribbles over the page] There's something terribly wrong here. I can't face it – the anger, the hurt, the pain, it's almost unbearable, but what? I'm trying my hardest to remember, but can't – what's wrong? Mr Karle, I don't mean to let you down. It's not that I don't trust you. I do trust you, more than anyone, more probably than the man I like, but I couldn't tell anyone. Sometimes I wish I could but he would laugh at me I think, and I suppose I know all the reasons or excuses why he wouldn't want to know me.

What do I do, Mr Karle? Can you help me, tell me what to do, how to cope with my feelings? If only I could find out how the man would feel, but how, Mr Karle, I don't know. How? Please help me if you can. [More violent scribbles]

I thought of various things that might have made me feel violently angry. Maybe Uncle Tom had his heart attack in front of me and died and it frightened me, or maybe we had an accident when going or coming home in the van, and I was frightened by it, but it doesn't feel right.

It seemed that she was finding herself caught in a cleft stick. She had desperately wanted to convince me that her improvement made her 'good enough' for me, but at the same time, such an improvement meant she would lose me because therapy would end. However, suspicious as I might be of the covert process in all this, I felt I had to take seriously what she was reporting.

Despite her great affection for this family and the happiness she had known with them, it seemed that she *now* was sure that an event had occurred which had distressed her and brought the happy relationship to an end. We agreed to use hypnosis to explore what had happened with Tom and Rene, Mavis's parents.

The Filthy Lie

Once again, as I suggested she go back through time, now to the age of ten, and to the weekend visit to Mavis's house at which bad things had happened, Mrs Collins seemed to shrink and become a child. In reply to my questions she told me what was happening, but after a while became intensely distressed and asked me to stop it. I suggested she let the picture fade away from her mind and come back to the present day, and bring with her only as much of the memory as she could tolerate. It took a long time for her visible distress to diminish and for her to be able to say that she had successfully closed the scene, switched off the 'video recorder' and returned to the present. When her eyes opened, she began shaking violently and then to weep. It was a considerable time before she was able to tell me what she had experienced.

I went back to them days. Mavis I had believed had fits and I found out one day how her Dad was supposed to be helping her get over these fits. One time, I decided to look to see how he did help her, in case I was ever with her alone and she had one I would know what to do. So I pulled the bedcover back and got a shock. I sat there stunned and shocked for a long time in disbelief. Her father was masturbating her, and she was enjoying it furiously. She'd never had fits at all. She was having this done. Then when she was finished, they tried to do it to me. I got a bit upset by this time and although my aunt came in, I realized she knew about it and was in on it. I thought I ran out, but I'm not so sure now.

There had been more that she could not bring herself to tell me, and she added that she thought there was even more that she could not recall. She felt strongly that she could not cope with uncovering any more about the incident. None the less, she could not leave the subject alone. Painfully, and with

93

intense shame and guilt, she began to recall that she had allowed Uncle Tom to masturbate her, and that she had enjoyed it.

She asked with mounting desperation how this could have been. Gradually the story was further elaborated. She now recalled what had been wholly forgotten before: that some time earlier, she had gone to Rene and told her of the abuse by Mr Baker. Rene had assured her that she would see to it that it did not happen again, and offered to help cure the vaginal soreness which had resulted. Meggie had accepted this offer and Rene had spread a cream on her vulva and within her vagina, and had repeated this in a somewhat lengthy way at each visit. Rene had then told the child that Uncle Tom could help her even more, since he was able to help Mavis with her fits, and again Meggie had acquiesced.

Mrs Collins became progressively more disturbed and demanding over the next few days. Six days after the last session, Heather, her social worker, telephoned me. Mrs Collins was 'very upset' and angry.

I was, at that time, in the habit of using the paper bearing my previous home address as scrap paper and had unthinkingly given a piece of it to Mrs Collins. She had assumed that the address on it was where I lived, and had telephoned the number given, leaving a message on the answering machine asking me to ring her back. Naturally, I had not done so, and she had become very angry, venting this on Heather before slamming the phone down on her. Heather had not left it at that, and despite Mrs Collins's angry insistence that she did not wish to speak with her any more, had rung repeatedly and tried to talk to her, until Mrs Collins had calmed down.

At Heather's insistence, I in turn rang Mrs Collins. She did not permit herself any expression of anger, but was politely disbelieving of my explanation of why I had not returned her call, and responded to my gentle explanation that I was not accessible to her outside the interviews with confusion and some contrition. She assured me she was now perfectly all right. My own anger at her attempted intrusion into my private life remained totally unexpressed and suppressed. I *was* angry, and I felt that at some level that had been Mrs Collins's intention. I thought that, quite unconsciously, Mrs Collins felt that if she could make *me* angry, then her anger at me would be justified, and if I were to express my feelings it would provide a vicarious discharge of her anger with me.

February–March, Year Two

The way in which the abused child becomes the abused adult was vividly illustrated in what happened when Mrs Collins came for her next interview. The receptionist, after welcoming Mrs Collins, forgot to telephone me to say that she had arrived. After a substantial interval, I felt safe in assuming that Mrs Collins had failed to attend as an expression of her anger towards and punishment of me. At last I thought I should check that she had not in fact arrived, only to find, of course, to my considerable chagrin, that she was waiting for me in the waiting-room. She was calm, composed and apparently relaxed, insisting it did not matter that she had been kept waiting. After all, I was a very busy man – and so on. And, of course, the session had to be abbreviated to accommodate my remaining appointments.

Mrs Collins began by speaking about her husband's death, saying that she felt considerable guilt still about Bert's death, principally that she had colluded with the doctors who had advised her not to tell Bert that he had cancer and was terminally ill, thus depriving herself and him of a proper parting. She then shifted to speak about her conviction that there were further gaps in her memory, particularly of the episode with Mavis and her family, and she wished to fill those.

I can't understand why I can remember some bits and not others and why I can remember the soldiers, but not the other rapes and assaults. I remember just bits and pieces. Sometimes I think it's not important to know any more and I just have to accept it, but Lee's been talking about when Bert died and not knowing what was wrong with him, and that's raising doubts in my mind again. It seems to be getting important again and it's annoying me not remembering exactly what or how I felt.

Sometimes it all feels it's been a waste of time. I've been a failure at everything I wanted to do.

At this point, she rummaged in her bag and gave me a sheet of paper.

Failed	*To have had a baby normally*
Failed	*To bring up my kids decently*
Failed	*To have a bike and go cycling with the kids*
Failed	*To have been a good wife*
Failed	*To have a good sex life*
Failed	*To have been able to touch a man*
Failed	*To enjoy life*
Failed	*To have coped better*
Failed	*To have met someone to enjoy life with*
	Failed

This was, of course, in part also an expression of her fear or expectation of failing in what was now so important to her: her relationship with me. Mrs Collins was now becoming aware too of the sadness she felt at the lack of so much in her life she had wished for.

But there were things on the credit side as well. She listed what she felt she had achieved: she was no longer taking psychotropic drugs; she had lost a great deal of weight; she felt that, despite her remaining anxiety about being able to relate to any man, and especially sexually, she actually wanted and felt she needed and might manage such a relationship. But ... she stopped short of a fairy tale ending with her Prince Charming. The neediness which prompted and fuelled these thoughts was vast, and the way in which she suddenly drew back from the brink at this point suggested that she had gained some intimation – like, perhaps, Sartre's 'glimpse into the void' – of the bottomlessness of the needs which she had been repressing for so long in order to survive. She had opened Pandora's box a crack, and had to slam it shut again.

In the course of the next two interviews, she told me the stories of both her father's death and that of Bert. Her father had had an exploratory operation some six years earlier, which had shown such extensive invasions that no attempt could be made at treatment. She and her mother had sat with him a week later while he died.

I felt guilty with Dad dying because I felt a sense of relief like I had with Grandad, and I didn't know why. I thought I loved my Dad, so I couldn't understand my feelings.

Dissociation still ruled. Even now, with the memories she had recovered and the associated feelings, she still could say, 'I thought I loved my Dad.' But then, that was the simple truth: she *did* love her Dad, just as much as she hated him, and as much as she feared him.

One of the central themes in Matte-Blanco's monumental book *The Unconscious as Infinite Sets* is that of the essential infinity of unconscious attitudes and feelings – that each and every feeling and thought in the 'unconscious' is necessarily accompanied by its opposite, and by the infinite gamut between. At that level, Mrs Collins – like all of us – loved, hated, feared, admired, despised, yearned for and fled from her father, but only one aspect and so far, largely the positive, of this infinite range of feeling could be tolerated within consciousness. And the diametric opposite, as indeed the full range in between, could be accommodated only unconsciously, symbolically or by displacement.

Then followed the story of her husband's dying. Not long after retiring, he had collapsed, and began to pass blood rectally. She rang for an ambulance and he was taken to hospital. In the course of the next few days, he was found to have a large tumour. The prognosis was bad.

At this point, a confusion came into the story. She first told me that she had insisted to the hospital staff that Bert was not to be told how serious his condition was, being sure herself that she knew he would not wish to know. Later, she told me that it was the doctors who insisted he should not know, and this became a point of intense anxiety and guilt, fuelled by the fact that her eldest child, who regarded Bert as his father, although knowing he was not, berated her for denying Bert the opportunity of fighting against his illness and thereby herself becoming responsible for his death.

Bert had had an operation and came home some time after it, when the family were able to go on holiday, although there were many alarums and excursions in the interim. Not long after their return, he had to go back into hospital, and a further operation was carried out. A month later, trouble emerged again, and it was found that the last operation had created new problems. A few days later, when she rang the hospital yet again, it was suggested to her that perhaps she should come there and then.

I knew things were worse and said I'd be up. My neighbour said she'd look after the kids, and her husband ran me up there. I didn't know what to expect, but I did think Bert'd be asleep, but he wasn't. There were about three or four nurses round the bed doing things. When Bert saw me he asked me what I was doing there, and I didn't know what to say, so I mumbled something about 'You know how I am, I couldn't sleep so I thought I'd come up.' I think I must have given the game away, he kept saying 'You must be tired, you should go home and get some rest.'

He'd doze off most of the time, I just sat there holding his hand. The doctor said things looked dodgy as they thought it might be his kidneys.

Then about 4.15 in the morning, the nurse asked me if I would like a cup of coffee and I went to the kitchen with her instead of staying with Bert, which I've always regretted. But I felt a need to talk to someone, or a break from sitting there feeling useless, so I went with her. I was talking to her about Bert and she was just stirring the coffee, when a noise went off and she ran out of the kitchen before I could think what was wrong.

She grabbed the crash trolley and ran back to the ward. I ran after her. Bert's lights were on and the screens partly round. As I ran I could hear the bed springs going on the bed. Sister was on top of Bert pressing his chest up and down. I panicked and ran to the patients' sitting room, crying and shaking.

A student nurse came in and talked to me saying that as they were there at the time he stopped breathing, there was still a chance, and I began to believe her. I wanted to believe her, but then sister came in and said she was sorry they hadn't been able to save him.

They gave me some brandy or whisky but I couldn't really believe it had happened and felt guilty for leaving him when I did. I asked to see Bert again, and I went and hugged him crying. When I looked at his face, one of his eyes had come open. I screamed. I felt Bert was blaming me for leaving him and angry with me for it.

The blame she believed she had seen in Bert's eye was still there, joining with the guilt she felt for not letting Bert know of the seriousness of his condition, and thereby, she felt, denying him a chance of life.

The following week showed a change. The detailed disclosure to me of this traumatic period had allowed her to re-evaluate how she had dealt with Bert's death.

I've suddenly realized I don't feel guilty any more. Don't ask me why, I don't really know. I think I did what I thought was right for Bert and myself and I know Bert wouldn't want me to have felt guilty. He always told me I should do what I thought was right or best. If you hadn't asked me I would still have avoided thinking about Bert and not realized I didn't feel guilty any more. I feel good to realize this, as I wanted Bert to die peacefully and not worry about me and the kids and be frightened of dying. So I feel pretty good realizing I did what I thought best for Bert's sake. Whether or not it was the right decision is not what matters too much. It's why I did it and that I thought and believe I did the right thing that counts.

The change which struck me was not only in her withdrawal from blame and guilt, but also in:

I feel pretty good ... I did what I thought was best ...

Something else struck me at this time: although Mrs Collins was still producing new memories and events for our sessions, the more recent were less salacious and apparently seductive, and had an air of greater reality. I began to feel less that she was prolonging therapy at any cost, and was reminded of the recurring couplet in Donne's 'Hymn to God the Father':

> When Thou hast done, Thou hast not done,
> For I have more.

With, I could now hope, the prospect of reaching the final lines:

> And having done that, Thou hast done,
> I feare no more.

Now Mrs Collins returned to the question of *why* she had been so appallingly treated both as a child and in her adult years. Her original assumption, that it was her intrinsic wickedness which had deserved such retribution, had largely faded, but she was aware that there was something about her that somehow drew abuse upon her. Now she seemed to recognize something I had suggested: that her fear of what men did to her, and her semi-conscious expectation of abuse, were sensed by a certain type of man, and drew them to assault her.

She told me that she had carefully sounded out one of her sisters, Lizzy, about Mr Baker. She had learned from her that Mr Baker had been well known for interfering with little girls. He had attempted to interfere with at least two of her sisters. Someone other than their mother must have been more responsive, since the police had trapped Mr Baker in the act and he had gone to prison. Mrs Collins felt an enormous sense of relief at discovering she was not the only one to whom Mr Baker had done these things, but the relief was heavily mixed with further confused feelings about, and incomprehension of, her mother's inaction. Her sister had said: 'Mum had no gumption, and she never wanted to know, and never said or did anything about Mr Baker.' Mrs Collins herself, however, side-stepped the consequences of this new information about her mother by once again herself taking responsibility for her mother's passivity.

I guess you could say that about me, really. I didn't say anything or do anything about Mr Baker, or anyone else, when I was a kid – apart from the first time with Dad.

Lizzy said that when Mr Baker tried it on her she told Mum but Mum didn't do anything about it. She was very hurt by Mum's attitude. She was about eight at the time, so I would have been at boarding school then. This really made my day. I know it sounds terrible, but to know I wasn't the only one really makes me feel less ashamed.

I felt this was something we should pursue strenuously, but Mrs Collins was determined on another direction: that of the gap in her memory concerning Mavis and her family. She had dropped into my lap this piece of information about her mother – which she obviously found quite unmanageable – but she simply *could* not look at what it meant to her. I acceded to her urgent and insistent request to explore the gap in her memory, once again yielding to subtle pressures and bypassing my own judgement.

She regressed in age once more. In reply to my questions, she told me what was happening, but after a while became intensely distressed.

I can't hear what they're saying. Tom's rubbing away at me and she's rubbing him, he's doing it harder to me and she's doing it harder to him. There's something on my legs.

At this point, the struggling movements Mrs Collins was making became more pronounced, and she moved her legs quite violently as though trying to escape.

He's sitting on top of me and I'm all wet. He's getting off me and Rene's saying something. Get her away from me! Get her away! Please get her away.

Then, with even more distress:

Get her away, Mavis, make her get away from me, make them stop, let go, please, make them stop.

I intervened here. Her manifest distress was becoming so great that I felt she could not tolerate any more. I told her to let her adult self provide the reassurance and comfort her child self so desperately needed. I added the usual suggestions of forgetting whatever could not be tolerated, and at length, she was calm again.

On returning to the present, Mrs Collins expressed real anger for the very first time towards her mother for having made herself inaccessible to her when she needed her protection and comfort. This, I thought, was the beginning of a major breakthrough.

After a great deal of hesitation, she went on to say that what Rene had done had been 'worse than what Mr Baker had done'.

The experience she had retrieved in this session was that, after she had discovered what Uncle Tom was doing to his daughter Mavis, she had been urged to 'let Tom do it to her'. Rene had come back into the room, and when Meggie appealed to her to stop this, Rene had herself urged her to 'let Tom', saying that it was time she learned about sex. She had continued to protest, and had been forcibly held down by Mavis and Rene while Tom attempted intercourse. He had ejaculated on to her thighs, and Rene had then licked his ejaculate away.

104

It was only after this that she had been allowed to escape, and had hurriedly dressed and fled the house, never to return.

It was Rene's behaviour which Mrs Collins had found the most horrifying. She could understand Tom's actions. In her view, men simply sought ejaculation by any means – but Mavis's acceptance of masturbation was incomprehensible, and Rene's evident pleasure in such bizarre perversity was beyond all possible comprehension. Homosexuality, especially between women, made her feel sick.

Mrs Collins was vividly distressed by this experience. We had a little time left to talk through this experience, and, promising that we would talk about this at our next meeting, I helped her calm herself enough to leave.

9

Mrs Collins could recall little of what had emerged in the last
session. She remembered she felt very upset at the end, and
afterwards, and thought that she had been rude to the receptionist in consequence. She was very apologetic about this,
but seemed otherwise wrapped in an impenetrable blanket of
defensiveness. Every time I asked her to go back to the 'orgy',
she talked about something else. First she spoke of redecorating
her house and described what she had done so far. It sounded
like a complete ground-to-roof refit, and I felt some alarm about
the risks of such exertions in view of her none-too-sound heart.
It seemed to me that the refurbishing of her home was a
symbolic re-enactment of the process that she was experiencing
in therapy.

No matter how much I tried to get her 'back on course', she
found something else to tell me: what her elder daughter had
been doing; Lee; the pain in her back; *anything* except Mavis,
Tom, and Rene. At length, I turned to another and urgent
topic: an impending break in our sessions.

At this time, my own health was deteriorating; it seemed
that I had returned too early to work after the operation in
December, and I had been advised to take a month away from
work to recuperate. I postponed this a little to allow me to give
as much warning as possible to my clients.

I was more worried about Mrs Collins than about any of my

other clients. Her early experiences of betrayal and her firm belief that she was of no importance made her seem more vulnerable than others, but an underlying feeling – which as usual was much easier to recognize in retrospect – was of my quite profound, if irrational, need to avoid her anger.

About half-way through the allotted hour, I changed the subject, and told Mrs Collins that there would have to be a break in our sessions in a few weeks' time as I would be away for several weeks. I said nothing of the reasons for this, careful not to re-arouse any fantasies of her involvement in my being unwell. She made very little of what I told her, and ignored or brushed aside my inquiries as to her reactions to the impending break. Ostensibly, she was not concerned about anything at all, and the interview trailed away in trivia.

In the days that followed, she began to alarm Heather again, both by her strange manner when visited and by her anti-pathetic and rejecting attitude when Heather telephoned her from time to time. Heather rang me on one of the days I was working at home, insisting that Mrs Collins was in a desperate condition and asking that I should ring her. With feelings of despair and anger, yet with considerable anxiety that Mrs Collins was playing the suicide-blackmail card once again and that if I did not respond she might go too far, I accepted this latest request to breach the boundaries of therapy.

I recognized within myself two additional pressures. The first, familiar – though perhaps not always consciously – to everyone engaged in this kind of work, is the fear that if a client attempts to die, let alone succeeds in the attempt, the therapist is under threat. The therapist may hear the Coroner's voice in his head, raised in disbelief that the therapist did not respond to such an appeal on the grounds that action on his part would transgress the 'therapeutic boundaries'.

The other was more personal. I had by now made a massive investment in Mrs Collins's story, emotionally, in terms of time and effort, not to say stress. Further self-damage or even suicide would invalidate all we had achieved.

So I telephoned Mrs Collins as Heather asked. She seemed to be in a very disturbed state, speaking incomprehensibly in broken sentences, expressing violent anger towards her parents. This was interspersed with apologies and contrition directed both at them and at me. I understood this as a manifestation of her reaction to the approaching separation from me, especially since I had been quite unable to get her to face up to her feelings on this score in our last session.

There were grounds for Heather's anxiety: Mrs Collins could very easily resort to self-damaging behaviour again, and might well create some sort of emergency. But at a less conscious level, it seemed that Heather also was reacting to an impulse that was neither objective nor professional: a 'mothering' impulse, one which was no stranger to me. Both Heather and I had allowed the definition of our roles to become blurred, and their boundaries to be broken: we had accepted the projections of 'Mother' and 'Father'. In consequence, we both felt pressures from Mrs Collins far beyond those appropriate to our professional functions: we were both too *personally* involved.

When Mrs Collins came next, she said that she had been looking at a framed photograph of her parents when I had telephoned her and that she had smashed it while speaking to me. She was feeling a great deal of anger towards both me and Heather too, and her ambivalence was transparent – but revealed only in the pages she gave me, and not in any single spoken word.

108

I'm pissed off with her questions, why this and why that, I'm pissed off because I want to hurry up and get to the bottom of things and deal with it, and get this knot of anger out and the hatred I sort of feel, and the bitterness. It wants to explode and I can't let it but I desperately need to. I wish I could but I can't do it alone. I'm afraid to. I might do something I'd regret. So what do I do? You say I have just to work and be patient even if I have to work till I drop. I hope I don't drop until I know everything, then at least I could drop in peace.

I feel hatred and bitterness at Mum at the moment. Hopefully I will get over that. I feel sorry for Mum as well, for being as she was, although I'm not sure what that was. Whatever it was, I don't want to be like it. If anyone says again I'm like Mum, I'll kill them.

Mrs Collins appeared indeed to be beginning to experience the hatred and anger towards her mother which I was so sure was present, but I was not at all sure that she herself fully recognized this yet. It seemed to me that her rage with her mother, however real in itself, was now actually a cover for similar feelings about me, but that mother was a safer target for them than myself at this moment. Therefore they were re-directed or displaced a second time. That all this was still not conscious for her was confirmed by the fact that Mrs Collins also complained now of various physical symptoms: a clear manifestation of the conflicts between her feelings.

Psychotherapists not infrequently inspire anger, scepticism, and rejection by what can appear to the 'outsider' to be a doctrinaire insistence that *everything* stems from psychic roots. My thinking of Mrs Collins's physical pain as demonstrating her inner conflicts could be seen as an example of this position. To be sure, acceptance of the role of emotional states in the aetiology of all physical illnesses is growing, but even so it can seem dogmatic and unrealistic to ascribe all illness and pain to the psyche. The middle path, expressed in one of my favourite aphorisms, perhaps resolves this: 'Things are rarely either-or. They are usually both-and.'

At this interview, Mrs Collins handed me the now weekly sheaf of paper. She told me that further memories had surfaced over the intervening week, and that she had written them all down, but did not want to tell me herself. I had told her repeatedly that I would not read what she had written, during the interview, and that we would discuss only what she told me in person. I also interpreted to her – yet again – that she was avoiding dealing with her feelings about me and my reactions through writing instead of talking face to face, and that writing had become a way of 'testing the water' without actually getting wet. It was not and could not be, I insisted, a substitute for telling me directly, no matter how difficult that might be. Bit by bit, she began to tell me.

The story was of a time in her teens when she had a date with a boy, and, while waiting for him, had noticed that she was close to where Mr Baker's shop had been. She had impulsively set fire to her dress to 'burn the dirt away', and ended with a brief stay in hospital. She went on:

Heather said once I looked upon you, Mr Karle, like a kind of father figure. She couldn't be more wrong. The last thing I want or need is a father figure. I don't mean that offensively. For a start, you're not old enough to be my father and I don't want a father. I had enough of my own one. I let her think what she wants as it makes her think she knows me. I feel so restless. I know what I want and

*I know I can't have it, so how can I live when I have nothing to
live for.*

*Sometimes I feel like two different people. One who's good and
understands and accepts things and wants to carry on. But the
second one feels so bad, so dirty and ashamed and feels it's all her
fault, and won't listen to reason. I don't think you've met that one
really.*

Once more, I turned over in my mind the vexing question of
whether this was an expression of her growing awareness
of her dissociative defences – her way of keeping intolerable memories and feelings out of consciousness by splitting
them off and removing them from awareness – and expressing this in a pictorial way, or whether it reflected her growing contact with an actual separate part-personality. And
again I failed to tackle her feelings about me and what she
wanted from me. 'I know what I want and I can't have
it.'

The following week, she told me that she had had a further
talk with her sisters about their childhood home and experiences. She had carefully and indirectly probed around the topic
of their father, and had been told without any special emphasis
that it was well known in the family that he had 'interfered
with' most of his daughters. Their mother had even seen him
fondling her stepdaughter. She had actually mentioned to one
of Mrs Collins's sisters that she knew of his abuse of Meggie,
and still had done nothing.

Mrs Collins's principal reaction was relief that it was not only
she who had been abused by her father. Despite considerable
probing on my part, she still seemed aware of no feelings about
her mother's inactivity when faced with the knowledge of

what was being done to her daughters. At last she began to speak of *feeling*.

I wish Lizzy hadn't told me about Mum. I think it's dragged me down and whatever confidence I was getting, I seem to be losing since she told me. It hurts like hell knowing Mum knew all along about Dad. She put me through hell because she wouldn't do anything about it, so my life was ruined because she wouldn't face it.

She was not angry, only hurt – 'like a knife being twisted in my mind and my insides' – at the knowledge that her mother had always known that she had been telling the truth. It seemed to me that the anger which was being expended on Heather and, more indirectly, on me, was connected with this information and Mrs Collins's powerful resistance to acknowledging any real negative feelings towards her mother.

And at last, Mrs Collins began to talk about what we had discovered the week before: the 'orgy', as she came to call it, with Mavis and her parents. She was determined to find out more of what had happened.

She could not see that it was this episode which had been causing her to feel greatly disturbed and to behave oddly and destructively during the preceding week. The photograph of her parents that she kept on the mantelpiece had similarly begun to obsess her. She had felt anger increasing inside her, but could not understand why.

In hypnosis, we used once again the 'TV' image, and I asked her to start the tape playing as before. I had asked her at the outset to give me a running commentary of what she saw, so that she would remain in touch with me.

Mrs Collins again described the memory, but this time con-

112

tinued from the point at which Rene had started to lick her and she herself had struggled and screamed – the point at which she had asked me to rescue her when we had 're-played' the episode for the first time.

She's not taking any notice of me, just going on and on as if I'm not there, just going on and on. I've stopped screaming now, just staring, staring at the light bulb and the light shade. I can't feel anything now, just staring at the light shade.

She's stopped now. I can see they're laughing at me but I can't hear. I must get out. I'm crawling to the door on my hands and knees. They've stopped noticing me now and they're just cuddling each other. I've got to get my clothes and fix my hearing aid so I can listen for them. Now I'm opening the door, looking and listening and running and running. I'm scared, very scared they might come after me.

I've opened the door and I'm crawling out. Now I'm running up to Mavis's room, and lock the door. I'm grabbing my hearing aid so's I could hear them if they come after me. I'm putting on my clothes, and I'm going to the door and listening there. I can't hear anything so I unlock it and run down the stairs and out of the house, all shaking and terrified.

At this point, I instructed Mrs Collins to intervene in her adult self, intercept the child, and provide comfort, reassurance and especially an awareness of her survival. I emphasized the importance of conveying to her child self that she and the woman who was comforting her were one and the same person. This appeared to be totally unsuccessful: Mrs Collins said the child was unmanageable, and added: 'She'll never be clean again.'

Mrs Collins clearly needed some further strategy to enable

her to overcome these feelings of irremediable contamination. I decided to try to use the 'Private Place' she had developed in our very first session, in the hope that she might react automatically to the suggestion of 'going there'. When I suggested she go to the fields by the church with the friendly lambs, and take her child self with her, she refused. I persisted, with as much persuasion as I could muster, until Mrs Collins reported that she had achieved this. There was obviously more work to do on this memory, but that would have to wait until a later occasion.

Mrs Collins seemed calm, although shaken and exhausted. The writing she did in the following week showed very clearly that her hidden rage was becoming more and more apparent. When would it emerge in my presence, open and without disguise, displacement or dissimulation?

10

For some time, Mrs Collins had been thinking more and more about paying a visit to her childhood home. At last, she asked if I would accompany her. With some reservations about spreading our contact outside proper interviews, I agreed. We were to discuss a date for this later.

In the papers she gave me, Mrs Collins had written even more clearly how much she wanted *more*. As soon as she had left the clinic after the last session, she felt a strong need to talk more about the last episode, and lacking this, she felt 'very bad', and unable to deal with what the session had brought up.

She was, however, able to express in writing what she would not articulate in person: her rage with her mother for failing her when she could have saved her daughter from all this suffering.

'If you can't trust your mother, whom can you trust?' She wrote that she had taken off her mother's rings, which she normally wore continuously, and added numerous apologies to me for being such a nuisance, and profuse thanks for what I had done so far, all of which seemed to me to be heavily disguised hints at further thoughts of suicide.

Among what she gave me the following week was the following passage:

I'm going to write a list of questions for you. Hopefully you may be able to answer some of them to me – that's if you remember. You know, you should get your memory seen to. I'm only joking, of course. I've only got my own problems to remember. You've got so many people's problems, and even maybe your own, so it's not surprising you've got a bad memory. For some things, maybe you should tape or write them down more. But then you'd probably forget the tape or paper. I'm not laughing at you here. I'm only joking about this, so please don't take this the wrong way.

Her ambivalence towards me was as intense as that towards her mother, the transference involving both positive feelings – affection, love, dependency, trust – and the negative counterparts resulting from the expected or assumed betrayal of those feelings: hate, distrust, and rage. The difficulty she had in actually telling me, either in person or through her writing, about the events that had taken place with Rene, Tom, and Mavis stemmed from a similarly transferred fear that I would reject her as 'filthy': I would be so disgusted with her that I would turn away from her just as her mother had done, perhaps even tell her that she was lying.

In consequence, her telephone calls grew more frequent: if I called back immediately, and she could feel that I was there for her, then she felt safer.

She also wrote extensively at this time about the importance of being truthful and her fear of being thought to be lying. These ruminations were related to the same theme and were a way, perhaps, of telling me that she was not lying, whatever I might think. She still believed, however, that the anger she felt, usually expressed only covertly, but occasionally explicitly, albeit usually displaced or somehow rationalized, had to be disguised by a careful insistence that she was 'only joking'.

A cornerstone of her feelings about herself and her mother was the latter's accusation of her lying about her father's molestation. In consequence, any question from me as to the truth of the stories she had told me would have seemed to her an exact replica of her mother's disbelief and would also make her feel that my offer of understanding was unreal, dissembled, and untrustworthy. Her repetitive insistence on her truthfulness was part of her anxiety about this possibility. Another aspect of the transference showed in her inability to respond to my invitation to her to explore the rage and hatred she was repressing. As a child, she had not been allowed to be angry; therefore she simply could not perceive that I accepted her anger. Being angry was wicked.

The theme of her longing for union with me was interwoven with despairing and suicidal thoughts.

I still want to shoot myself, but won't (well, at least not yet). I must be fair. I owe you a lot and should give you the chance to convince me. I owe you that. But please don't ask or expect me to spend the rest of my life on my own. I couldn't do that. You've helped me this far, so I'm relying on you to help me the rest of the way. I will fight as long as I've got some hope in me, and I've got hope in you, so that will keep me going for now.

'Look after me and make me better, or else.' Quite openly too she was saying that this was a life-long expectation: 'Don't expect me to spend the rest of my life on my own ... I'm relying on you to help me the rest of the way.' If I did not respond to her telephone calls, then this was evidence of my not caring about her. This grossly needy child appealing to be nurtured and loved was all too real, and painfully so.

The transition from dependence to independence is difficult and painful enough as the natural process of childhood and adolescence; it was far more difficult and painful for Mrs Collins, who had no *positive* experience of dependency and its resolution on which to draw.

It seemed to me that Mrs Collins might go on discovering more and more traumata, both to keep my attention and concern, and to divert us from the painful task of looking directly and openly at the relationship between us.

Recognizing *now* some part of the collusive avoidance which had been taking place, I resolved that, when she next came, I would spend some time reviewing where we had reached, and determined firmly that I would bring the transference into explicit focus now.

My good intentions and firm plans again came to nothing. The pressure of the demands she was making, my fear of upsetting her and increasing the risk that she would overdose or otherwise injure herself and thus end therapy prematurely – and expose my inadequacy as a therapist – seemed to combine to dilute whatever control I attempted to take.

It is highly probable that my marked post-operative ill-health at this time stemmed at least in part from the stress of the daily intrusions that Mrs Collins made. And equally the reverse was true: my own debilitation weakened my efforts to re-focus therapy.

Mrs Collins again asked whether I would go with her to visit her childhood home, and we agreed on the following week. We met at the hospital and took a taxi to the end of the street where she had lived until she had finally left home. Mrs Collins was very composed as we made the journey, but her composure was quite visibly maintained only by effort. I had taken a camera at Mrs Collins's request to record the visit.

We made non-committal conversation as we were driven to our destination. At the end of the rather run-down and seedy street, we left the taxi and walked through the market which still filled the upper end of the street as it had done in Mrs Collins's childhood. The street was littered with piles of wrapping, boxes – rubbish of all sorts. Mrs Collins gave little grunts as though of recognition as we picked our way through the detritus of market trade, and then she began to point out landmarks she recognized until we reached the site of the row of houses in which her family home had stood.

That was now an open space. Mrs Collins stopped, and looked through the fence around the area gazing without expression at the empty space where the scenes of her childhood had been played out. We went into the site, explaining to a workman there that this had been where Mrs Collins's childhood home had stood which she was revisiting after thirty years. The man knew little of the history of the place, although he had lived in the area for many years himself: he was not sure when the houses had been demolished. We walked to the exact area of her one-time home. Mrs Collins stood on the spot where the kitchen had been, her face still completely expressionless, and then walked to the wall that now separated this area from the railway cutting at the back.

Here had been the fence with the nails on which she had cut herself when climbing over to get to the railway lines and the coal yard beyond; there the tunnel through which the trains had approached; there the site of the coal yard, now a derelict piece of waste land; that was where the water tower had stood, in which her brothers and sisters had swum, and where she herself had once swum. Now, of course, the trains

119

were electric, but in those days they had been driven by steam. The memories flowed, Mrs Collins maintaining a rigid control over the feelings that accompanied them.

I found it difficult to picture the row of houses in so small a space, especially as they had also had the back gardens which had figured so vividly in her memories of her rabbit. We left the site and walked further down the street.

There was the alley in which she had hidden so often, curled into a ball to try and block out what Mr Baker had done – wet, cold, hurt, and alone, utterly alone. Or was it that one? Perhaps it had been further along. And there had stood the wooden platform on which the small lock-up shops had stood, the platform under which she had hidden for several days and nights after that final, especially horrifying, assault by Mr Baker. Still not the slightest sign of reaction. Her control held, her comments made in a flat tone as though describing something of no especial interest or importance.

She showed more signs of feeling when we walked to an adjoining shopping area, especially when she pointed out the shop that had been Mr Baker's. She sat down on the bench opposite for a moment, but did not want to linger, and readily assented when I suggested it was time we left.

We walked back up the street, through the market, and looked for a taxi to take us back to the station where we would each catch a train home. As we travelled back, she began to relax, and by the time we reached the station and parted, she seemed in full control again.

On my return to work early in May, Mrs Collins told me of the other efforts she had been making to gather more information about her childhood. She had been to the Council offices and had obtained copies of documents and photographs of the area, and had approached the Social Services Department to trace any records of the time she had spent in care.

Despite this, she had felt even more suicidal during the break. She had telephoned my home at least once, clearly not believing that I had gone away, and had spent many hours on the telephone to the Samaritans. She despaired even of my reading what she had written – and she set a trap for me. In the middle of a passage about the visit we had paid together, she wrote:

You know, I don't know if you read any of this half the time. For all I know, you may glance at it and throw it away. Not that I'd blame you, but I'd be interested to know if you do. If you get to this page, I'll know you really read all this. If you answer this, I'll know you do. If you don't, I'll know you don't.

The visit to her old home had, after all, not laid any ghosts. If anything, it had made her *more* desperate, *more* unhappy, *more* angry. And she had become even more mistrustful of me, and reprimanded me for what she saw as a deception:

You said you was going to be away two weeks, but it was four, to the day. I won't tell you what I'm thinking right now, you wouldn't like it. So don't ask, you wouldn't like the answers.

But when we actually met – not a word of reproach at the supposed deception, no anger, nor indeed anything but a polite conviction that I had been deliberately avoiding her. The only topic she would speak about was her back pain, even though what she had written was much to the point. Repeatedly and insistently, I asked her to tell me what was in the bundle of papers rather than leave it with me to read later – but to no avail. Later I read:

121

The Filthy Lie

I don't know if I'm going to be here when you get back, Mr Karle. It all depends how soon the doctors will help me. I don't intend to wait another 35 years to get the right help. I can't. Do you understand?. Surely I don't have to suffer any more. I wish you was here so's I could talk to you about it. I know you would say I should live, but can you tell me why?

How do I stop this? Please tell me what to do. I don't know if this pain is real any more. It hurts like hell, it feels real, but is it? If it's in my mind, can't you get rid of it for me? All I can do is wait – for you, for the doctors. That's the name of the game – wait. That's been my whole life – wait and see what happens. WAIT, WAIT, WAIT, that's all I hear.

I should count myself lucky I got your help, Mr Karle, and that you've put up with me and that you've helped me so much. I'm just sorry I got this back pain to come along and get me down and cause me to feel so low.

In an envelope, she enclosed the following letter:

Mr Karle

I'm going away, but before I go I'll try to write the rest of what I remember. It's not going to be easy for me, but when you've read it, you'll know why I had to go, remembering something about myself. I was and still am such a coward, I had to go do whatever he said. I was too scared for my life.

I'll post it to you before I go. I'm going to a place where I used to find some peace. Maybe I'll find some peace again.

You know what they did, but you don't know what I had to do. I can't face anyone knowing what I had to do for him.

When we met for the next appointment, she said nothing of

all this, nor showed any response to anything I suggested. Her only overt reaction was when I told her, yes, I had read what she had written. For a moment, she could not remember the trap she had set for me, then she was able to laugh. I tried to make her talk about her feelings about my protracted absence, but as usual without any success at all. She would only talk about various difficulties with members of her family, but the reference in what she wrote was obviously to her feelings about the way she felt I was treating her. She described her resentment at the way she was automatically expected to help any of the family who wanted anything, and at finding herself feeding them, at letting them use her telephone: resentment at the exploitation in which she indulged them without any effective restraint. The parallel was patent: she was exploited and abused, unable to establish and maintain her own boundaries, and exploited and abused me, who in turn could not insist on my own privileges of that kind. Her ambivalence was very obvious, yet totally hidden from her. Mine was equally there: I was angry and resentful at her refusal to *say to my face* what she had written, at her evasion of the topics which she herself had expressed in writing and towards which I was trying to direct her.

We got nowhere. The change from her greater openness before the break to this apparently impenetrable resistance was a statement. The implication was obvious to me: she felt betrayed by my going away and was angry in consequence. I made this explicit several times and in different ways, but the interpretation was roundly rejected. No, of course she was not angry, after all I had my life to lead, I needed a holiday and deserved it – with the nearly explicit implication that she of course would not be so entitled, whatever her needs might be.

I felt I was being well and truly punished and was vividly aware of some degree of irritation myself.

I was genuinely concerned about my own health and well-being. I was putting and had put a great deal of time, effort, thought and care into her treatment, and felt no small resentment at her 'lack of cooperation' and her dishonesty in denying the feelings which were patently present. My irritation was heightened by the way in which she could express anger more openly, and occasionally quite explicitly – even if always 'explained away' – only in writing. The fact that I had found no way of enabling her to bring it fully into the open between us, even by reading out to her what she had written, made me feel frustrated, and therefore angry towards her. Since interpretations, and my willingness to receive her anger and thereby enable her to acknowledge it, were proving futile, I sat back and waited until she could bring herself to be more open. It seemed that nothing I could do or say would facilitate the acknowledgement of her confused and ambivalent feelings.

I had long since begun to regret suggesting that she write her thoughts and memories down, as this had become so effective an evasion for her. Although I had not fallen into her trap, and did refer from time to time to what she had written, the feelings of which she wrote were somehow a secret between us: she knew that I knew – and that was all.

I know it may sound a rotten thing to say to you, but right now I hate my mother more than those who did me harm. I feel that if she'd helped or listened to me in the first place I may not have had to go through all that filth and pain and maybe a lot of others would not have had to go through things as well.

When I quoted this to her, she would attend only to the last point in it: had her mother listened to her, then other children would not have been molested by Mr Baker. The more personal reference – especially to her feeling of hatred – was shrugged off, diminished, played down, almost denied.

There seemed to be so much understanding and real insight when she was writing, and it all appeared to be going to waste because she could look at what she knew in her heart only when alone. It showed so clearly what is in all the textbooks and was wholly familiar to me from my own experience: that it is not enough to know, to understand, when alone. Insight is ineffectual unless it is shared with the therapist, and in person. For the umpteenth time I cursed my apparent inability to help her to bring all this into the sessions.

Mrs Collins returned now to a theme from her adult years. She had been living alone in a rented flat and working as a nursing auxiliary in a hospital, when she had been visited one evening by one of her brothers and a friend of his, Chas. At the end of the evening, her brother had gone home, but Chas insisted that he was too tired to go home, and he would sleep on the sofa. During the night, he had come into her bedroom and crept into bed with her, assuring her he meant no more than to get warm. Before long, however, he had insisted upon intercourse. He had not actually forced her physically to consent, nor had he actually threatened violence if she resisted, but potential violence was implicit, and in any case automatically expected by Meggie.

She had become pregnant. The pregnancy had carried very mixed feelings. It reassured her that she was normal, but she had not been a willing partner in its conception. She now would have something of her own, someone to love, but the baby was also a living reminder of her shame and weakness at permitting Chas to have intercourse with her.

This mixture of feelings was very plainly visible in her handling of Lee. She could never be firm with him, or do anything he might throw back at her as rejection, not only because of her own unsupported childhood, but because of her guilt at her actually violently rejecting feelings towards him as the product of and testimony to her 'cowardice' and shame. It was, of course, her guilt at the one time she had been really firm with him that had led to self-mutilation, and the disclosure which had launched us on therapy.

And he was, of course, a male. Her horror when a visiting social worker had commented on the fact that her way of playing with Lee when he was beginning to grow up seemed to be rather sexualized had made her stop this 'play-fighting' at the time, but she was still heavily embroiled in what was evidently a highly eroticized relationship with him. Her horror at her own semi-conscious recognition of the sexual elements in their relationship served to intensify her ambivalence and fear.

This seemed to be related to the anxious ruminations about her supposed submission and lack of resistance to Mr Baker in the newly discovered events at which she was hinting in her writing at this time. It also related to utterly confused feelings about Rene, which had assumed even greater strength than before. Mrs Collins had some insight that there was a connection between these feelings and her refusal to see Heather or to talk to her, to trust her in any way, but could not avoid reacting to Heather quite automatically with anger, hostility and feelings of betrayal.

11

The following week, Mrs Collins was in a great deal of physical discomfort, and complained that the pain she was experiencing in her back and one leg was getting her down badly. The rheumatologist had told her that one of her intervertebral discs had narrowed and that this was causing the pain. She was offended because he had told her she should lose weight – apparently he was either unaware of or unimpressed by the amount she had already lost. Her pain successfully blocked my attempts to move towards more purposeful work. In the end, I capitulated and suggested that we use hypnotic techniques to reduce the pain she felt. I thought that this would both convey my concern and reassure her enough to allow us to resume therapy, quite apart from the direct benefit of pain reduction.

She responded well, and was pleased at the increased comfort she gained. The following week, this effort seemed to pay some dividends: Mrs Collins was ready to talk more meaningfully and to the point about herself again.

She took me aback by asking if I would explain the facts of sexuality of which she was ignorant. For example, what was orgasm like, since she simply did not know if she had ever experienced one? She enjoyed my pointing out that I was the wrong gender to describe this adequately. She wanted to know if satisfaction and ejaculation were synonymous for a man,

127

what it was a man needed, what a woman's part in intercourse should be, and so on. There was no mistaking the invitation to intimacy: intercourse – albeit verbally and by proxy – with me.

Mrs Collins's manner of relating to men in her everyday life was vividly illustrated in that session. Her apparent seductiveness and flirtatiousness were probably just as strongly signalled to other men. However, if anyone acted upon it, Mrs Collins would undoubtedly and, to herself quite realistically, have screamed 'Rape'. The behaviour she had learned to adopt in order to elicit affection from men was indistinguishable from an invitation to sex. Her confusion had its origins in the fact that she had never had the opportunity, as a child, to learn the difference between affectionate contact and inappropriately sexual contact.

Another question eventually came: how does conception relate to satisfaction or its lack? She was apparently confused because she had conceived her first two pregnancies through rape, but had been unable to conceive when she wanted to in her first marriage. Although there was a strong seductive undertone in all this, the resumption of apparent trust and contact was important to foster. There seemed also to be something in the questions that involved some sort of decontamination for her of the whole subject of sex. This seemed too valuable to ignore or to discount in favour of articulating her flirtatiousness and clarifying the nature of our relationship, and I felt that we could do both: remove the odium from sexuality *and* establish the nature and boundaries of our relationship at one and the same time by talking through her questions objectively, dispassionately, and impersonally.

I did not know then that at the very same time as she was

talking with composure and confidence, she was experiencing highly disturbing upsurges of memories or part-fantasies concerning Mr Baker, Aunt Rene, and her landlord in her early adult years, and that these were increasing. She was, as I realized in retrospect, presenting one of two quite separate aspects of herself, as a result of the pressure of her ambivalent feelings towards me. I was her friend, saviour and protector on the one hand, and on the other, she expected imminent betrayal and exploitation. This ambivalence, or more precisely, the tension generated by that ambivalence, seemed to trigger off the recovery of similar experiences in her past, like that with Rene, whom she had loved and trusted and who had turned into a monster of depravity.

During the following week, for the first time, her writings reflected grief at Bert's death, his absence, and her feelings of missing him. Perhaps becoming able to talk more openly and courageously about sex – something which had until then been coloured exclusively with overwhelming self-disgust, shame, and loathing – had allowed her to gain access to more positive and loving feelings.

The interview in which she had asked me so directly for sexual information took place on a Friday. At four o'clock on Sunday morning she telephoned my home, and was answered by my recording machine. She later told me that she had tried the number she had used before, my previous home, and been given my new number. She did not leave her name, but I had no difficulty in recognizing the voice when I played the tape. For some time she simply sobbed into the microphone, and then brokenly spoke odd words which, pieced together as best I could, sounded like: 'He didn't rape me again,' repeated over and over.

Two days later, Heather telephoned me to say that she was more concerned than ever that Mrs Collins was seriously planning suicide. As I had an appointment with Mrs Collins on the following day, and there was no way of intervening if this was a serious plan, short of compulsory admission to hospital under the Mental Health Acts, I insisted to Heather that she should not do anything.

When Mrs Collins came to see me the following day, she was taken aback that I had known of her suicide arrangements and had nevertheless not telephoned her. I reminded her of our contract, that she had tested it almost to breaking point once before, and that no further leeway could or would be given. Her controlled and defensive façade crumbled at last, and she broke down completely.

Throughout the rest of the interview she spoke fragmentarily of her feelings of guilt at permitting Tom to touch her and even worse at enjoying it, and equally of her guilt at failing to flee from Mr Baker on at least one occasion when she could have done. I could not work out what this complete change of mood meant, or indeed what had motivated the preceding period of calm preparation for suicide. Her threats of suicide persisted during the following week. She succeeded in creating panic in all around her, and eventually the GP was called in by Sharon.

Mrs Collins told me this at her next appointment. Her manner was somewhat different: she seemed angry rather than *distrait*, and told me that the GP had spent a long time with her, allowing her to talk. She had apparently told the doctor all the story she had so far told me, and expressed her rage at what had been done to her. The GP had been sympathetic and concerned, had indeed spent a long time listening, but had then suggested they should pray together.

130

In the course of this prayer, she had asked that Mrs Collins should receive the strength to forgive those who had harmed her.

This pious plea had done the trick. Mrs Collins was furious, and her rage seemed to break her out of the consuming mass of guilt that had plagued her for weeks. *Forgive* Mr Baker? Never! I made encouraging noises, and she appeared to become more and more convinced of her right to be angry. Then she broke out again: Heather had been away during that week and had sent a colleague, a young man, to visit Mrs Collins instead. Mrs Collins had spoken with him at length about the various incidents with Tom, Rene and Mavis, and this man had asked her whether she was aware of her own lesbian tendencies.

It was my turn to be taken aback. Did this interpretation indeed come from the social worker, or was he a stalking horse being used by Mrs Collins to test out a perception of her own? The latter seemed the more probable, but tentative inquiry produced only furious rejection of the whole idea. Whatever direction I attempted to steer Mrs Collins into, she came back every time to the question of why she had enjoyed being masturbated by Tom, and her self-condemnation for this pleasure. This had been, she said, the background to her decision to kill herself. Using minimal interpretation, I tried to help her to see the incident as she would have done as a child of the age she was when these events had occurred, but as soon as she came near to recognizing the desperate need for any kind of affection and comfort that must have swamped her at the time, she changed the subject to the ever-present and interwoven theme of why she had not fled from Mr Baker when he had called to her from the doorway of his house, a point she had touched on repeatedly but without telling me any more. I did not know what episode this had been, although apparently Mrs Collins took it for granted that I did.

When she asked insistently yet again *why* she had not run away, I suggested firmly that we should now find out without any more discussion. She agreed.

In hypnosis, she regressed to age ten and the time when she was on her way home from school and saw Mr Baker standing in his doorway beckoning to her. When she showed physical signs of being highly distressed, I asked her to tell me what was happening. She made no response, and appeared to be wholly engrossed in what she was watching or experiencing. Repeated questions on my part similarly went unheeded. The episode went on for a very long time. The time allotted for the interview passed, and I was warned by telephone that my next client had arrived. My suggestions to her to return to full consciousness fell on deaf ears. Eventually I gave her very authoritative instructions that she should move forward to the time of her release by Mr Baker and then meet her adult self in the street and receive the comfort she needed.

Once out of hypnosis again, Mrs Collins retained a vivid picture of her own internal state of mind at the time of this event: she had been wholly paralysed by fear. Calm now, and with the distracted ruminations over her guilt and dirtiness apparently gone, she seemed able to recognize her own helplessness in the face of the aggressor who had hurt and terrified her repeatedly over so many years. She said she simply could not tell me what had happened on that occasion: it was too horrible to speak of.

I was very puzzled by what had been going on. Mrs Collins's ready acceptance of my suggestion of hypnotic exploration was out of keeping with the provocative and resistant games she had been playing for several weeks with everyone around her, including me. On the other hand, it was very much in keeping with the scene we had just explored: compliance with the adult male's demands.

This seemed paradoxical to me. The trauma was founded on her helpless acquiescence to a man's domination, and yet appeared to have been neutralized as a result of acquiescence to instructions from a man. At the same time, it seemed that using hypnosis gave Mrs Collins an indirect and slightly detached, less self-committing way of communicating things to me which she found too distressing to speak of directly: that she could use the vehicle of hypnosis to tell me about what was preoccupying her, when simply telling me was too threatening.

I thought also that her provocative behaviour over the last few weeks was an indirect demand that I should take a more directive approach in her treatment.

A week later, Mrs Collins arrived for her usual session completely drunk. Her speech was slow and slurred, and she was barely capable of coherent thought. She admitted that she had gone to the pub for 'Dutch courage', and had simply 'overdone it'. Apparently she often used drink to calm herself. From time to time she came very near to tears, but I made no attempt to do any work: one cannot do therapeutic work with a client who is drunk. Any material covered or insights achieved would be either denied or actually forgotten subsequently.

We had already arranged to meet twice during this week, so I was able to see her again two days later. She was sober when she arrived, purposeful and determined to pursue and settle finally some specific questions. It was these that had made her seek courage at the pub two days earlier: she had found the prospect of telling me what was troubling her so daunting that she could not face the interview unaided.

First, she gave me the written account of what she had recovered two sessions earlier, of the occurrence in Mr Baker's house. I asked her to tell me about it but she refused, saying that there was something else she was anxious to deal with. While I was not content to accept this at face value, it appeared at the same time a positive and purposeful attitude which was very welcome.

She reminded me that she had told me that she had been raped by the landlord of a flat in which she had lived some time after leaving home, of which she had been so disturbingly reminded when examined in the ward by an Indian. She was now determined to recover the memory itself. This was a very clear example – and one from her adult years rather than from childhood – of the apparently amnesic gaps in her memory. She could recall that the rape had taken place, and that she had become pregnant as a result, but *how* it had occurred was a blank. Interestingly, she was unable to remember the name of the man, referring to him only as 'the landlord', or as 'Lil's husband'. She insisted she wished to fill this gap, and to do so by means of a hypnotic 're-play'.

Additionally, she still wanted to explore the reasons why she had found Tom's masturbatory attentions pleasurable, and whether this related in any way to the pleasure she had experienced when making love with Bert. She also wanted to get a clearer understanding of why she had allowed Chas to make love to her again once or twice at least after the initial rape. I speculated within myself on the more immediate relevance of all this: a message to *me* that she could be sexually responsive?

The Filthy Lie

We settled on the landlord as the first target. The rape had occurred when she was twenty.

As always, she went easily into hypnosis. I asked her to go back to when she was twenty, and living in a room in the house of her friend and the friend's husband. Without difficulty, Mrs Collins answered questions as to what was happening until she reported that the landlord had entered the room. From then on, she showed increasing fear and distress, weeping copiously, making pushing movements with her hands, and writhing on her chair, until finally she seemed almost to collapse. She seemed unable to reply to my questions as to what was happening, so I suggested firmly that she would now come back to the present, to my room in the clinic, that she would be able to remember only those portions of the event that she could tolerate, and that she could forget anything in it that caused her excessive distress until such time as she could cope with the memory.

On regaining normal consciousness, Mrs Collins seemed shaken and was very weepy for a time. She was both horrified and relieved at having recovered the memory of this event. She said she could remember it all now, including the name of her assailant.

I had moved into a furnished room in Tooting. Lil, the landlord's wife, got me a job where she worked, and Lil and I became friends. I used to stay in my room at first in the evenings but after a few weeks, Lil invited me down to sit with them to watch TV and chat. I was glad to do this at first, but I never liked her husband, Rasheed. He was as far as I was concerned shifty-looking and always seemed to be watching or looking at me. It made me feel very uncomfortable. I would tell myself I was being daft, then I'd think there was

135

something wrong with me, but I didn't like or trust him.

This Saturday, I got back and Lil wasn't in so I went to my room. I just supposed she was held up and would be late, so I settled down for the night and went to sleep.

Next morning, Sunday, I was sleeping and I heard my door open and when I went to sit up in bed I saw it was Rasheed, Lil's husband. He said Lil had rung up to say her Mum was bad and she was staying there with her and would probably be back Sunday evening if her Mum was better. He had a cup of tea in his hand and he was staring at me, which made me feel uneasy. Then he put the tea down and said 'I'm going to rape you.' With that I froze. I managed to mumble 'Please don't' but he said he'd waited a long time for this chance 'so don't fight and you won't get hurt'. I was just frozen stiff.

Thus began an ordeal which, from the detailed description Mrs Collins later wrote, must have lasted several hours. Rasheed left nothing undone. He had raped her repeatedly and in every possible way, with every possible humiliation and degradation. Apart from an initial weak verbal protest, she had not resisted. She had been unable to move, 'frozen stiff with fear'.

Following this horrifying ordeal, she had fallen ill, and been utterly confused. At last she had told her mother, who immediately asked whether Meggie had resisted. Hearing that she had not done so, her mother had been furious, and among other things had called her a 'weak, stupid, gutless coward', saying that she had 'deserved everything she had got'.

The fact that she was pregnant was discovered only when she had collapsed at work and been taken to hospital.

When I came out of hospital I moved and left my job while Lil and Rasheed were at work. I moved to Wandsworth, got a small flat and a job in a canteen but I didn't want this baby. Funny, I'd always wanted a baby, and now I was having one I didn't want it. To me it was dirty, a constant reminder of what Rasheed had done and how gutless I'd been.

I hated the baby inside me, I wanted the baby to die and I wanted to die too but again I didn't have the guts to do it. That day will live with me for ever. I killed her as surely as if I'd stuck a knife in her. I wished it dead and I got my wish.

The child was born dead after a long and very painful labour. She had felt utterly responsible for her baby's death, and repeatedly returned to her mother's condemnation of her as a coward. During this session Mrs Collins struggled to force me to share this view of her.

The following week, Mrs Collins gave me her usual sheaf of paper, among which something new and unexpected appeared. In the middle of a passage reflecting on the previous session, there occurred a passage written in a quite different hand: crude, sprawling and ill-formed.

No I can't

Little Meggie was little so she couldn't do anything but I wasn't any more

Anyway, Little Meggie died a long time ago and bigger Meggie tried to live now and failed She was twenty now, she should have had some guts but she DIDN'T She'd buried Little Meggie then she had to bury Twenty-year-old Meggie somehow but she couldn't if she had the baby but when she lost the baby the guilt was too much for her and she didn't feel any less ashamed and humiliated and dirty even when she lost the baby now. She had more shame and guilt so she tried to cut the dirt away but even that she ...

Alright I write it but don't say I didn't warn you you may not

The Filthy Lie

*think shameful about Little Meggie but you will with Twenty Year
Old Meggie she was grown up or should have been ...*

*I didn't want to write the details of Bigger Meggie for fear of
what you'd think of her she had a choice Little Meggie didn't.*

What was this? Neither the phrasing of this passage nor the
writing were characteristic of Mrs Collins. Little Meggie I knew
about, and Big Meggie was, so I thought, Mrs Collins herself.
Now a new 'Big Meggie' – and 'Bigger Meggie' – had come on
stage. In an intuitive leap, I guessed that Big Meggie was
another separate personality, dating from the time of the rape
by Rasheed when Mrs Collins was around twenty, and not Mrs
Collins herself. Mrs Collins had been amnesic for all but the
fact of the rape, and had recovered the memory only in hypnosis – by, it seemed to me, going back twenty years – and so
accessing the memories of a part-personality split off during
the rape. Who 'Bigger Meggie' – mentioned in 'Big Meggie's'
writing – might be, I could not even guess.

There now were three personalities: Mrs Collins of today,
'Big Meggie' and 'Little Meggie'. Until now, it had seemed that
'Little Meggie' could be reached or could act only while Mrs
Collins was in hypnosis and we actively sought her out. It now
seemed that another 'secondary personality' could emerge
spontaneously while Mrs Collins was absorbed in her thoughts
or in writing.

However, when Mrs Collins came for her next session, I
knew nothing of this. We talked round and round what she
had discovered of the rape, and had partly revealed to me. The
constant theme was that she was a coward and deserved
everything she got.

I said: 'There's a test psychologists use to see how many

words a child knows, and one we ask about is the word "brave". Most children say that it means not being frightened. D'you think that's the right answer?'

'Yes, of course: if you're brave you don't get frightened, only cowards get frightened.'

'Well, actually that's not the whole answer. Brave people go on without giving up even when they *are* frightened: that's what makes them brave. They don't give in to their fear, but they certainly *are* afraid. After all, only fools are not afraid when things are dangerous. The brave thing is to face up to whatever is frightening and endure it. Was your mother really right when she said you were a coward?'

'*Course* she was, I *was* a coward, I *always* was a coward, so it *doesn't* matter what happens to me. *Gutless*, that's what I am.'

I probed more and more into her mother's judgement and condemnation. Once again, although she had on many occasions been able, just about, to acknowledge anger towards, and even criticism of, her mother, my challenge to her mother's attitudes, her perfection, still made Mrs Collins increasingly angry and intensely anxious. At the same time, there was a glimmer of something else: even if she was a coward and in the wrong, perhaps her mother should still have comforted her. There was a hint that she was getting just a little nearer to some slight recognition that her mother had failed her.

She was perfectly sure that her own reaction as a mother would have been quite different: if one of her own children had been raped and had told her, she would have tried all she could to comfort the girl, even if she had felt that the girl should have struggled more, or screamed.

I tried to explain the concept of a learned or automatic

response – a conditioned reflex – but it meant little to her. I tried the image that had proved useful to her before, that of 'the child inside'. Mrs Collins was insistently asking me *why* she had been so passive. Using analogies of rabbits frightened into paralysis by a stoat, birds 'mesmerized' by a snake, all ideas that she had met before, I pointed out that she had used the phrase 'frozen stiff'. I said I thought that Little Meggie had learned helplessly and hopelessly to 'freeze' when sexually assaulted, and that in a sense Little Meggie had been present when Rasheed said 'I'm going to rape you.' Not only had Little Meggie been present, but the close similarity between that situation and those terrifying events of childhood had triggered off the by now familiar reaction of 'freezing', with the result that Big Meggie – her identity at the time of this rape – was helpless. She was mesmerized, paralysed, incapable of thought or action, swept up in a replay of past events: a little child in the power of a monster once again.

Intellectually Mrs Collins could see this, but it made no difference to her feelings: she was a coward, her mother was right. Her mother *had* to be right.

In retrospect, my attempt to re-shape her reaction to and interpretation of her own behaviour twenty-odd years earlier may well have contributed to the emergence of separate 'personalities'. At those times, later, when I periodically became sceptical again of the reality of 'multiple personality', I blamed myself for introducing the concept. It could be argued as I often did, both with myself and with colleagues, over the succeeding months, that the identification of part-selves, of separate groups of reactions, feelings and behaviours, might have stemmed at least in part from the imagery and language I had used to Mrs

Collins, in the therapeutic endeavour to give her a means of 'handling' her experiences.

At other times, when the more vivid and powerful episodes of different personalities 'taking over' occurred, I felt instead that I had intuitively sensed and responded to something real: the presence of hidden but powerful 'sub-personalities'.

Much of Mrs Collins's life had been rendered unconscious – dissociated from the mainstream of her consciousness – and then repressed – *forced* out of awareness. Her experience of recovering memories in hypnosis must have been possible at least partially because the hypnotic ritual in a sense gave *permission* for her to articulate memories, thoughts, and feelings which otherwise were too distressing or too dangerous to be admitted to herself, let alone told to me.

12

Mid June, Year Two

As usual, Mrs Collins presented me with a sheaf of paper when we met the following week. Again as usual, I pressed her to *tell* me what she had written, and this time – gradually, with much leafing through the pages as though to refresh her memory – she did so.

To be truthful, I felt very disappointed with myself last time. I had hoped that I might find out that I had at least tried to resist or scream but I hadn't. It was a brutal rape. I can understand Little Meggie's fear. She was only a little kid but I was supposed to be grown up by that time. I should have at least tried but I didn't. I was like a lump of meat taken out of a freezer, frozen and stiff, and scared as hell. The rape wasn't as bad as some of the things that happened to Little Meggie, but it was bad enough and the fear was just as bad if not worse. Why do I always give in to fear? I wanted to know what happened. Now I know, I feel shame and humiliation.

One good thing I felt, was knowing that I didn't tell Lil because I didn't want to hurt her. That was the only decent thing I did do. Mind you, I guess I was also afraid she'd blame me for not resisting or something. I also know it wasn't my fault, but at the same time I think if I had resisted or told him I'd tell Lil he might have backed off. But I didn't, so in some way it was partly my fault, for not doing or saying anything. I don't think it would have made any difference to him and I know in some way my resisting or fighting wouldn't have helped me, but at least I wouldn't have felt a coward. I think I was also afraid of Lil.

Courage, or the lack of it as she saw it, remained a prominent theme. I felt that Mrs Collins was showing immense courage in pursuing anamnesis – restoring to consciousness what had been 'forgotten' – striving to recover the memories which had been so deeply buried, but she could not acknowledge this.

Mrs Collins had begun to behave more and more strangely at her visits to the clinic. The receptionists became increasingly anxious when she arrived sometimes nearly mute, or weeping and uncontrolled, or acting in various odd ways. They had become very concerned about her, knowing a little of her story.

Not long before Mrs Collins had begun to see me, a special team had been formed to work with children who had been sexually abused, and the whole subject was in the forefront of discussion. I had sought advice and help from my colleagues, and some of her story was, therefore, known to them. There was a great deal of sympathy for her. The receptionists, despite their agitation when Mrs Collins was especially strange in her manner or behaviour, were tremendously caring. She was looked after while waiting for me, or in the periods she sat in the waiting-room after her interview with me, with the utmost care and kindness.

At times this was difficult. Mrs Collins would arrive apparently confused and unable or unwilling to speak. She would wander around the waiting-room and the adjacent corridors, looking lost, asking where she was but not appearing to take in the replies she received, weeping, and appearing totally disoriented. At times, she behaved more like a very disturbed small child than an adult.

She frequently telephoned asking to speak to me, always in a highly distressed state. Since it was very rare that I was actually unoccupied during my sessions at the hospital, and I applied a rigid ban on telephone calls when a client was with me, the receptionists bore the brunt of this pressure. They were marvellous; always patient and caring, with a concern which was wholly genuine, and they took great pains to provide what comfort and support they could. However, on many occasions, Mrs Collins could not be comforted or eased by anything except that which she craved: time with me. Whatever I gave her in the way of attention, support, reassurance, and comfort was never enough, and *could* never satisfy her, no matter how much I gave.

What she demanded from me was not, of course, what she *really* wanted, or needed: her actual need was for her *mother's* love, care, protection and comfort, and that more than three decades ago, not now. Anything anyone gave her now would be coming from the wrong person, at the wrong time – and so could never fulfil her need.

The restriction of contact with me to the formal and arranged appointments felt increasingly irksome to her and she made stronger and stronger efforts to spend additional time with me. There was usually a substantial space between the end of her appointment with me and the arrival of her transport, and she waited, of course, in the clinic waiting-room. Frequently she would ask the receptionists to ensure that I would speak to her when I came to a space between appointments. Since the waiting area formed part of the passage between the consulting rooms and the clinic office, she could also buttonhole me herself if I passed by. On occasion, she would appear too distressed to

144

leave when her car arrived, and I would be put under great pressure to give her more time.

The more she achieved some contact in these ways, the greater, of course, was her use of these pressures. Consciously, however, she felt great reluctance to 'bother me', giving way to her anxiety, depression of mood, distress and so on only when she could not bear it any further.

Unwisely, Heather had actually encouraged Mrs Collins to telephone me whenever she became additionally distressed. This was largely the product of Heather's own anxiety, but at this time, she and I had not established any form of regular contact in order to coordinate what we were doing separately with Mrs Collins. As a result, we found ourselves re-enacting another aspect of Mrs Collins's earlier experiences: the lack of cooperation and hence consistency between her parents.

Mrs Collins gave many indications of suicidal intentions, and in any case her manifest and intense distress called out the protective and caring impulses in everyone she met, while at the same time exposing those who tried to help her to feelings of total impotence and inadequacy. We could not do what she wanted because it was impossible, yet we all wanted to help her.

The 'abuse' Mrs Collins was offering us was, of course, typical of those who have been themselves abused in childhood: the victim of abuse will later re-enact that abuse in different forms with all who try to help, or exert power over them, especially at an emotional level. Eric Berne, in *Games People Play*, describes a very similar process in the 'Game' he called 'Uproar': a child whose experience in life has been of chaos, fear, violence, and total insecurity creates those conditions around him or herself later in life.

145

At the next interview, Mrs Collins produced a bulky envelope and a number of letters. The large envelope, so it transpired after much coy refusal to answer my question, contained all her jewellery, and some letters to her children, a further letter being addressed to me. She opened the large envelope and removed her rings, earrings and other ornaments from it and put them on herself again, tore up the letters, and deposited them in the waste-paper basket.

I caught myself feeling angry at the provocative game that she was playing with me. Why could she not simply say to me: 'I had decided to kill myself, but now I have chosen to live,' instead of performing this charade? How much *easier* it would all be if she could be 'up-front' with me! However, I could not but be pleased too at the message I thought her play-acting was intended to convey: that this phase was at an end, that she had moved on to a more positive plane.

Mrs Collins seemed to have worked out that the time I was most likely to answer the telephone at home in person was on Sundays. On the Sunday following our last meeting, however, I was away conducting a training workshop. She was therefore answered by my telephone answering machine, and she left a message, speaking in a distraught voice and sounding thoroughly confused.

'Little Meggie and Big Meggie are fighting' was the gist of the confused recording I heard on my return in the evening. I rang her back, and told her quite gently that she should not disturb me in this way, especially since she had an appointment with me very shortly. She seemed to be uncomprehending of what I was saying, and continued to talk in a rambling, confused and apparently highly distressed way about the two

146

Meggies fighting inside her. I too was confused, but managed to calm her.

Two days later, we had our next meeting. Mrs Collins was still very distressed and disturbed, and she spoke vehemently of a fight going on inside her, directed as much against her as between the two protagonists, Big and Little Meggie.

'They want to die and I don't.'

I asked what *she* meant by Big Meggie, and she explained that it was her identity at age twenty, around the time of the rape by Rasheed. She insisted that these two identities – herself as a child of about eight, and the other, a young woman of twenty – were trying to force her to kill herself so that they too could die. It was obvious that she believed firmly and clearly that there were two other personalities inside her own body, in addition of course to the person she thought of as herself. Her identities at these two principal times of trauma were, as far as she was concerned, still as they had been, with their own thoughts, feelings, impulses and wills.

She told me that she had felt fine after our last interview and for all the following day. She had been visited by Heather, and had enjoyed the visit. She had gone to the cemetery to visit Bert's grave, and had coped well with that.

The problems had started when she went to bed, and she had woken feeling this battle going on inside her. In the end, desperate, she had telephoned me. The conversation we had on the telephone when I rang back later had calmed the battle, but she was aware that it could start again at any moment – and she was terrified, feeling that she might very well be forced against her will by these apparently independent identities to kill herself. She was insistent that this wish for death was now alien to her: she wanted to live, had so much to live for, but felt that she could not tolerate the inner assault that had been mounted on her, if it were to return.

At one level, this sounded like nothing more or less than a return of the same suicidal threats and gestures which had marked recent weeks, albeit in the disguise of metaphors and images I had used in therapy. It felt to me as though this strategy were intended to protect her from any accusations that she was continuing the earlier suicide threats. In effect, she was saying: 'You must help me – *they* are trying to kill me.' However, it was as renewed suicide threats that this sounded in my own ears when I discussed the whole situation later with a colleague, and certainly how he interpreted it. At the same time, when actually in Mrs Collins's presence, the story was convincing. There was no doubt at all that she herself utterly believed the reality of what she felt, even while expostulating that it did not make sense and was not possible. As she continued to describe this experience of inner strife personalized in this way, I quickly carried out a mental review of recent events, and of what had emerged in therapy.

I decided that my remaining doubts about the 'reality' of the separate personalities had to be put aside, and Mrs Collins had, in any case, firmly adopted this interpretation of her own experiences. At worst, if it were a misinterpretation, it could still perhaps be turned to good effect as a therapeutic device. I therefore suggested to Mrs Collins that I should talk to Little Meggie directly myself.

This took her aback: the concept was being accepted more directly than she had expected. So far, all 'contact' with Little Meggie had been inside her own head; now I was asking to enter directly into the process. She said she could not understand how this could be done, but agreed to go along with my suggestion. We agreed to carry out this plan the following week.

13

June, Year Two

Mrs Collins told me at the next interview that the war between the hidden personalities and the outward one was still raging – 'They want to die, and I don't.' I made no comment, but reminded her immediately of our agreement to allow me to meet Little Meggie directly.

I went through the hypnotic induction with her, and suggested that the adult Mrs Collins should allow herself to become completely detached from control of her body, but remain in contact so that she could observe what happened, listen to what was said, and that when asked, she could take part. Mrs Collins needed considerable reassurance that she could take control again, and that she would not, by relinquishing control during the session, lose it altogether and be 'taken over' permanently by Little Meggie. When at last she had become comfortable with all this, I asked Little Meggie to talk with me.

Over the next minute or two, Mrs Collins began, as she had before, to look in every way like an overgrown little girl. This time, there were two differences: her eyes opened, and she looked especially distraught and fearful, repeatedly putting her hands to her ears and fumbling with the top of her dress until I realized she was 'looking for her hearing aid'. As a child she had been profoundly deaf and, although aware that I was speaking, would not have been able to hear what I was saying without her aid. I immediately fetched out a Speech Trainer I

150

keep to hand for interviewing profoundly deaf children, and offered her the head-set. She seemed to recognize the apparatus, put the headphones on and adjusted the microphone to stand in front of her mouth. We now became able to communicate.

Little Meggie wanted, naturally, to know who I was. I identified myself as a friend who wanted to help her, and began to explain that all the things that troubled her, frightened her, and made her feel bad had happened a very long time ago, even though it seemed to her that it was still all going on now. Mr Baker and Uncle Tom were now dead, they had died many years ago and that she need no longer be afraid of them.

She became more and more agitated, insisting vehemently that these things could not be, I was wrong, she was bad and stupid. I repeated my insistence that all the people concerned were dead. She then became angry, saying that it was bad to say things like that, I must not say these things – it was dirty and bad.

I suggested that perhaps the grown-up woman she had become should talk to her, at which her agitation grew further. I then addressed myself to the adult Mrs Collins and asked her to explain to Little Meggie how much time had passed and that what I was saying was indeed true. This seemed to have no effect, so I spoke to Little Meggie again. I told her that I knew what her father had done to her when she was seven years old, and what he had done later when she was older. Her agitation rose again.

Speaking as I would to a young child about being abused, and choosing my words with care to ensure they would be within her vocabulary at this age, I explained the reality of the event, the true location of responsibility, and especially my understanding of her feelings about these events. Throughout this, she was agitated and distressed, making whimpering sounds and expressions of protest: 'No, No, it's not true, it's me, I'm dirty, bad, Mum said so, Mum told me,' and the like. I told her that her sisters had also been molested by her father and that they had told her mother; that her mother had actually seen him do things like that with one of them; that her mother had known that what Little Meggie had told her was true, even though she had denied it at the time.

This produced a violent paroxysm of protest and denial. She cried desperately that this could not be true, that her mother had told her she was telling filthy lies. I reminded her that *she* knew she had been telling the truth: her father had indeed done bad things to her and that there was no doubt of that in her own mind: she could *remember* it. She seemed to yield a little, but still refused to accept this. 'I'll go under the shops, I'll be safe there. I mustn't talk to people, mustn't tell anyone': an implicit admission of the truth of what she knew and what I had been saying.

I went on to explain that she need no longer hide or run away, she need no longer be afraid or want to die: it was all over and would never happen again. As determinedly and reassuringly as I could, I tried to persuade Little Meggie that she could now be at peace. Her protests lessened a little, but she clearly did not wholly believe me.

I asked her again to allow her adult self to speak to her, but this seemed to be meaningless to her. If the conventional wisdom concerning Multiple Personality were true, then Little Meggie should have known of the adult self who had developed, but it was clear that this was not the case here. She had no idea that time had passed and that she, or a part of her, had indeed grown and developed into an adult.

I therefore spoke to the adult Mrs Collins, speaking with all the authority I could muster, and instructed her firmly to find Little Meggie and introduce herself. She was to ignore any protests from her child self and gather her up in her arms and comfort her, repeating what I had told the little girl and insisting on its truth.

This seemed to work, given considerable repetition and encouragement. The 'little girl' in the chair in front of me gradually seemed to calm down, close her eyes, relax and then look quite peaceful.

I asked Mrs Collins to 'take over' again and to return to her normal waking state. When her eyes opened, she fumbled at the head-set and took it off, looking at it in some surprise, and asked what it was. I explained, saying that Little Meggie had seemed unable to hear what I was saying.

She told me she had had a very clear picture of her child self hiding under the platform that supported the market shops, the hiding place she had so often used as a child. The child had been too far back for her to reach: with her adult girth, she had been unable to crawl underneath the platform herself! She had, however, been able to talk reassuringly to the child. She said: 'She was afraid of Mum. I don't understand that, because I never was.'

I expressed some doubt, and pointed out how much of what she had told me of her childhood spoke very clearly of a very strong fear, both of her mother's disapproval and, above all, of her rejection. Mrs Collins half-accepted this, but went on to talk extensively about her childhood. The manner in which she spoke made it clear that many of these memories had not been available to her before this session: it seemed as if this new contact with her dissociated child self had restored access to some of her own hitherto lost history.

Then Mrs Collins asked quietly but insistently that I should there and then read the account she had written of the rape by Rasheed. I was very vividly aware that she would note every flicker of expression on my face, and of how she had interpreted the expressions she had seen on Heather's face recently while she had read what Mrs Collins had written about the abuse of Little Meggie. I modulated my facial expressions with extreme care, and when I had finished reading, told Mrs Collins that I understood how difficult it had been for her, and how much courage it had taken, to write this account, give it to me and then witness my reading.

At the end of our allotted time, Mrs Collins was calm and composed. She seemed distinctly more in control of herself than when she had arrived, and said how much better she felt, although now very tired. The interview had seemed curiously long to both of us, much longer than the hour it occupied.

Over the following week, Mrs Collins wrote at length about this session. Much of what she wrote seemed to be an attempt to get an intellectual grip on the confused and confusing experience of finding quite separate people inside her – Little Meggie, Big Meggie, and herself.

She was confused especially by the apparent fact that, although Little Meggie had been 'blocked off', she was nevertheless able to exert considerable influence on Big Meggie and to make her 'freeze' when threatened by Rasheed.

One theme in the material she produced during this time, but which she was still not able or willing to talk to me about in person, was an increasing awareness of anger at her mother.

Even though it was there, it was still somewhat muted.

Mum was so wrong and weak. So very very wrong. She hurt me and my sisters. I wasn't the bad one. She was. I didn't want to blame Mum, but when I think about it now, it was in fact Mum and Dad – but Mum more – who were to blame for my actions in life.

The battle continued inside her. She had become aware of behaving oddly for periods of time after which she could not recall what she had been doing, especially because her children remarked upon the fact that there were times when she had not seemed to know them and had behaved 'strangely'. She believed, although it 'made no sense' to her, that she *became* either Little or Big Meggie on these occasions.

The confusion over *who* she actually was remained intense. It was increased by the intensity of her feelings about me.

I know this is going to sound ridiculous but sometimes when I feel I can't cope and I can't reach you, it's (I know it sounds crazy) like Little Meggie needing Mum's help and can't get it as she doesn't want to know, that she doesn't want to know what's happened, or care how you feel. You've just got to deal with it or let it drive you crazy, and sometimes when I've not been able to reach you, I've been sort of glad because in a way it's like Little Meggie needing to talk to Mum but then when she's thought about it she was glad she didn't because she was afraid of how Mum would react.

Please don't think I'm insulting you by saying this. I'm not, at least that's not my intention, I wouldn't insult you by thinking you were like Mum. I'm just trying to explain how I feel when I feel that, how it in some ways brings back Little Meggie's feelings of needing help.

The unsophisticated and exceptionally direct insight this remarkable passage conveys was a marked step forward. However, although Mrs Collins recognized the transference on Little Meggie's part, she had not yet fully recognized many of her *own* reactions towards and feelings about me. Still less, of course, could she recognize that much of what she felt about me was transferred: from mother on to me, and I still bore the brunt of the emotional pressure of her attacks. I could fail her, and my failure would confirm all that was bad in Mrs Collins's feelings about herself. If I made myself fully available: able to talk to her or see her at any moment that she felt the need – that is, to play the role of the perfect mother she wanted me to represent – the pressure would go up and up until in the end I too would not be able to meet her demands, as, for example, at four in the morning. And then I would have been 'just like Mum': I didn't care, didn't want to know. I too would have rejected her.

And if I insisted on proper boundaries, on confining contact to our contracted interviews, then equally obviously I did not care what happened between sessions and, by extension, did not care about her and was not ready to help her when she most needed help: just like Mum again. Heads we both failed to win, tails we both lost. This would be a difficult passage to negotiate, and the only way to free both of us from this impasse or 'double bind' would be to help her to recognize the mechanism that underlay it: the projection on to me both of her hopelessly inadequate real mother, and of the 'good mother' she had so longed for and needed.

This is the core of analytic therapy, of course: the process whereby the patient re-experiences in the relationship with the therapist the significant feelings and relationships of infancy and childhood, so that they can be brought into full – adult – consciousness, and therefore understood and dissolved.

'All very well in theory,' I muttered to myself while considering how to tackle this problem effectively, 'but a bit different in practice sometimes.' I had repeatedly tried to work with the transference, and had repeatedly run into a solid brick wall. Despite her frequent explicit and heartfelt *written* statements about her anger at me, Mrs Collins in person unfailingly denied any negative feelings towards or even vaguely about me. These denials were accompanied by admissions that, of course, when she was feeling low and couldn't reach me on the telephone she did feel a bit annoyed, but really it was of no significance. I was really wonderful the way I put up with her, she was so grateful to me, I was the only one who had helped her, of course she understood that I could not always be there to answer the phone to her, but yes she did feel occasionally that perhaps I did not want to talk to her, especially if I did not ring her back when she had left a message saying she was upset, but then, I was a busy man and had many other concerns. Round and round, like trying to catch a piece of thistledown in a high wind.

As usual, by the time she came for an interview, the intervening week had been filled with a great deal of work on her part, always in writing. This meant, of course, that what I had in mind as the next step was already quite out of date, or on a different track from what she wanted or was ready to explore with me. When therapy goes well, and indeed often when it appears to be going badly or to be stuck in the doldrums, more work is done by the client in between sessions than is carried out in the sessions themselves. This was very much the case now with Mrs Collins.

Her present focus revealed a great step forward. She had learned from her contact with Little Meggie that there were previously unrecognized feelings within her: love, fear, and hate, all directed at her mother.

I never realized how much fear Little Meggie had or got from Mum's attitude towards her. How badly it made Little Meggie feel. She loved her Mum, but Mum made her feel so bad about talking about Dad, and punished her, so that she feared Mum too much to turn to her when Mr Baker raped her on the stairs. She feared Mum now, but she hated Mum as well because she needed Mum's help so badly. Every time Mr Baker hurt her, she hated Mum more and more and at the same time, she loved her. Every time Mr Baker hurt her, Mum was hurting her too in her mind, because she needed Mum's love, help, and comfort but was too scared to tell her for fear Mum would punish her and tell her she was bad, and dirty.

She was so confused by so many feelings – fear, hate, love, need, pain. She wanted them all to hurt and die, like they were hurting her, yet she loved Mum. The guilt she felt about wanting people dead, people she loved, was too much for her. She couldn't stand feeling like that about Mum. She had to blame someone, so she had to blame herself.

All that hurt, she thought it was her punishment for talking dirty to Rene, her punishment for feeling she wanted all these people hurt, to hurt the way she felt. The people she loved hurt her so much, it had to be her fault. It had to be she was bad, otherwise they wouldn't hurt her like this. So she grew up with those feelings about herself. I think I could say that she became obsessed that it was her, that she deserved all the beatings and the things her husband said. She couldn't believe anyone could love her. Although she didn't realize till now, in a way the beatings he gave her was punishment for being bad even though she wasn't doing anything wrong to deserve the beatings. She made no attempt to defend or stop him as she thought she deserved it and was too bloody scared anyway.

The consistent use Mrs Collins made of the pronoun 'she' was quite emphatic: she was talking about *another* person, not herself: a person with whom she had become as familiar as any one of us is with him or herself, and yet 'she' was not Meggie Collins.

Her account was an extraordinarily clear description of the reactions typical of the child who has been sexually abused. Let me emphasize that I am *not* saying that Mrs Collins is right, but rather that Mrs Collins is telling us that the books have got it right. The secrecy demanded of the child by the abuser makes it crystal clear to the child that what has been done is wrong. The child almost invariably concludes that the wrong, the dirtiness, is hers or his, and not the adult's. After all, to the young child, adults are by definition right in all they do. The only exception seems to be when several children in a family are abused by the same adult and share this knowledge. This sharing, however, is much less common than Meggie's experience: secrecy, enhanced and protected by the shame and guilt the child feels. Everything from then on is *her* fault, everything bad or painful that happens to her is due punishment.

In a very real but deeply unconscious sense, pain, suffering, humiliation, and shame are then actively sought as a confirmation of identity, of personal existence. A wicked self is the only self. Reality *is* suffering all these things, and without them, there is no reality, no *being*.

What she had written was an unmistakably profound and

crystal-clear insight. My reaction on reading these passages was one of admiration and respect for this exceptional woman, mingled with relief, and some pride: all my fears and anxieties were, after all, groundless, and I *had* got it right!

14

July, Year Two

In the next few interviews, Mrs Collins gradually demonstrated a change in her feelings about Little Meggie. She began to speak and write about the child's courage.

I think really she was brave. Maybe not so brave as she would have liked to have been, but in her own way she was brave, to have lasted through so much for so long. And she did fight in the only way she knew how, even though she didn't know it. No, that doesn't sound right, does it? How can you fight without knowing it? Oh, I don't know. Was it fighting, or retaliation, or what? All I know is that she didn't know what to do really.

That led on to telling me that when her mother died she had felt very guilty, but at the same time was aware of quite different feelings: relief, freedom, and *joy*. At that time, she had found herself able and wanting to respond sexually to Bert more than ever before. She was just then recovering from kidney surgery, and intercourse was not possible for them. To her joy, she found herself able to masturbate Bert – something which he had often wanted but which she had been quite unable even to contemplate.

Her new-found freedom had led her to study some of the girlie magazines that Lee had in the house. She had bought Alex Comfort's book *The Joy of Sex* and had asked Bert to read it with her and then 'to try something different'. He, however,

161

had expressed disgust at the book, and this initial reaction had made her feel very guilty again. He had, though, eventually been willing to try 'something different': he was prepared to try fellatio. This, predictably, as she herself could not recognize, had revolted Mrs Collins.

Mrs Collins was also beginning to have rather different feelings about Little Meggie's experiences with Uncle Tom. She insisted still that it was all wrong, wicked, and dirty, but now she could feel that it was understandable that a small child who had experienced nothing but violence and pain at the hands of adult men should accept the gentle attentions of Tom despite their inherent 'dirtiness', and that she should have been deceived by him. After all, she had been told that Tom 'made Mavis better', and how should she – Little Meggie, that is – have known any better? Changes seemed to be taking place almost daily.

Mrs Collins had occasionally asked me how long it would be before she could reasonably expect to have become free from the turmoils and troubles that beset her. Now she asked again how long would our work take? My immediate thought was that she was looking forward to a time when the professional relationship between us could be ended so that we could move into a more personal mode. This, of course, needed to be tackled and worked on. At the same time, however, I read her question as suggesting that she was beginning to look forward to *living* instead of undergoing treatment.

One of the – all too numerous – difficulties inherent in psychotherapy is that the treatment and the relationship with the therapist can take over and substitute for the whole of the client's life. As treatment progresses and an end can be foreseen, the client is likely to shy away and retreat for a time into a re-play of past problems or discover new ones in order to postpone the fearful prospect of becoming independent of the therapist and ceasing to see him regularly.

Sometimes, when psychotherapy is explicitly 'open-ended', one can wait for the client to work towards his or her own ending. One hears and reads accounts of therapy going on for ten and more years, and one wonders whether it will ever end. Children in therapy often make their own endings, reflecting perhaps the fact that their damage and their problems are less entrenched than in older people, and the fact that the processes of normal maturation and progress towards independence are easier, stronger and more natural in childhood and adolescence. With adult clients, 'termination' must be on the agenda, and in the minds of both therapist and client, from the first interview onwards, and worked towards consistently. When the client looks forward constructively, perhaps even impatiently, to becoming independent – and this is not a manoeuvre to distract the therapist from an imminent and painful issue – the therapist can feel reasonably sure that they are approaching the last lap.

However, I was not at all certain that Mrs Collins's question represented this hopeful stage. None the less, I thought her question, asked rather more insistently and with a more positive feeling than in the past, was a good sign. I welcomed it also because I felt that setting a finishing date would exert a very constructive pressure on us. I had already arranged to take a sabbatical year beginning in the spring. If we planned to finish in December it would give us four months in which to deal with any aftermath, unsettled issues, or residues of the transference. I told her that we would conclude treatment at

Christmas. Mrs Collins seemed pleased at a date being set, but would not discuss her feelings about this at all.

Predictably enough in the light of our discussion of a termination date, Mrs Collins had back-tracked in the interval before the next interview, and once more resisted any implication that her mother could have been wrong, or that she herself could be anything but a coward. In the course of the previous eighteen months I had touched on her mother's failure to protect Mrs Collins on many occasions, always meeting total resistance marked with a great deal of distress and guilt on Mrs Collins's part. Now I found myself attacking Mrs Collins's mother quite violently, with a rage which was at first simulated, but gradually became wholly real.

'She's a fine one to call you a coward! You – with the courage you had as a tiny child, let alone now. Look. You had the sheer guts to go on and on going to Baker's shop even though you knew damn well what was going to happen, in order to keep what little good there was between you and Mum, and then when it got so that no living creature could have stood any more, you had the guts first to run away, and then to do the only thing you could. It took a hell of a lot of guts to jump into the river from the bridge. Then you had the courage to stand up in court and stick up for yourself and say you did not want to go back home. But look at your Mum. She had no guts at all. She knew what that fine husband of hers was doing to her daughters, and what did she do? *Nothing*! That's what she did. Damn all. Who's she to talk about anyone being gutless, or a coward? She had no guts, no courage, and that's why she said *you* didn't have any. It was *her* cowardice she was talking about.'

I actually *felt* furiously angry, and let that show. I had

no personal reasons for feeling anger towards Mrs Collins's mother: it was *her* anger that I was expressing so vehemently on her behalf, through the 'protective identification' so well described and analysed by Casement. Perhaps, too, some of the anger was quite clearly directed at Mrs Collins herself for the submissive cover she was so skilled at using in order to disguise her covert manipulation of me. I allowed my anger to show: I was aware that that was to some degree stage-managed by Mrs Collins; that partly it stemmed from feeling that control of the whole process of therapy was slipping a little from my grasp; but it also gave a route by which I could re-establish greater control of the therapy.

Mrs Collins was more than a little taken aback by this onslaught. As I expected, she rose to her mother's defence, only to find herself betrayed and trapped by her deeper awareness of her mother's failure to protect and support her. She began, of course, by protesting that I must be wrong, her mother was no coward, her mother had been right in saying that she could not be sure that she was being told the truth when Meggie had told her of her father's molestation. That was easily scotched: Mrs Collins now knew without any doubt that her mother had already known of her husband's vile behaviour before Meggie had told her. She had to agree – yes, her mother must have known it was the truth but she must have been afraid of tackling her husband about it.

Gotcher! Which of them now was the greater coward? Mother, who knew her little girl, and other girls in the family, were being abused by her husband, their father, and did nothing, because she was afraid? Or the little girl, helpless, in the power of adult men who threatened her very life, and yielding to them, *unable* to do anything else?

Of course, common sense and logic have little effect on unconsciously determined beliefs and attitudes, but the impact of the logic of all this was massively increased both by the depth of the relationship that had developed between us over the months, and by the vehemence with which I presented and pursued this interpretation.

I had no great hope that it would break right through the barrier of defences around Mrs Collins's feelings about her mother: I would have been more than content with widening the breach that had been there for some time already by just a little. If we could also get a slight glimpse of the grief which I was sure must also lie alongside the rage, we would be much further along the road we were so sluggishly traversing. I left the interpretation at that, and let Mrs Collins work on it. It seemed, however, that the notion that, as a small child, she could not have been expected to defy grown men or to cope with the terror that had been roused in her made no difference.

She reverted to a previously held and briefly abandoned position: she had acted wholly wrongly in allowing Tom to touch her, and in enjoying that, in exposing herself to abuse by Rene and Tom. No, it was her fault, her weakness, her essential badness.

I found myself in a curious paradox: I was trying to explain to the victim of gross childhood abuse what it feels like to be a child experiencing such abuse. Her denial of what I presented to her, although it followed very closely what she herself had written over and over again, made me feel quite helpless at times, and frustrated at the apparent impenetrability of her resistance. Tackling this fundamental presupposition about herself was like trying to kill the Hydra. As soon as one head was lopped off, another would take its place: presumably exactly the experience she was undergoing in the increased militancy of her defences.

The aggressive and invasive manner in which I pressed Mrs Collins at this time to break down the defensive idealization of her mother came very close to being an assault on her, and she might well have experienced it as that. It came perilously close to fulfilling Mrs Collins's worst expectations. I was, without doubt, mounting a powerful assault on the self-condemnation she had learned as a child. At a deeper level, however, the assault was directed quite explicitly at the 'false self', the self-loathing, self-condemnatory persona she had developed, in the service of freeing Mrs Collins's healthy self from the prison in which she had locked herself – but feeling to *her* simply an assault on her *self*.

What was especially noteworthy about this interview was the absence of the powerful emotions that Mrs Collins had previously shown in reaction to the slightest hint of any criticism of her mother on my part. Those defences seemed to be weakening, at least in that the fierce protectiveness towards Mother as a defence against her own rage was now absent. There would, of course, be more lines of defence, like the serried ranks of bastions around a castle.

What would be the most effective way of dealing with these? Could we use the Little Meggie identity to go directly to the heart of the matter? Would it be possible, perhaps, to treat each separate identity in a multiple personality as an individual needing therapy? We could, for example, treat Little Meggie as a grossly abused eight- or ten-year-old, as I had done in one interview already, and then treat Big Meggie as a young adult, the victim of rape, with a background of abuse in childhood.

These questions I would have to solve soon: time was beginning to run out.

15

In the next two interviews, Mrs Collins spoke directly for the first time about being actually frightened by the apparent 'taking over' of her body and mind by Little and Big Meggie. She had found pages of writing in their handwritings and styles after periods of time for which she was amnesic. At the second interview, she described 'coming to' to find herself holding a kitchen knife and, she thought, trying to stab herself in the abdomen, discovering that she had already inflicted a number of cuts on herself. Apparently, Big Meggie had 'taken over' and was trying to kill herself.

I spoke again about the need to bring Little Meggie and Big Meggie into direct contact with her central self and to heal the split between them, the need for her own part-selves from the past to be reunited into a single self.

Mrs Collins expressed complete incomprehension. Bearing in mind that the secondary personalities would in all probability be listening closely to what I was saying, I explained what I meant over and over again, using a variety of analogies and metaphors.

I knew that one of the things that the few writers on this subject agree is that it is essential to bear in mind in the treatment of this condition that the secondary personalities are afraid of being destroyed by successful treatment and see the therapist as a threat. Very carefully and with much repetition,

I made a point of insisting that Mrs Collins *needed* Little Meggie and Big Meggie: that they were essential parts of her. Equally, they needed her if they were to be complete, and the aim of what we were going to do was to free them from their isolation and from their constant distress and struggles. In no way were we going to destroy them.

By the end of the interview, Mrs Collins was once again saying 'Well, I don't understand it at all, but you do, and you're the doctor.'

The following week, she opened the interview.

I've been fighting fear all week, and building up a brick wall in your mind tires you out. I remembered something last week and I couldn't cope with it, so I had to block it out somehow. It must have been something bad, because sheer fear was in me, and fighting that off tired me out. I felt so ill. Come to that, like Little Meggie again, I couldn't eat or anything. I just wanted to hide away and sleep.

I'm trying to think what could possibly be behind this wall. Could it be Little Meggie or Big Meggie? It can't be that bad, surely, we've learnt everything, I think.

You don't realize how much I've felt like hurting myself this last week and it's been a battle, I can tell you. You say I'm in control but you don't know just how hard it is, fighting Little Meggie, Big Meggie, and in a way Mum as well. It's me against them and it's bloody hard work. Rather, I've got to make friends with them, or help them understand, or calm them down somehow.

That, I felt, was a move in the direction I believed to be necessary. But before I could intervene, Mrs Collins began to talk pressingly of other and present-day concerns, and it was some time before I could break in. At last, I suggested firmly that I should now speak directly to Big Meggie. She accepted this, and we went through the usual hypnotic induction. Once she was in hypnosis, I began by making emphatic suggestions to her of calmness, feelings of security, confidence in her ability to resume control at any time she chose, and, especially, that she would be aware of the whole of the session and remember it clearly afterwards. I asked her to let go completely, and to allow Big Meggie to 'take over' for the time being so that she could speak to me directly.

'I'm talking to you now, Meggie Lawrence, and I hope you will talk to me. You can take over now and come out into the open. Please will you talk to me?'

On each occasion in the past when I had used this technique in treating other patients with multiple personalities, I had observed a curious struggle that occurs when a secondary personality 'comes out' and takes control. The struggle is manifested by convulsive movements, violent grimaces, and a general incoordination which then gradually fades. Mrs Collins showed all these features, and, as had been the case when we had gone back to childhood experiences, her whole appearance changed. Her face looked much younger, with an expression of resentment, anger and fear.

When she spoke, her voice too was quite different, her diction much less clear and with a different intonation. She asked who I was and why I wanted to talk to her; after all, she did not know me, and no one ever wanted to talk to her. I reminded her that she had written about me on a number of occasions, and that she knew that her other self came to see me regularly. At first she denied all knowledge of this, apparently terrified that I would be angry. I told her I knew how badly she had been hurt, first by Rasheed, and then by her mother. It seemed as though she did not know which part of this to respond to, but became very angry. She raged at me that I could not possibly know anything about Rasheed: no one knew about him except herself and her mother, and neither she nor her mother had ever told anyone else. She was equally furious that I should suggest she had been hurt by her mother: that was rubbish and a wicked thing to say – she loved her mother.

Yes, I told her, I knew what Rasheed had done. Very gently and without detail, I repeated enough of the story to convince her that indeed I did know what had happened, and that I understood why she had been paralysed with fear and so been unable to resist, and that she was innocent. She replied in the terms that had become so very familiar: no, it was her fault for being a coward, that she should have fought, that she did not resist because she was dirty. After all, her mother had told her this, so she knew it was right.

I persisted. Inside herself she had resisted, screamed, protested, even if outwardly she was frozen, frozen with the terror that Mr Baker had inspired.

She was shocked, and a little frightened: how could I possibly know all this? I explained how her grown-up self, twenty and more years later, had told me in detail all that had happened. She was totally disbelieving.

I insisted then on questioning her assumption of guilt and cowardice. Bit by bit, as she seemed to become able to accept a little of the offer of friendship I was making, she began to speak of feeling some anger both at what Rasheed had done and at her mother's failure to give her any support or backing. Time was running out. I suggested that she should now give way to her adult self again, and that we would talk again next time we met, and she became tearful and expressed resentment at being 'shut away all the time', and admitting now that she

complaining lately that sometimes she's talking to me and I'm what she calls 'not here'. It's just that I don't hear her.

She also noted an episode during the week when she appeared to have been 'taken over' while Heather was present. In the course of talking to Heather she had apparently got up and left the room without a word, and had woken up some hours later in bed, quite unaware of the interval.

The following week she again changed tack when she arrived for her next session. It was Tom and Rene's turn now, with a renewed upsurge of guilt: it had all been *her* fault. Up to this time, Mrs Collins had believed that *Rene* had suggested that Meggie should allow Tom to 'make her better', in the way that he had helped Mavis's supposed fits. There was now apparently a sudden awareness of why she was so angry about this event: it seemed that in reality Little Meggie had *asked* for Tom to 'make her better quickly' as Rene was 'hurting her'. So when he started stroking her, 'she'd asked for it', asked for Uncle Tom 'to make her better and love her like he did Mavis'. The whole ordeal with Tom, Rene and Mavis turned out to be 'Little Meggie's fault'.

This strongly suggested that she was almost aware that what she was asking of me closely resembled what she had asked of Rene and Tom: to 'make her better quickly', and she therefore felt threatened by me in case I too should abuse her instead of help her. The interview went round and round, leaving both of us feeling frustrated and more than a little despondent. We seemed to have entered another set of doldrums.

Perhaps I should have drawn this parallel then and there, but, confused as I was between wishing to speak with Big

Meggie again and work towards a reunion between her and Mrs Collins, and the return to the problem of Little Meggie's culpability in the 'orgy', I simply did not recognize that opening.

The shift to the 'orgy' theme seemed to me to act as an effective defence against confronting the Big Meggie issue. It seemed to me that at a no more than semi-conscious level, she felt that so important and absorbing a topic would take precedence, and so would postpone or even avert what she apprehended as a threat. Yet this topic was closely interconnected with that of the reunion of Big Meggie with herself, since that would 'make her better'. That interconnection made confrontation much more difficult, and so provided a highly effective set of linked defences. While I felt that, with sufficient effort and determination, I could single out one strand at a time and perhaps circumvent the maze in which we were struggling, I still felt diffident about the reliability of my choice: I could not be sure that choosing reunification of the dissociated part-selves, for example, was a free and objective action on my part, or whether it would distract us from what might be more important and urgent areas. A very effective *embarras de richesses*.

Mrs Collins had undergone one of her rapid mood changes by the following interview. She was cheerful, positive and optimistic, seeming very much in charge of herself once more. She felt that at last she had some understanding of what I had been saying about the way in which Little Meggie and Big Meggie had become separated from the mainstream of her life and personality and the need for them to become fully integrated with herself once more. She was clearly less disturbed by them now, feeling that this intellectual grasp of their nature gave her an explanation of the frightening experiences she had of being 'absent' for periods of time.

I found this reassuring. If the secondary personalities were in any way aware of what was going on in the primary, then the latter's hostility towards them would make them alarmed at any attempts to bring them out into the open, and they would not believe in my goodwill or that of Mrs Collins herself. They would probably refuse to emerge and, even if they did communicate directly, would disbelieve that I was trying to help them, believing instead that, as the primary personality's 'doctor' and friend, I was motivated to destroy them.

It now became clear that the function of her writing had changed. It had become a rehearsal of what she wanted to tell me at the next interview. The papers she gave me on this, and indeed on many later occasions, were in two parts: the 'prepared script' formed one part, the personal ruminations and those sections apparently written by the secondary personalities formed the other.

Having given me the bundle of papers, she began to talk about a visit she had received from her oldest sister, Julie, with whom she had talked about old times. Julie told her that she had herself, as a child, known that their father 'interfered with' the girls in the family, and that their mother had been very well aware of her husband's proclivities, as well as of identical behaviour on the part of her own father and brother. Julie had also told her that their mother had an affair with another man before she met her husband, and that she had taken this up again as soon as her husband died until she remarried.

Mrs Collins said that she was shocked at her mother's behaviour, and that she had known nothing of all this. Her mother had apparently told everyone except her.

The more I learn about Mum, the less I understand her. Julie said she never trusted Dad and always felt uneasy with him. She also said that Mum couldn't face that her husband was going with other women and interfering with his own daughters. She said after all it's not nice or easy facing something like. I don't think I'll ever understand Mum or Dad. And Mum never.

I want my children to be decent, hard-working children who will work for what they want, and not cheat, lie, or steal, not like my family. I want them to be straight and honest. Maybe I want too much from them, I don't know, but it's what I hope for. Julie said times were hard in them days, but that doesn't give the right for fathers, or men and women in my case, to interfere with or rape their own or anyone else's children. I've had a hard time all my life. But it didn't stop me from helping my children and it wouldn't have stopped me killing Bert if he'd done anything to my children or anyone else's.

And then, back to Rene and the 'orgy'. Round and round again, until it led her to mention a conversation with Heather, who had said that she, Mrs Collins, had successfully left her family and its awfulness behind her, unlike her brothers and sisters who had all in various ways remained caught in a life of criminality. This had made Mrs Collins feel guilty: she had 'deserted' them. The whole session seemed empty.

Early in my clinical training, it had been impressed upon me that the wholly understandable feeling of need to be active in therapy – to *do* something – had to be recognized, and resisted. That was the *therapist's* need, and therapy was about the *client's* needs. This principle came back to mind as I reviewed the last few sessions with Mrs Collins. It was quite clear that, as in some other periods in the course of the last year, we were

177

in a sort of impasse, a pause, and that we were not making any kind of obvious progress – but *why* did I feel that I must *do* something? Mrs Collins had recovered into consciousness so many horrifying and previously repressed memories, that there needs must be a lengthy period of assimilation and, even more, of adjustment or change in her self-view. Furthermore, she had become aware of an extremely disturbing reality – the fact that she could be rendered unconscious and her body 'taken over' by a mysterious 'other self', Big Meggie, who, for all that she *was* herself in earlier years, was still an independent entity – outside her own control.

There was no hurry, and indeed there *must* be no hurry. When she was ready, Mrs Collins would begin once more to move forward. The need to *do* something was mine, my own need to feel in charge, in control, 'doing therapy'.

In the middle of the writing which Mrs Collins gave me that week was another instance of Big Meggie's work. The writing changed in the middle of a page into a large scrawling hand.

He's not ashamed and says he wants to be my friend? That's a laugh. Who wants to be my friend, knowing about me? He says it's not my fault? Try telling that to Mum. She'd say differently. She's already told me what I am and she's ashamed of me. Why shouldn't he be even more? He doesn't know me. Why shouldn't he be ashamed? Anyone would, I am, Mum is. I need someone to talk to but no one really wants to talk to me or be my friend. You're all lying. No one wants to know me, by rights I should be dead. If I had any decency and guts, I'd be dead, but I haven't, so I'm not decent or got any guts, Mum said so. Mum will be very angry with me talking to you and Meggie telling you about me. No one must tell her, she'll be really angry.

And then the writing changed back again into Mrs Collins's normal hand, following on the previous train of thought and apparently unaware of the interpolated passage.

At the following session, despite my resolve to wait for Mrs Collins to take the initiative, I felt that the passage which Big Meggie had apparently written was a direct message to me, asking for more contact. I therefore suggested to Mrs Collins that the interview should be devoted once more to talking with Big Meggie.

She was easily recalled, and less hostile than on the first occasion, although extremely guarded. After much reassurance from me, she began to tell me events she could remember from when she was younger, especially about setting fire to her dress 'to burn the dirt away'. I pursued that theme, suggesting bit by bit that by talking through the things that made her feel dirty we would be able to remove that feeling. Doubtingly, Big Meggie asked me whether she could ever become free of her dirtiness. I assured her that we would work towards that the next time we spoke together.

Her mood gradually changed to one of grief and sadness, then returning to an anxious confusion about how she and Meggie Collins, and perhaps this little girl called Meggie, could *all* exist. She asked how it was possible for there to be parts of herself that she did not know. I tried to develop a metaphor which would give both her and Meggie Collins an image by which to explain the process they had undergone, and which we could also use to facilitate their reunion.

'People are a bit like rivers. Can you imagine a stream, starting up in the mountains from a spring and running down the valley?' Big Meggie agreed that she could picture this. 'As it runs down the valley, more water joins it so that it gets

179

bigger and bigger. That's like a person being born and then growing and learning. When the river gets to a rough bit with rocks, the water gets all disturbed and churned up, just like you when bad things happened to you.' Big Meggie nodded, her eyes still closed, but clearly picturing what I was describing and becoming wholly engrossed in it.

'When there's an especially rough and difficult bit, with big rocks, sometimes a bit of the water gets turned off to the side and then goes round and round like a whirlpool. Can you imagine that? A bit of the river going off behind a rock and getting trapped there so that it just goes round and round while the rest of the river goes on, not even knowing it's left a bit behind?' Yes, she could imagine that.

'Well, that whirlpool will just go on and on, going round and round, quite on its own. It does not know that it is really part of the river itself or that the river is there and flowing on. The water that's in it is now quite separate from the rest of the river, although it is still part of the river and belongs to it. What it needs is to get out from behind the rock and stop going round and round so that it can become part of the river again. That's you, stuck going round and round and not getting anywhere, but needing to get right back into the river, the whole person of whom you are a part, an important part. You need to join up again, so that Meggie is all one again and not divided up into separate parts.'

She had been following closely, absorbed in my description and, I thought, the image I had called up.

'Can't you put us together again?'

I hoped my sigh of relief was inaudible.

I spoke of my hope that *we* would be able to do precisely that, but that it would take her, and Meggie Collins, and Little

180

Meggie as well, to work together with me to achieve this. She agreed to allow Mrs Collins to 'take over' again, accepting my assurance that we would talk with each other again. This all seemed very satisfactory: Big Meggie appeared to have grasped that I was not an enemy, was not ashamed to speak to her, and above all that there was hope for her in union with her older self.

However, in the papers Mrs Collins gave me the following week, there was another passage apparently written by Big Meggie. The writing again was large, poorly controlled, with erratic use of capitals, and lacking in punctuation: all quite different from Mrs Collins's usual style. Oddly, this passage was written with a different pen from the pages which preceded it.

so Doctor let me interduce myself
Im Meggie Lawrence and your Mr Karle she says and you want to help us stop fighting so you can help her not me
sure she's told me what your both trying to do and what she's told you in Detail in writting
she says shes told me about this courage lark you must be jokeing thats not courage that's hiding behind paper
anyone can write on paper not that she had a right to but shes got no guts anymore than me, if she had guts or this courage why doesnt she tell you herself no she cant can she so wheres her courage she has'nt got any
she thought she knew everything but she doesnt does she
she hasnt said anything about Rasheed Rapeing me a second time has she,
how come she never mention that to you or could'nt she take any more of this learning as she calls it you know why because shes so ashamed and discusted with me about the first rape rasheed did and

cant face the other one so wheres her courage
and from what she's told me about what she calls Little Meggie she
was done a lot of hurt and nasty things but she ask for the last lot
did'nt she, Meggie does'nt seem to knew herself for sure about this
Little Meggie with Aunty Rene and Mavis you said what happened
to this Little Meggie was why I froze so Ive got her to blame have
I and Mum Meggie says no but then she doese seem to be sure she
says she thinks theres something about aunty Rene but she doesnt
know what that's a lot of good is'nt it I do'nt fight her she fights
me
I try to Die to be Decent but she stops me she says thats because
she wants to live and wants to help me to a bit bloody late for that,
if you've been working together for as long as she says then how
come it took you so long to talk to me,
well I'll tell you why cause really your only trying to help this little
Meggie and her not me you dont really

The blue ink and the better formed handwriting resumed at this point.

She's lying. There wasn't any second rape by Rasheed and Rene
didn't interfere with Little Meggie. She's just lying to make me feel
bad you know she's lying, don't you Mr Karle? Tell me you know
she's lying.

Then there was another line interposed in the cruder writing.

she didnt tell you about rasheed raping her a second time in the
liveing room did she so she's got to be lying

The clearer writing resumed again, although somewhat shakily continuing the pleas for me to tell 'her' that 'she' is lying, and then the rough hand resumes, heavily scoring the paper.

so your calling me a liarer now
well think about this the Armchair in the Liveing Room [followed by a rough drawing labelled ARMCHAIR] *REMEMBER NOW you wanted to know everything well remember this and see whos lying*
you cant help me or little Meggie
its a bit fucking late for that you only want to bring out our shame and dirt to help you Meggie youve said theres three of us in one body, thats impossable
I'm me Meggie Lawrence no one else and stuck in the darknes cause you wont let me die
its very confusing I dont know how you know so much about me but you dont know it all do you, you did'nt like it did you when I wrote about Rasheed rapeing me a second time did you well its true so for someone who reckons they now all about me shows your lying
if I was part of you you'd know that its me that suffered the shame and degraded me he hurt me that froze me that was dead till she disturbed me so why should she worry why should she bother

You sounded sincere but are you, you dont have to kid me your just as revolted as Meggie and mum and even me you said it wasnt my fault alright so your right with the first rape but do you think that takes any of the dirt and degraded feelings but the second one was
you dont fucking care anyway so whats the difference anyway its my dirt and shame and not hers so why should she or you bother

and like I said before she does'nt want to know and doesnt want you to know
No one can help me or little Meggie but if you are really sincere and want to help us some way you can by
Whats the use

There followed several more pages of abuse of Meggie Collins for her 'cowardice' in not really wanting to know the truth, and further demands to be left alone.

Fuck off and leave me alone I've got enough of my own cowdardness and I dont need yours as well

Despite the irresistibly convincing appearance of Meggie Lawrence, I began to have doubts about her again. The way in which she accused Meggie Collins of cowardice because she could or would tell me only in writing the more embarrassing or distressing things about herself and her life suggested to me that Mrs Collins herself was using 'Big Meggie' as a screen or disguise behind which she could express her own feelings. It also seemed to me to be something of an accusation: that *I* did not have either the courage or the genuine concern to facilitate her telling me the full truth face-to-face.

How much, I wondered, was I colluding with a defensive manoeuvre which somehow displaced, or even fictionalized, Mrs Collins's experiences? It was all very well for Mrs Collins and me to be understanding and sympathetic towards this supposedly separate person we called 'Big Meggie', but were we thus avoiding having to face directly and explicitly that it was *Mrs Collins* who had been raped, once or more often, by Rasheed, and had not fought to defend herself?

A great deal of the to-and-fro between Meggie and Big

The Filthy Lie

Meggie sounded like the internal dialogues most of us have with ourselves at times, and the picture of Mrs Collins sitting at her table writing alternately in one and the other personality was difficult to take seriously. And yet the internal dialogue and the multiple monologue addressed to me were strikingly reminiscent of the fictionalized accounts of cases of Multiple Personality Syndrome, *Sybil*, or *The Three Faces of Eve*. My own internal dialogue continued as unabated as Mrs Collins's.

16

It was only the following week that I recognized a major error I had made in the previous session. When talking to Big Meggie, I had not thought of asking her to open her eyes and look around. This meant, as it transpired later, that she did not know what I, my room, or even the clinic itself, looked like. When I went to the waiting-room to collect Mrs Collins, I found her standing in the middle of the room, staring vaguely around her. She ignored my greeting, and seemed to be startled, looking totally confused when I went over to her and repeated it. I said, 'Let's go to my room,' and led the way. She followed automatically, looking around her with a strangely bemused expression.

It was some time before I realized what was happening. Big Meggie had 'taken over'. After some time she agreed that she recognized my voice from last week. When eventually she agreed to sit down, she sat as far as she could from me, ignoring my gesture of invitation towards the chair in which Mrs Collins invariably sat.

Then she began to berate me for lying to her. I had told her I knew all about the rape by Rasheed. I could not know all about it because no one except Rasheed and she herself knew. She had not told even her mother all the details.

I assured her I had not made this claim, but rather that I knew all that she, in her other identity, had told me, and asked

186

if she would like me to go through all that I knew, so that she could be sure of what I did and did not know. She did not want me to do that, and became plaintive again. I asked her to give way to Meggie Collins as I wanted very much to talk with her, assuring her that we would talk again soon. This was another error, one that was to be rubbed in later: I had forgotten that I had promised to help her to get rid of the dirty thoughts and feelings.

She agreed to retire, and Mrs Collins reappeared, her posture, facial expression and voice changing as dramatically as always. She looked around the room expressing astonishment: she had no memory at all of coming here and was wholly taken aback to see where she was. She could remember getting ready to come to see me, but could recall nothing of the period following that.

I told her of the conversation I had had with Big Meggie, and discussed with her the image that I had already described to her the previous week. In a somewhat befuddled way she thought it made sense, but was not at all sure about the desirability of integrating Big Meggie into herself: she had had 'enough aggro' in her life without taking on any more. She agreed though that unification might be a great deal easier and less disruptive of her life than the present tug-of-war over her body. The interview passed, filled with little more except rambling complaints about how difficult, confusing and distressing all this was.

Two days later, Big Meggie came to the clinic. She gave her name to the receptionist as Mrs Lawrence and demanded to see me. The receptionist remarked later that, while she knew perfectly well that it was Mrs Collins she had seen and spoken with, she had looked so different, and behaved and spoken so differently, that she had actually doubted her own eyes.

On this occasion, however, Big Meggie was less angry. She asked me to explain what was going on, how apparently she and Mrs Collins could occupy the same body. Once more, I explained the concept of Multiple Personality, quoting the analogy of the river I had used before. She seemed altogether less aggressive and desperate than previously, and listened, asking for further explanation here and there, and for the first time accepted that I actually knew her personal history in considerable detail, including a great deal of information that she had believed no one but herself possessed.

She asked, as she had done earlier, about the reunion or fusion of her and her other part-selves, but found the concept extremely confusing and quite incomprehensible. Very poignantly, she expressed considerable longing for an end to the strife between her and Mrs Collins. We were by this time at the end of the allotted appointment. I suggested that, as we did not have time today and she was still distressed, she should sleep from now until the following Tuesday when we would meet again. She agreed, stipulating that she would remain asleep as long as Mrs Collins did not bother her, and as I talked soothingly and reassuringly, she appeared to fall into a relaxed sleep.

When Mrs Collins reappeared, I summarized for her the conversation I had held with Big Meggie, emphasizing that Big Meggie had withdrawn into sleep, but that she had insisted that Mrs Collins must leave her alone and not try to search out more memories.

The following week, Mrs Collins arrived as herself and was very composed and determined: today we were to try to bring about the reunion of her self with her separated twenty-year-old part-self.

I had planned to use the 'Empty Chair' technique while Mrs Collins was in hypnosis. I explained the idea to Mrs Collins. She would picture Big Meggie, who of course would look as she herself had done twenty-odd years earlier, sitting in the chair opposite hers. She would tell Big Meggie all that she knew of her traumatic experiences and destructive feelings, her understanding of how Big Meggie felt, and especially of her sympathy for her. She was to get closer and closer to Big Meggie until she could put her arms around her and then allow their two selves to merge and become one. Mrs Collins expressed some scepticism and considerable embarrassment.

She said: 'I'll feel such a fool talking to an empty chair like that, let alone pretending to put my arms round someone who isn't there, but I s'pose you know best, so I'll try.'

I reminded her how vividly she always experienced whatever she pictured in hypnosis and that it would not be 'pretending' at all, since she would be doing something very real: warmly embracing and accepting a part of herself that belonged within her and needed to be reunited.

We went through the induction. I repeated the suggestions I had already made about what she was to do, and that she was to return to ordinary wakefulness when she had completed the task, and then sat back and waited. Looking back, perhaps it would have been more effective had I asked Mrs Collins to speak aloud in both roles.

Various expressions flitted across Mrs Collins's face as she sat silently: anger; sadness; occasional tears appearing at her eyes; impatience. After a long time, she moved forward in the chair and began to lean towards the chair opposite her, then moving back again. Once more, she slid forward and reached her arms towards the other chair, held them out for a while and then sat back again. After an interval, she opened her eyes.

She didn't want me to get near her. She kept saying it was all lies, that what I told her about getting married to Bert and having the kids, that it was all lies and that I was trying to trick her.

I asked how she had felt and what Big Meggie had seemed to feel.

She was a bit angry, in fact she was angry with the both of us. She was angry with you 'cause you'd said you'd talk to her yourself, and that you'd let her down. You'd said you would help make her clean and take away the dirt. And she was angry with me for telling her what she said was lies.

It was only then I recognized how I had allowed myself to be swept along with the drama of all this. This strange and unusual situation seemed to have dislodged me from my habitual way of working: I would not normally have forgotten to fulfil a promise to a patient made in one interview for the next, in the way I had done with Big Meggie. Her questionable existence as a real person seemed somehow to have shaken loose my normal patterns of behaviour. I had determined much earlier to regard each of the secondary personalities as people in their own right and that I would try to carry out the interviews with them as real people. I had let that principle slip, and Big Meggie was right to be angry with me for doing so.

Mrs Collins was somewhat disappointed that we had, she felt, failed in this session, but was markedly impressed with the feeling of reality she had experienced in this very strange exercise. To her, it had been a wholly real conversation with a wholly real person whom she knew well, more intimately perhaps than most of us ever know anyone, but who was at the same time, she felt, independent. Most people have the experience of talking to themselves, and of replying, but such internal dialogues lack the dimension of separateness that Mrs Collins felt. We ended the interview agreeing to repeat it next time and hopefully take it further.

She had brought some papers with her, but was not at all sure whether to give them to me. She had not, as far as she was aware, written them herself, and she did not think they would be much help. All the writing had been done, apparently, by Little Meggie. It seemed to me, especially when I looked at them, that Little Meggie was feeling rather left out of things and becoming jealous of the attention the 'others' were getting.

The sheaf of papers was covered in a very childish hand, heavily scratched into the paper.

I want to die   help me to die
Love hurts to much [criss-crossed out]
I hurt so much   dont believe in nothing no one
*   why dont you let me die   God help me*
*   Ive no future*
Musternt hate mummy   it want mi falt   Im bad
*   thay just puneshing me for being bad   teralk bad*
didernt meen to   didernt no it was rong
mummy sorry   woant agane
mummy plees doant let them ceep herting me
plees mummy stop them plees   I woant teralk

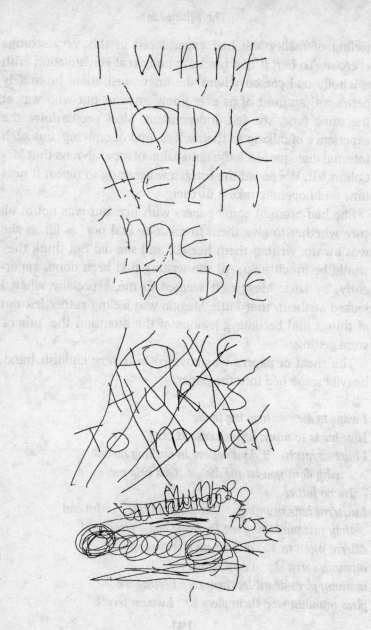

dirty and bad agane   plees plees
[In a somewhat larger scrawl] *Hate you all   Hate you*
Hate you all   Hate you
Mummy plees help me   that herting me so mutch
*   plees plees plees   mummy help me*
mummy I wish I was ded
Mummy Im so friten so scered
I hert so mutch   I wish I cood teralk to
I wish you forgiv me   I didernt meen to be bad and talk
derty   bout daddy
mummy mummy help me   mummy Mum

A real child, preserved in limbo for thirty-odd years, still suffering the torments which had been inflicted on her, still pleading for the help which had been withheld all those years ago – which to her were a continuous moment of eternity?

Or an adult woman pleading in what she intuitively felt to be the only acceptable way of pleading her own felt neediness?

Or an adult 'hysterical personality' manipulating her therapist's naïveté to gain the attention and interest she felt she could not get any other way?

And is there a difference?

Late that evening, the telephone rang. 'This is Meggie Lawrence. Is that Mr Karle?'

'Yes, Mr Karle speaking. Hallo, Meggie.'

'I'm in Eastbourne and I don't know what to do, it's all different from how I remember.'

My astonishment was total. I live not far from Eastbourne, and despite Mrs Collins's discovery of my home telephone number, I had not anticipated that she would find out where I lived. By questioning her carefully, I established which telephone box she was using. It was not far from the railway station, so I suggested that she should catch a train and go home, but she became very agitated and said she did not know where to go, she could not go home because her father was so angry with her. That ruse clearly was not going to work.

Thinking quickly of how she could be intercepted and guided home, I suggested that she should go to the railway station and wait there until either I or someone else would come to meet her. After considerable hesitation, she agreed.

I telephoned the railway police, and asked if they could intercept Mrs Collins and look after her until either a social worker or I could collect her.

Then I telephoned the Duty Officer at the Social Services Department of Mrs Collins's home area. After some initial resistance to becoming involved in this difficult situation, he agreed that if I would ensure that Mrs Collins caught a specific train, he would see to it that she was met in London and even escorted home. That encouraged me: whatever happened in Eastbourne, she would at least get home safely.

I drove to Eastbourne station. The Sergeant on duty was very anxious – and curious – about the rather strange, uncommunicative, and withdrawn lady whom he had found wandering around the station.

They agreed to let me see Mrs Collins, or Mrs Lawrence as they knew her, alone in another room. I was taken to see her, slumped in a chair over a cup of tea on the Sergeant's desk. She seemed relieved to see me, but looked very vague and could not be persuaded to speak.

Once settled in a separate room, we sat and talked. 'Mrs Lawrence' took out a packet of cigarettes, and then rummaged in her handbag, discarding the lighter she found, which Mrs

Collins normally used, and eventually finding a box of matches with which to light her cigarette. She explained that she had been disappointed and angry not to have seen me earlier in the day. She had gone to the clinic and asked the receptionist when I would see her. She had of course been told that I had already done so, and that I had now gone home. She had no memory of having seen me that day – which, to be sure, *she* had not done – and had therefore been very upset. She had then decided to go to Eastbourne because, so she said, she had happy memories of living in a hostel near there when she left school. When she had arrived, however, she had become completely confused because the town was not at all as she remembered it. She had looked in her handbag for cigarettes, and found a piece of paper on which was my name and a telephone number, so she had rung me.

I had told her repeatedly in our previous conversations how difficult it must be for her to cope with life in the world of twenty years ahead of her time, without Mrs Collins's knowledge and understanding of it, but never before had I had so apt an illustration. She seemed, for the first time, to accept that perhaps what I had been telling her – about the changes that had taken place in the world since the time in which she believed herself to be – was actually true, and that she was indeed somehow, in a way that she could not grasp, dislocated in time. She complained of it all being too confusing and that she was so very tired. I suggested that the best thing she could do would be to go to sleep and let Mrs Collins deal with things for both of them until our next meeting. Mrs Collins, I said, would be able to get home without difficulty.

Meggie immediately became distressed again. She could not possibly go home, her father hated her and would be angry if she were to do that. Slowly and carefully I again explained that this was no longer so: she had a house of her own, where her children would be waiting for her, worried about what had happened and why she had not come home by so late an hour. No! She had no children, I must not say things like that!

It suddenly struck me how odd – and completely outside normal psychotherapeutic practice – it was to be having a conversation like this, sitting in the Railway Police office, in the middle of the night.

As persuasively as I could, I suggested that we should leave all further discussion until our next meeting, but that she must realize she had somewhere to live, even if she did not know where it was. She accepted this, and finally also the repeated suggestion that she now let Mrs Collins 'take over'. I asked her to close her eyes, to relax, and gently to go to sleep. When she seemed to have followed this instruction, I asked Mrs Collins to 'take over' and open her eyes. She was both alarmed and confused at the unexpected and strange surroundings in which she found herself.

I explained what had happened. She was a little amused, and very apologetic about the disturbance and inconvenience she had caused me, expressing much gratitude for my coming to her rescue, and some anxiety about her children. I explained the arrangement with Social Services, telephoned the Duty Officer then and there, and told him which train Mrs Collins would catch. He assured me that a car would meet her train.

With Mrs Collins safely on her way home, I left for mine.

Mrs Collins kept her appointment the next week, very apologetic for the trouble Big Meggie had caused, but quite unwilling herself to accept any responsibility for the event. She was full of questions about what Big Meggie had said and done, but I would not allow her to spend any substantial part of the interview in this diversionary way, and insisted we had work to do: our time was beginning to run short.

We agreed that the first part of the session should be given to Big Meggie, but that Mrs Collins was to listen to the conversation and to take part and talk with either Big Meggie or myself whenever she felt it necessary.

Big Meggie emerged as soon as I addressed her, after Mrs Collins had relaxed and entered a light hypnotic trance. We talked about her visit to Eastbourne and the difficulties she had encountered there. She explained the excursion rather differently now: she had wanted 'to go into the sea' and had indeed tried to do this, but the sea 'was angry and wouldn't have her', because she was 'so dirty'. She said she had tried repeatedly to walk into the sea but had been rejected by it every time.

I reminded her that she had not been in the least wet when I had seen her at the station, so the endeavour had been minimal at most, but she ignored me when I pointed this out. When I challenged her euphemism of 'going into the sea', she agreed that she had wanted to drown herself.

She was apologetic about having troubled me and making me come out so late in the evening. She claimed that she did not know where I lived, a claim later repeated by Mrs Collins, who also expressed surprise that I had been able to find Eastbourne and get there so quickly. I said that I *had* been angry that she had been so silly, had taken control and got herself and Mrs Collins into so much difficulty, as well as causing her children such anxiety. She was perturbed when I mentioned being angry, and asked me if I was still angry with her and would no longer want to help her.

The Filthy Lie

This was a golden opportunity. We talked about anger and the fact that one could be angry with someone and still care for them, could be angry indeed *because* one cared, and that there need be no desire to 'take it out' on them – an explanation which seemed to reassure her. I used this episode again to emphasize the importance that Mrs Collins, with her experience and knowledge of the contemporary world, had for Big Meggie, and the need for the 'split' between them to be healed. I had a momentary feeling once again that Big Meggie was a masquerade, however involuntary, used by Mrs Collins – a masquerade which, Mrs Collins felt, needed to be maintained if she were to warrant my continuing time and attention.

Big Meggie again seemed to have lost the concept of reunion or fusion, and expressed her fear that what I really meant was her own extinction. This refusal to take on board something that had been repeatedly explained, discussed and apparently grasped seemed artificial and wilful. Suppressing my irritated reaction that extinction was after all what she had so assiduously but ineffectually sought in her suicide attempts, I recalled to her the image of the river and its whirlpools once again. Seeming only partly to accept this, she again returned to the theme of her irremediable dirtiness. I explained that when she and Mrs Collins had become one, she would no longer feel this because she would then be able to understand so much more than she did at the moment with her ignorance of the past twenty years.

I suggested that she should avoid intruding or 'taking over' for a few days but could remain aware and observe the day-to-day life of Mrs Collins, learn something of her history, get to know her children and so on. At this point, she pleaded with me: '*Please* don't make me go to sleep again.'

I felt the same conflict in myself once again over the contradiction she seemed to be inviting me to take up. I was
fairly confident that her suicidal wishes were not a deliberate,
purposeful search for death, but represented more her desperate feelings and a violent appeal for rescue. I also felt that
Big Meggie was actually a wholly real aspect of my client,
Mrs Collins, who would never be intact if this part-self were
suppressed again.

On top of these considerations, however, I was also aware
of my own irritation at being manipulated by Mrs Collins, and
of my impulse to take Big Meggie at her word when she spoke
of wanting to die.

In retrospect, when thinking over this interview, I felt I had
been mistaken, and that I should have explicitly challenged
her suicidal gestures and histrionics then and there, since a
better opportunity could hardly be envisaged. I could very
properly have tried to *make* Big Meggie face the fact that,
whatever she *said* about wanting to die, it was obvious that
this was not what she meant. Not only had she failed to drown
herself, but she also rejected the equivalent: going to sleep.
The threat was actually empty, and meant something quite
different, even though I did not see what at the time, and I
would not take it at face value. What she was saying between
the lines of her actual words was something like 'Please make
it all right' – work some magic which would relieve her of all
the burdens, all the pain, all the rage and hatred 'at a stroke'.

As we were discussing the idea of uniting the two part-
selves, Big Meggie interrupted herself to say that Meggie Collins
wanted to say something, and asked if she should allow it. She
accepted my reassurance that she and I would talk again in a
short while, whereupon Mrs Collins's voice now appeared. She

had apparently been monitoring the conversation and was not at all happy about the suggestion that Big Meggie should remain awake and observe her daily life. She asked that I should get Big Meggie to go to sleep again until our next appointment – whereupon Big Meggie 'broke through', the voice changing back again, to plead with me once more that I should not 'make her go to sleep again'.

This three-handed conversation continued until I was as confused as Mrs Collins had always said she was. In the end, we all agreed on a plan. Big Meggie said she would remain awake and promised not to interfere, and Mrs Collins agreed to permit this and not fight Big Meggie as long as she behaved herself. We were to meet again in two days' time.

It was 'Mrs Lawrence' who kept the next appointment, arriving two hours early. When I collected her from the waiting-room she remained mute, looking confused and extremely distressed, eventually wandering around my room in an agitated and aimless fashion. When I insisted that she must either respond to me or I would have to end the interview, she agreed she was Meggie Lawrence. I chided her for breaking our agreement: she had 'taken over' when she had promised not to do so. Then she explained. 'That woman' had allowed things to be done to her that she, Meggie Lawrence, could not tolerate. Mrs Collins 'had let somebody touch her'. It transpired that Mrs Collins had attended the Physiotherapy Department earlier in the day, had taken off her outer clothing there, and had permitted the physiotherapist to manipulate her back.

With many an inward sigh, and strenuous efforts to restrain my impulse to tell her to stop trying to make a fool of me, I explained why it had been both necessary and totally acceptable that a woman should touch her in this way, that it was a completely proper medical procedure, and very necessary to reduce her physical pain. I still had a very strong feeling of being played up, but could see no other way of preserving the ground we had gained. By the very concepts and images I had employed much earlier, I had fostered the framework in which we were operating and I was now hoist with it, albeit in a far more concrete form than I had envisaged.

We talked at considerable length of her feelings about being touched in any way by a woman, but when I connected these with her reaction to the abuse by Rene, Meggie became increasingly distressed, and brought up another grudge or anxiety. She had been observing Mrs Collins's life, and so had noted a visit from Heather at which the latter had mentioned that she and I were shortly to meet to discuss Mrs Collins. Mrs Collins had been consulted about this meeting, and although a little anxious about why we should wish to meet and what we would say to each other, had consented.

But Big Meggie was very angry at what she regarded as a breach of confidence. It was barely all right for Mrs Collins to talk to *me* about such intimate things, but it was by no means all right for me to pass on these confidences to yet another person. She would not accept that Heather's knowledge of her life was as intimate as mine, and that indeed Heather had known Mrs Collins for very much longer than I had done.

I speculated, silently, about the disturbing effect of physical contact with another woman, recalling too Mrs Collins's violent feelings when asked about 'lesbian tendencies' by another social worker. It seemed complex: Mrs Collins seemed to have been denied affectionate contact in childhood, and, from the picture given by her of her mother, probably from birth onwards; the physical contact with Rene had been initiated as a pseudo-mothering; there was reason to suppose that Mrs Collins had experienced sexual arousal when manipulated by Rene; apart from the intrinsic abusiveness of this, the whole thing became part of a grossly abusive and terrifying episode. *Ergo* what would, to most people, be innocuous or even pleasing – comforting, healing, gentle touch – had become eroticized, and inextricably linked with disgust, shame, and terror. To speak of 'not having come to terms with her lesbian tendencies' would be a travesty, but close enough to the mark to be grossly disturbing.

Big Meggie filled the whole interview. She refused to allow me to take up her earlier demands for help with her feelings of being unclean, or indeed with anything, and persisted in talking about her anger at Mrs Collins about the physiotherapy, and at me for my unreliable confidentiality. In the end, with considerable pressure from me, she agreed to retire again so that I could speak briefly to Mrs Collins.

I noted that Big Meggie was every bit as determined as her *alter ego* of the present day to prolong the interviews well beyond their allotted span, and it seemed to me that Big Meggie was fully aware that I would have to cut Mrs Collins's 'own' time with me short as the interview was by then already running over. Jealousy of Heather, my other clients, even of Mrs Collins herself – perhaps all this was an expression of *Mrs Collins's* jealousy of anyone who had my attention, of anyone with whom she had to share me.

During these weeks when I was heavily engaged with Big Meggie, Little Meggie was writing furiously and at length. What she wrote was addressed primarily to her mother and was no more than an endlessly repetitive expression of her ambivalent feelings, and appeals for rescue, but it emerged in such large volume only when my attention, and of course that of Mrs Collins, were turned away from her. The whole situation felt and looked exactly as if Mrs Collins's three part-selves were all competing for my time and attention, and each resented the attention and care I spent on one of the others.

Rather belatedly, I brought the interview to a close. It had seemed a rather fruitless session, and I felt that Mrs Collins, although she said nothing, felt much the same.

17

September, Year Two

Mrs Collins kept the next appointment, her primary personality apparently well in control. She was very subdued in manner, and responded to none of the openings I gave her. She was extremely defensive about anything to do with Big Meggie, assuring me that she had had no significant difficulties since our last meeting. She talked at length about her desire to have a break and to spend some time at the seaside.

I tried suggesting that perhaps she was finding it difficult to talk because of her resentment at my impending meeting with Heather, and her feelings of betrayal about the threat this represented to her. Nothing. The interview wore on without any breach of the wall around her.

The following week, I found Big Meggie in the waiting-room, no longer confused about where she was or who I was, and angry – very angry. The tirade that poured out when we got to my room sounded more like Mrs Collins's anger even though spoken in Big Meggie's voice.

She was angry that I did not allow her to telephone me whenever she wanted or needed, that I would not see her more frequently and for longer sessions. She berated me for having said I was angry with her for going to Eastbourne and calling me to her rescue. Gradually, however, she began to speak of her mother, that she was always and necessarily right and that she, Meggie, loved her mother, respected her views and actions and so on. The transferential split was all but explicit.

I challenged this quite directly, telling Meggie that she was lying and knew she was doing so. I said firmly and baldly that her anger at me was in fact anger at her mother's failure to be available and willing to help her. I insisted that there was no point in her trying to convince me that she thought of her mother in this idealized way, but that she was doing so in order to avoid admitting to herself the anger, disappointment, and even hatred that she could feel inside herself and which made her feel overwhelmingly guilty. Those feelings she was displacing on to me.

She denied that this made sense or could possibly be true. I pointed out to her that her experience with me contradicted her experiences with her mother. Although I was not available all day and every day for her, I *was* there regularly and consistently and offered her unconditional and unqualified acceptance. When I was angry with her, I continued to be concerned and to offer the help she needed; when she was angry with me and could allow herself to tell me so, nothing bad happened. I did not reject her because of her hostile and angry feelings towards me, and even encouraged her to express them. In addition, her feelings did me no harm: I was not damaged by them.

She could – or would – neither recognize the connection I was making, nor grasp the generalization I sought: that her negative feelings were not dangerous. The interview went on and on without seeming to lead anywhere. Eventually I pointed out that we were approaching the end of our time, that I must recall Mrs Collins and that she should give way to her. She did not dispute the need, but spun out the time in a transparently deliberate way, and would not cooperate – she would not stop talking even for a few moments – until the time for the end of the interview had come and gone, and I had been warned by telephone that the next client was waiting. Then at last she agreed to give way.

All I said to her in the course of this interaction had been concerned, caring, designed and intended to help her to break free from her pain – but it was all abusive, too. I was 'battering' her – in the most caring way, to be sure – but nevertheless fulfilling her expectations. Her view of the world was vindicated.

This understanding, as so often, came only in hindsight, however. Even with the advantage of that viewpoint it is difficult to see how else I could have responded. I could have waited, allowed Big Meggie and Mrs Collins to arrive in their own time at the understanding I was trying to *make* her grasp. To say that time was running out sounded – and still sounds now – like an excuse.

Mrs Collins re-emerged, weary, complaining of many pains, especially in her chest, back and legs, and ignoring completely all my efforts to focus on what had happened and why we were meeting. She expressed suicidal wishes. All this pain and trouble were too much for her, and she showed me the razor-blades she had bought that morning. Severe and continuous pain certainly can lead very readily to thoughts of suicide, but the fact that such thoughts were back again had more to do with the rage which was central to the interaction we had just had. Unable to do anything else at that moment, I had to insist that she had already overrun her time, and that any discussion of all this would have to wait until the following week.

There were, apparently, no writings to give me this week. I wondered who would attend the next appointment.

In the event, it was Mrs Collins who came. She was reluctant to talk about anything except her pains, her weariness of the whole business of resolving her problems, her anxiety about whether she would be permitted to continue the voluntary work she did for Social Services, the unhelpfulness of Heather and her department over getting her the weekend break she needed – all the diversionary tactics she could command. Eventually, she agreed to allow me to speak with Big Meggie.

Fruitless though the last session had seemed at the time, some change had occurred in Meggie's attitudes. She was no longer angry, accusatory and complaining, but generally much more positive and cooperative, although I had no idea as to why the change had taken place. She seemed to have accepted the fact that the year was what I had said it was, even though it still seemed quite incomprehensible to her. This was not surprising. After all, she had no knowledge at all of the years between her 'own' time and the present, nor of any of the events during that interval. It seemed impossible to her that she should, for example, have given birth to four children without knowing anything about it, but admitted reluctantly that it seemed that this must be true.

Once more I tried to convey to her the nature of the 'split' that had taken place in her own personality, around the latest time that she could actually recall – the time she thought it still was. I described the way in which she had been able to dissociate herself from things that were actually happening by, for instance, focusing all her attention on some object such as a light bulb, so that she became numb to what was happening. I explained that the horror of what she had been forced to endure – by Rasheed, by her mother when she had told the latter of the rape, through the pregnancy and the miscarriage,

207

and in her feelings of responsibility for and guilt about the death of the baby – all this had caused her to need to enter this detached and isolated state.

With enormous reluctance, she seemed to accept this formulation. She was in an impossible situation: twenty years must have gone by, but it simply could not be so. Here was an explanation which, however far-fetched, complicated and difficult to grasp, seemed at least to make some sense of what she was experiencing. In the end, she yielded without difficulty or resistance to Mrs Collins, on the understanding that our earlier agreement of non-interference and observation still stood.

I felt that I had been expected to repeat all that I had just previously discussed with Mrs Collins with this other 'version' of the same client, and that I was being tested for consistency. I had a strong impression that Mrs Collins was using this device to see if, when faced with herself as she had been at the time of the rape, I maintained the same attitudes, or whether I would reject and condemn her as her mother had done. It was as though she were using the transference in her own way.

Usually, the therapist interprets the client's reactions towards him, and her feelings and behaviour in the therapeutic situation, as a re-enactment of her behaviour, relationships with, and feelings towards, emotionally important people in her childhood. Mrs Collins seemed to be doing this in reverse – in dramatized form – presenting the actual persona she had been at the relevant time, *in* the therapy room and *in the presence of* the therapist.

The next appointment was kept by Big Meggie. We began by speaking of her mother's part in her history. For the first time, her protests were feeble, and then faded away completely.

Sadly now, she seemed to accept the truth of what she heard and at least in part made it her own by paraphrasing the essentials of what I had said: so much of what she had suffered had happened because of her mother's failure to protect, comfort and succour her. At last, reluctantly and playing hard for extra time, Big Meggie gave way to Mrs Collins.

The next week, we discussed what had transpired in the session. Mrs Collins felt just as Big Meggie had felt by the end of the session: sad at her mother's failure and betrayal, but with no evident anger. I re-called Big Meggie and took up the same thread, but Mrs Collins seemed unready at any level to face the issue of what had happened to her angry feelings as yet, except when writing alone at home. Big Meggie was as always very reluctant to yield to her *alter ego*, pleading for more time with me over and over again.

Mrs Collins told me as she was leaving that Social Services had now come up with a short holiday for her: a weekend in Eastbourne. I was startled at the unwisdom of this arrangement, but there was no way in which I could question it, as she was due to go at the end of the week. It so happened that I went away for the weekend myself.

On my return late on the Monday evening, I found the tape on my telephone machine was nearly full. Meggie Lawrence had called repeatedly; there were half a dozen calls from the Samaritans in Eastbourne, whom she had approached and who were in turn anxious to reach me; the police surgeon in Eastbourne was anxious to contact me about a lady she had been called to examine, a Mrs Lawrence, who had been picked up by the police wandering along the shore and periodically walking into the sea; the consultant psychiatrist at the hospital in Eastbourne, who had admitted Mrs Lawrence, wanted to speak to me. They had all been told by 'Mrs Lawrence' that she was seeing me and that I would deal with everything. Finally, there were several calls from Sharon anxiously asking if I knew where her mother was.

I returned only one of the calls – that from Sharon – to tell her that her mother had been admitted under the name of Lawrence, explaining that that had been her name in her first marriage. I suggested that she should contact the hospital and perhaps speak to her mother herself.

The next day I spoke briefly with the nursing staff on the psychiatric ward, told them Mrs Collins's real name, gave them her address, and explained my involvement and, very tentatively, my diagnosis. I also spoke to the consultant psychiatrist, and heard from him much the same account of what had happened from him as the police surgeon had left on my answering machine.

The consultant clearly believed that the wool had been well and truly pulled over my eyes by this client. He and his colleagues considered her to be 'depressed, having difficulties in coping with life, and lonely' – to quote the words of the report he sent to me later. That, of course, was much the same reaction as Mrs Collins had aroused in psychiatrists throughout her life, and it was, of course, true – but superficially so, in appearance only, and only if one failed to *listen* to her. She had been admitted compulsorily, but after brief observation it was thought that she was not really at risk of suicide and she was to be discharged in a day or two, on the understanding that she would return to my care.

'Meggie Lawrence' telephoned me herself from the hospital that evening. I told her firmly she had only herself to thank for her predicament and that it was up to her to resolve it. She had to deal with the situation she had created herself. I pointed out that this was yet another instance of the disastrous effects of her attempts to dominate Mrs Collins, and that the best thing she could do would be to give way to Mrs Collins. That, however, aroused only fierce opposition.

I reminded her of our appointment the following day and ended the conversation, refusing explicitly to 'come to her rescue'. Her predicament was of her own making, and the solution was in her own hands. To myself alone I said that I was her therapist, not her mother.

Was Mrs Collins as 'innocent' as she claimed, or had this been another challenge to me to see whether I really did care as much as she wanted me to? I also wondered to what extent this escapade represented a desperate attempt to get me to become her mother in all the ways in which her mother had failed her: an attempt to get me to take over total care of her – as though she were a baby?

The appointment of which I had reminded her was duly kept by 'Mrs Lawrence'. She said nothing of what she had done to make the police detain her and which had precipitated her compulsory admission, and she became evasive when I told her that I already knew what she had been doing. Once again, I used her distress and her inability to cope with life as indicating her inescapable and vital need for Mrs Collins, the central self of which she herself was a separated part, emphasizing, as I had done on the telephone, her responsibility for *her* actions.

At long last, her anger began to appear: initially at me for my apparent refusal to speak to her on the telephone – she seemed not to have recognized my answering machine as such and was convinced that I had answered the telephone in

211

person and then refused to speak to her, understandable in that such machines had not been as common in 'her day' as they were now – or to come to her rescue over the weekend. I had let her down, just as Mum had done. At last she seemed to have made the connection and it made sense to her. In return for my promise to re-call her and help her deal with these intolerable feelings, she yielded to Mrs Collins.

Mrs Collins had no knowledge of anything since catching the train for Eastbourne the previous Saturday. As far as she was concerned, she had moved straight from that moment to the present. I told her in outline what had happened, making it clear that I felt the responsibility for all that had occurred was hers: Big Meggie was her responsibility, part of her, and could 'take over', as I had always insisted, only with her consent or collusion. Big Meggie's actions were in all truth essentially her own, and sooner or later the 'split' between them must be bridged if she were not to go through the rest of her life in this destructive fashion.

As an aside, I found it puzzling to note that Mrs Collins described the events of the weekend in writing a week later. It appeared to be a clear memory, but since Mrs Collins claimed categorically that Big Meggie had 'taken over' before she had started the journey to Eastbourne, I could not make sense of the fact that it was *Mrs Collins* who remembered and recounted the story. The memory should, one would think, belong within the Big Meggie personality and therefore be inaccessible to Mrs Collins, and at that time, no reunion of Big Meggie with the primary personality, Meggie Collins, had as yet been carried out. As Mrs Collins once wrote: 'Confused? Join the club!'

In contrast to Big Meggie, Mrs Collins's concern was not for the events of the weekend at all, but for Little Meggie, whose distress and shame, and especially guilt, over having enjoyed what Uncle Tom had done to her, still plagued her. Believing that this was an avoidance tactic, I insisted on sticking to her feelings about her mother. I used the phrase, 'your mother inside you' as the source of her feelings of shame, cowardice, dirt and so on, and this provoked a powerful reaction.

'I don't want her inside me, I want to kick her out!' But eventually she agreed to start work with Big Meggie.

My plan was to substitute comfort from Mrs Collins's adult personality – the comfort which Big Meggie had sought and failed to obtain from her mother immediately following the rape by Rasheed – for the rejection she had experienced.

In hypnosis, Big Meggie reappeared. I carried out an hypnotic induction with her and asked her to go back to the time immediately following the first rape by Rasheed. It seemed a curiously and awkwardly roundabout procedure, and more than a little bizarre: to 'hypnotize' a secondary personality who emerged when I hypnotized the primary. Furthermore – to conduct age-regression therapy with the *secondary* personality was something I had never read in the literature.

Yet it seemed to make sense. If Big Meggie actually was a separate personality, then she could be treated as such, despite the curious fact that she was not the only persona inhabiting the body in the chair.

Big Meggie began to describe her despair as she washed herself and cleaned up her room after Rasheed had at last left her alone: the feelings of utter helplessness and degradation, her desperate need to be comforted and supported. Eventually, and with enormous effort, she talked of her anger at her mother for her mother's failure to meet her needs in any way, offering instead only contempt and condemnation. Her emotions were clearly visible in her face and movements.

She began to rage violently, her face working, her fists clenched and moving around spasmodically as though looking for something or someone to strike. As this rose to a crescendo, I asked Mrs Collins, who I hoped was monitoring the procedure, to intervene and to provide explanation, comfort and support to her younger self. Bit by bit, the movements of her hands and arms became less violent, and her face and body slowly relaxed. When she reported that she was able to visualize Mrs Collins present and offering comfort, I asked her to let herself be embraced, and as she felt Mrs Collins's arms go round her, she could let all the disgust, degradation, dirtiness, pain and horror fade away, soon to be followed by the rage at her mother's inadequacy, weakness, and failure.

It seemed to work. Mrs Collins's arms went out in front of her and around an invisible other, then folded against her chest. At first she was stiff and tense, but gradually her whole body and face relaxed again.

Big Meggie, in a markedly less distressed voice, told me that she was now feeling better, at ease, and no longer in distress, and Mrs Collins confirmed that she was able to cuddle Big Meggie with comfort. She was visibly more at ease.

Using once again the image of a river with an eddy forming a backwater, I suggested that Big Meggie and Mrs Collins allow themselves to merge together, to become one, and then to return to the present, to my room, and to normal consciousness. After a little while, she opened her eyes.

We talked a little about what had happened. The whole episode had been very vivid and real to Mrs Collins, and she spoke in a reflective and gentle way about what clearly had obviously been very moving to her.

The Filthy Lie

When you told me what we was going to do to try to get Meggie and me as one, I knew that I'd have to work extremely hard if it was to work. I was afraid Meggie might not though, as I didn't know if she was willing. Luckily it worked, and my feelings to live was stronger than her thoughts or plans to kill herself.

I made a mental note of the fact that she was still talking of 'Big Meggie' in the third person, when suddenly, before I made any comment, this changed: it seemed to me at that moment that the reunion had actually taken place.

The anger and hatred was so intense, it hurt so much, and I had this terrible urge to lash out. I wanted to smash, break, and hurt everything around, including you. How I didn't, I don't know. It was so bad, I can only put it down to you that I didn't. You said I was a very brave lady. I think you were very brave too. You'll probably never know what I mean by that. But your calmness and voice helped me keep control of my temper, and as the anger and hurt began to come out, I could see the whirlpool opening up and begin to run slowly into the river like the water draining out of a bucket into the river.

Slowly the whirlpool seemed to get smaller and smaller, until I could see myself. Then the river seemed to run straight, and the whirlpool had gone, and I was hugging myself and I felt calmness and peacefulness come over me, and Meggie and I became one.

18

Mrs Collins was very cheerful when she arrived for her next interview. I gradually realized that she had had recourse to 'Dutch courage' once more. All had been well, so she said, over the preceding five days, without any of the disturbances that had plagued her for so long.

Even allowing for the drinks she had so obviously taken before coming, this seemed just a little too good to be true, the more so because she deftly avoided talking about anything except what was happening in her life currently. She fetched a large pad of her usual paper from her bag and began to leaf through it. In a distinctly flirtatious way, she explained that there were some parts which she did not wish me to read. She did, however, begin to speak of her feelings towards me, which, she said, were now 'more than just friendship'. It was obvious that her imbibing had been intended to give her the courage to tell me this – the disinhibiting effect of alcohol was patent.

I tried to take up this topic, and we spoke for some time about the intimacy which therapy can induce. Mrs Collins found it difficult to grasp the distinction between a relationship that develops spontaneously between two people in the course of everyday life, and the relationship fostered in therapy.

I reminded her of the various emotions she had felt towards me, such as anger, resentment that I did not give her enough, fear of betrayal and so on, all of which were 're-plays' of her

216

reactions to her mother. I pointed out to her that she had actually recognized herself that some of her reactions to Heather were of the same kind: that they had nothing to do with Heather herself, but were a re-play of how she had felt towards, particularly, Rene.

My explanations fell on deaf ears. As far as she was concerned, her feelings were real. That is, of course, unquestionable: feelings *are* real. I tried at length to articulate that the feelings themselves were real, true, and indeed valuable and good, but that the supposed *object* of the feelings was not true or real. I emphasized over and over again that it was not *me* she felt for but an idealized representation of what I stood for. I felt I was putting more effort, more energy, and more sheer work into this than I had felt myself expending at any other time with Mrs Collins.

Most of it, however, made no sense to Mrs Collins. From her point of view, she was deeply attached to me, even 'in love' with me, although her courage did not extend to so explicit an avowal. She also saw me as caring about her, as accepting, appreciative of her qualities, patient with her when it was necessary – almost all that she wished for in a man. That my caring for her, my attention, the time I gave her and so on, should be my professional responsibility, but not *ipso facto* false and a pretence, was an insoluble puzzle to her – as it is to many in her position.

Mrs Collins had known for several weeks that we were due to have another break in our sessions, as I would be away on holiday during the following fortnight. As always, she could not admit that she resented my absences, or that she was made anxious by them, except occasionally in her writing. She showed her feelings only very indirectly, through her insistence

217

on talking superficially, about current events only, and by endeavouring to prolong the interview beyond the set time: suddenly remembering, as we were closing the session, one after another 'important' point that she insisted on raising. Her evasion of the real issues of an interruption in our contact was both obvious and unbreached.

While I was away, Mrs Collins wrote rather less than usual. There was more rumination about what had really happened with Rene and Tom, ending with a plea that, by using age regression, we should clarify what had *really* happened, and especially to discover whether Rene's attentions had been at least in part intended to help her or whether it had been entirely for Rene's own perverse pleasure.

Another passage mourned the fact that she was unable to tell her elder daughter what it is like to give birth to a child, since all her children, except the stillbirth, had been delivered by Caesarian section. This seemed to be a disguised expression of a deeper conviction – that her inability even to give birth normally was proof that she *herself* was not normal. Then there was a description of yet another upsetting set-to with Lee. He had given her a 'love-bite', which had upset her greatly. She felt that she could not stand him, was afraid of him, and yet she loved him.

This was where we had come in. These thoughts – the self-condemnation for her 'bad mothering' of Lee when she had thrown him out of the house the year before last at Christmas – had been the trigger for rubbing paint-stripper into her legs.

The date we had planned for the end of therapy – Christmas – was coming measurably nearer, and her anticipation of the separation naturally increased the intensity of her feelings about termination. Perhaps too the fact that her therapy was to end almost exactly on the anniversary of her self-mutilation/self-punishment had something to do with this.

The increasing sexualization of her feelings towards me was reflected in some of the questions she had asked me in various interviews. For instance, she had asked me some weeks earlier, insistently and repeatedly, whether any man could want to have a physical relationship with her if he knew her history. When I asked her to explore this question, she side-stepped. These questions were quite obviously intended to disclose whether *I* was sexually repulsed by her, and so whether she could be sexually attractive to me. The discussion in her writing, and to a lesser extent in the sessions, of the eroticized aspects of her interactions with Lee, also carried overtones of sexual display.

Our first meeting on my return was very difficult. Mrs Collins smiled pleasantly, and denied any problems. All was fine, there were no difficulties, she was perfectly happy. The defensive screen seemed impenetrable. I chipped away, asking repeatedly about her reactions to my absence, suggesting that her acceptance of my going away was not as genuine as she made it out to be, until bit by bit she felt safe enough to talk about being angry that I should go away to enjoy myself when she needed me so much.

The next step, linking her feelings of being let down, betrayed, unloved, to her relationships in the past, was even more difficult. The defensive smile was back in place, and her response to all I offered was summarized in her passive-aggressive: 'You're the doctor. You'd know better than I.' From time to time, the real Meggie Collins, with her wit, directness, and courageous honesty, showed in brief flashes, only to disappear again behind the aggressively polite and passive façade.

We got nowhere. I pinned my hopes on the fact that I would be able to see her twice weekly for a few weeks and so could, perhaps, increase the pressure to break through these intensified defences. I was, however, also aware that the greater frequency of contact would also enhance her attachment to me.

I reminded Mrs Collins that our time was beginning to run out, and that we were now barely two months from the planned end of treatment. This too was accepted with the same outward equanimity and calm. There was no visible sign of any reaction or feeling, and I wondered what form her reaction would take when it did emerge. Somehow, despite her defendedness, the interview threatened to continue beyond its allotted space, but I firmly ended the interview at the set time.

What she wrote after this session showed that she had experienced this properly-timed interview as abbreviated – 'I was sorry our talk today was so short.' I felt that she had experienced it to be short because I had not prevented her from keeping the content to trivia: that she had been able to fend off my attempts to address her real feelings. She had also assumed that her anger at my taking yet another holiday had actually been communicated to me, and clearly thought that I had 'shortened' the interview for that reason.

When I read what she wrote in the following few days, I found myself oscillating between rage and frustration. On paper, she spelled out what she felt and what she thought in detail and without dissimulation or hesitation, but in person – little or nothing. For example, she wrote of avoiding Heather when the latter wanted to visit, lest she see the mark of Lee's 'love-bite' and be angry.

*I told you I'd refused to see Heather the first week you was away.
I didn't really know why I felt that way at first, but after a few
days I'd been trying to figure it out and discovered I was afraid of
her. I think I was afraid she'd see the mark on my face and neck
what Lee had done by force, and more than likely I thought she'd
have a go at me over it, like Mum had done over Rasheed. The mark
was making me scared and panicky, so for a while I was down over
that, but I've gotten over it now. I guess when I worked it out or
realized that Heather was not Mum, I arranged to see her at the
office, though she was unable to keep the appointment.*

A most encouraging insight, to be sure. We had spent a considerable amount of time some weeks earlier talking about the
concepts of projection and transference without Mrs Collins
being able to grasp them, but now she had, in her own way
and at her own pace, understood the ideas and made them her
own. But how could I build on such an insight when it had
not been articulated openly in person?

One thing, however, I felt I could take up from her writings:
the anger which she expressed in person towards men who
abused children. Reports of such incidents appeared almost
daily in the newspapers, and her rage was wholly appropriate.
Good, healthy anger – and directed outward, not on to herself,
but there was still the same need to disown her anger towards
me in her fear of reprisal or reaction on my part. Not only did
she repeatedly disclaim her anger with me – 'Honestly I was
not angry with you', 'I don't mean to be', etc. – but she even
went a step further, in a final paragraph, by describing herself
and me as allies in a common fight against evil when referring
to the planned book.

Mrs Collins was more her normal self when she arrived for

our next session. The noncommittal and distant smile was absent, but for a long time she would talk only of her current difficulties with Lee. This continuing saga had served many times to divert from her immediate feelings, while at the same time enabling her to talk about her attitudes to him and probe my reaction to them.

Lee's way of life, his attitudes, and his behaviour towards her represented the unacceptable parts of her self: deeply buried and denied. Her 'public face' was the converse: gentleness, submission, self-abnegation, patient suffering, acceptance, and tolerance of deprivation. Lee personified the dark side of her own personality: demanding, assertive, angry, aggressive, violent, and sexual.

Bit by bit, we worked on the problem of Lee and her relationship with and reactions to him, especially her difficulty in reconciling her need to exert some real control over his domination of herself and her home. She needed to avoid at all costs rejecting him in exactly the way that she had been rejected by her own mother, but she seemed quite unable to respond at all to the interpretations I made, however gently and carefully phrased, that this was really about herself, and that Lee in this context represented the disowned aspects of herself.

Gradually, however, she moved towards her feelings of anger towards her mother. This had often been expressed quite openly on paper, but Mrs Collins still shied away from speaking openly about it. She had been able for quite a time to speak of being *disappointed* in her mother; she had begun to feel more comfortable at admitting that her mother had been inadequate, and even wrong.

On the rare occasions when Mrs Collins had spoken of her anger towards her mother openly, she had spoken calmly, sometimes a little plaintively, but never with real feeling. Her anger was somehow sanitized and abstract. The release and experience of that rage was the next and major task ahead of us, and I told Mrs Collins so. Without a hint of the 'I'm sure you know best' compliance, Mrs Collins accepted this – but she was quite sure she could feel nothing of the kind.

Yes, her mother had been wrong in what she said and did, both when Little Meggie had been abused by her father, and equally when Big Meggie had confided in her about the rape by Rasheed – but she could not feel any anger. I kept my disbelief to myself. Mrs Collins quite clearly did *not* feel conscious anger explicitly at her mother. She was quite unaware of displacing her rage on to others: on to Lee, on to myself, sometimes on to Heather, and especially towards herself, in one or other of her personae. I replied that her anger *was* there, but disguised in various ways, and that until it was freely and openly experienced and acknowledged between us, she would not be free from it.

At the thought of the release and discharge of her anger, Mrs Collins said with some humour that *I* might not be afraid of what would happen then, but *she* certainly was. The mood lightened somewhat, and I found myself promising that when she let it out in my presence, really giving it vent, I would give her a bottle of champagne in celebration. She became much more relaxed, and left my room in a positive frame of mind, however doubtful of the wisdom of really letting go of her stored-up anger.

I should have realized that her reaction would be delayed until after the end of the interview. An hour or so after I had said goodbye to Mrs Collins, I came down to the reception area and found her there, struggling violently with one of our doctors. When I went over, he explained to me, between his endeavours to control Mrs Collins, and through the breathlessness of his struggle with her, that she had suddenly tried to stab herself with a screwdriver, and he had intervened. He had been trying since, unsuccessfully, to break her grip on the screwdriver, and even while we were both restraining her she was trying to force the tool towards her stomach.

Between us, we managed to prise her fingers off the screwdriver and take it away. She was completely unresponsive to anything that was said to her, struggling until the screwdriver was removed, and then making frantic and uncoordinated movements of her arms, and dashing around like a trapped animal, making little sounds of distress, but not speaking. It was obvious to me that Little Meggie had returned.

I talked continuously and persistently, as close as I could to her ear, addressing her as 'Meggie' and speaking as though she were a little girl. She slowly began to calm a little, and my colleague retreated with obvious signs of relief. The car driver arrived, and was asked by the receptionist to come back in a little while. He looked more than a little curious about what was going on, seeing Mrs Collins dashing about the waiting-room, closely followed by me wherever she went. Fortunately, no other clients were in the room at the time.

Eventually I was able to get her to sit down, and then began an hypnotic induction. Slowly she relaxed, the tension and frantic movements fading away. Still addressing the little girl, I told her that we would talk properly next week and that I would be able to help her then, but that she should sleep now so that she could have relief from all that troubled and frightened her. Like a frightened child, she snuggled down and visibly fell asleep. After a few moments, I asked Mrs Collins to open her eyes.

She was more than a little surprised to find me sitting beside her. She complained instantly of a fierce headache and was obviously in a very confused state. What had happened? I explained briefly, and then, pointing out rather firmly that she had already made me miss two trains, insisted that she must now go home. Mrs Collins was distressed to hear she, or Little Meggie, had given so much trouble, but it was only with some difficulty that I could persuade her to leave without holding another interview – yet another consequence of the inde-terminate boundaries that followed inescapably from that unstructured start of her therapy.

Mrs Collins was struggling. I was struggling. But worse was to come.

Shortly before Mrs Collins was due to see me next, Heather telephoned me to tell me that she had been promoted to a more senior post in her department. This was disastrous timing. It meant that she would no longer be able to visit Mrs Collins and seemed yet another illustration of the principle that for people like Mrs Collins, 'Sod's Law' seems always to apply. In this case, it meant that Mrs Collins would be losing two of the most significant relationships in her life within a month of each other.

Mrs Collins arrived rather drunk. In a passive way, she expressed considerable aggression. No, she had not taken any drink. No, she was not upset about anything, why should she be? No, she was not angry, certainly not about the fact that Heather was moving to another post and would not be seeing her any more. No, she had no feelings at all about the fact that before much longer she would not be seeing me any more.

225

Why should this upset her or make her angry? I had other and more important things to do than to talk with her, and anyhow, everyone dropped her in due course, so why should she have any feelings about this, or indeed about anything else?

Eventually, she began to drop her defensive posture, sobered, became more her usual self, and at last I was able to move into the programme I had planned for this session.

I short-circuited her attempts to discuss what had happened after our session the previous week and insisted that we must work on the task of reuniting Little Meggie with her adult self. I must therefore speak now to Little Meggie. Perforce, she agreed, and accepted the instruction that she was to listen throughout the conversation, and be prepared to intervene when asked. Little Meggie emerged.

She began to weep immediately I addressed her. She sobbed heart-breakingly about her rabbit, her only friend. 'They' had killed her, and, with mounting distress, she finally cried: 'They *ate* her!' The sound of that heart-rending cry raised my back hair, and has stayed with me ever since.

I responded as one would to any child who had just experienced such a horror: with sympathy and understanding. I then told her that the event had taken place a long time ago, more than thirty years earlier, and that she was no longer the little girl she thought she was. The more I emphasized all this, the more agitated she became, denying fiercely that any of it could possibly be true. I suggested she look at her hands: they were not the hands of a little girl but of a grown mature woman. She looked, then became even more agitated, tore the rings off her fingers, and hurled them away from her shouting: 'I didn't steal them, I *didn't!*', and curled herself into a protective ball on the chair.

I told her that no one would claim she had stolen them because they were indeed *her* rings and that it was right and proper that she should wear them. I retrieved the rings from the corners of the room and put them into her hand. She hurled them away again, crying as before: 'No, *no*, I *didn't* take them, I *didn't* steal them, I didn't!', and then got off her chair, crawled under a table in the corner of the room, and curled up again.

I asked Mrs Collins to intervene to comfort Little Meggie, explain to her the relationship between them, and persuade Little Meggie of the reality of the present. She remained curled up under the table, mute and unresponsive until, as I became conscious of the approach of the end of our time, I suggested that Little Meggie should go back to sleep until the next time I asked her to emerge.

Gradually the tension in her body ebbed and Mrs Collins re-emerged, astonished to find herself tucked into a ball, far under the table. She extricated herself with none of the agility she had demonstrated in getting there, and said she had been unable to make any impression on Little Meggie, who had taken no notice of her attempts to speak to her and had remained locked in a state of apparent panic.

Mrs Collins had completely dropped her air of bored detachment and was working with me again. Her inability to make close contact with Little Meggie was, of course, a little suspicious in the light of her many hints that she wished to prolong therapy. I thought also that her feelings of responsibility for the murder of her rabbit were a reflection of her fear that Heather's departure so soon, and mine expected not long after, were also to be blamed on her. She felt, at some level, that it was her proper deserts to be dropped: a natural and inevitable consequence of her badness.

Her open grief over the rabbit, although appropriate in every way to the child she had been, seemed to be a displaced way of grieving over the loss of Heather and of myself. I felt an appreciable degree of anxiety. Which of us would win the battle over terminating at Christmas, and would we be able to complete the work of reuniting her dissociated part-selves, and therefore her personal rehabilitation by that date?

A week later, Mrs Collins was as defensive as ever. I continued to probe for anger, anger at both Heather and myself. The only hint she allowed to slip was in her description of a recent event. Heather had offered to take her on a visit to her old school, and had also asked her to make a short tape-recording relating something of her childhood to be played to a support group for victims of incest. The visit, so Heather had said, was 'a farewell present', but Mrs Collins described it as 'a bribe' to get her to make the recording. The sheer venom in her voice when she spoke of this was vivid – but absolutely denied.

The sense of despair I felt at her blandness was short-lived. During the two days which intervened before our next meeting, Mrs Collins had clearly been working hard. She arrived in a more positive and forward-looking frame of mind than I had seen for some weeks, and was prepared to speak openly of her feelings: the betrayal by Heather, whose offer of a 'bribe' only confirmed Mrs Collins's view that everyone was unreliable, dishonest, and at bottom certain to lie, and finally to reject her.

Yes, she *was* indeed angry with Heather, no matter how understandable was the latter's ambition and search for promotion, and however unreasonable it was of herself to think that her needs should have some weight. Yes, she was angry that Heather was leaving her. In an abstract and dissociated way she also saw the connection between Heather's desertion and her desertion and betrayal by her mother, Aunt Rene, and indeed all women. And at last, yes she *was* angry because we were approaching the time when I too would abandon her and leave her on her own again as she had been all her life.

The anger was there and expressed clearly in *words*, but uttered without any feeling in tone, volume of voice, choice of words, or in her manner and actions. Over and over I pointed out the discrepancy between what she was saying and how she was saying it. Wryly, and in a very positive and mature way, she admitted that the anger was there, that she could even feel it, but that she simply could not 'let it go': she simply did not know how, and was in any case terrified of what would happen if she did discover how to give it free rein.

I was aware that there was some ground for her fear. Even on the occasions when I was explicitly confrontative, I had always been a little careful to have reassurance ready. She would necessarily have sensed my cautiousness, and even apprehension – the unconscious is extremely astute and perceptive – and this would have confirmed her fears of her own destructiveness and made her more afraid. If *I* was nervous about it without even experiencing it, then how much more should she be so, who did? Later, when I read what she had written about her feelings towards Heather, and then read between the lines of what she reported, what Heather had actually said and done, it seemed that Heather too had felt this anxiety, and that she too had gone to considerable pains to offer some sort of palliative for the unpleasant truth of her imminent departure. Mrs Collins's unconscious, and sometimes not so unconscious, fantasies of her own power to hurt and destroy were not altogether fantasies. She was, it seemed, actually experienced by others as threatening and as potentially destructive. We were all a bit afraid of her.

As we reached the end of the session, the anger still only *spoken of* and not directly felt, I reminded her of my promise: that when she did release it, become able to experience it fully, and so become free from its domination, I would give her a bottle of champagne in celebration.

'Do you really want me to let it out? I might hurt you, or damage your room or something.'

We talked briefly about my assurance that there was no danger, of damage either to me or to the room and its contents, an assurance that she still could not wholly share.

Forty minutes later, I was summoned to the waiting-room. Mrs Collins had again gone into a 'strange state' and was behaving in a bizarre way. I could not see her when I entered the waiting area, and went in search of her. I found her in one of the lavatories, banging her clenched fists against the mirror. I restrained her, fearing that she might break the glass and so injure herself, and led her out, not without considerable difficulty, towards the waiting-room.

Repeatedly, she evaded me before we reached it, ran back into the lavatory, stared at her reflection in the mirror and then began pounding at it again, her eyes tightly shut. It seemed that 'Little Meggie' had taken over, and that the sight of a middle-aged woman looking back at her from a mirror had been intolerable to that child.

Once again, by talking gently, persistently and with massive reassurance, I was able to get her to slow down a little. At first, Little Meggie kept making gestures towards her ears, as though to indicate that she did not have her hearing aid fitted, and so could not hear me. I took the hint and spoke from close by one ear in an emphatic and especially firmly articulated voice. Once I had gained her attention sufficiently, I began making suggestions of increasing fatigue and her need for rest until she began to slip into a hypnotic trance, ending with suggestions that she would now sleep until I called her to waken. At last, I was able to 're-call' Mrs Collins, and to give her a brief résumé of what had been happening, before dashing off myself to catch, as seemed to be becoming quite usual on the days of Mrs Collins's appointments, a later train than I had planned.

19

November, Year Two

In the course of the last few months, Mrs Collins had been weighed occasionally, as she had been at the last appointment. She was then down to sixty-four kilograms – ten stone – little now above her target weight. At least we were well on course to achieve *that* aim.

I was now more than ever conscious of the fact that we had contracted to complete treatment by the end of the year. I had also told Mrs Collins that I was going to leave the hospital – and the country – for a year beginning in the following spring. It was therefore explicit that, whether or not treatment was successfully completed by the New Year, there was no possibility of extending it. There would be a great deal of work to do to enable Mrs Collins to detach herself from me emotionally so that her past experiences of being deserted and abandoned were not re-enacted.

It was even more important that her inevitable fantasies of having somehow compelled my departure, of being unmanageable, of having damaged me, and of having repelled me by arousing in me the disgust she felt for herself, should not be allowed to go unchallenged and unresolved.

She had written at one time of her belief that I would be relieved not to have to see her any more, and much of her written ruminations were filled with thinly disguised and occasionally quite open convictions of being directly responsible for the deaths of the people who had been important in her life. However unconsciously, she was similarly afraid of destroying me.

The agreed plan to produce a book about her life and therapy made a bridge into the future, albeit an ambiguous one. It gave her some assurance that she had not destroyed me, but at the same time undermined her ability to detach from me and turn her emotional life outwards to the world.

When Mrs Collins's next appointment arrived, I was called by the receptionist to come down to the waiting-room. The staff were unable to get Mrs Collins to speak or respond to them. When I found her in the waiting-room, wandering around distractedly, she made no response to my greeting until I went right up to her, when she started, looked closely at me as I spoke to her again, and then gestured to her ears. I spoke clearly and in front of her so that she could 'lip-read' and asked her to come with me to my room.

I handed her the headset of the Speech Trainer, and she donned it without hesitation. Now when I asked her what was going on, she replied immediately, in the childish voice and slightly distorted diction characteristic of 'Little Meggie', and using childish language, that she was upset about the rabbit that had been killed.

I said immediately that the rabbit had been killed more than thirty years ago, and that she was no longer the child she had been at the time. She tore the headset off and folded her arms around her body, began to rock backwards and forwards on the chair, and wept copiously. I raised my voice, and asked her to replace the headphones, and when she complied, repeated that the rabbit and all the other distressing things that troubled her were long past. She looked appealingly at me through pouring tears: 'They hung her on the washing line!'

I had difficulty in suppressing tears myself: the grief of the little girl she had been, the vivid picture she evoked of her beloved pet and friend, slaughtered to make a meal and its skin pegged out to dry, was almost overwhelming. I decided that I would again have to meet Mrs Collins on her own chosen ground. I asked her how old she was.

'I'm nearly eleven – there's a rabbit!' (getting up and dashing to the opposite wall where a picture of some rabbits hung).

'Tell me about your rabbit.'

'She let them kill her. I *hate* her! It's my fault, my fault.'

'Why is it your fault your mother let them kill your rabbit?'

'I'm bad, bad, Mummy says so, I'm bad.'

'Why do you think you are bad?'

'Mummy says so, she *says* so!'

'I don't think you're bad.'

'I don't want to grow up, people are wicked when they grow up, I don't want to be grown up.'

'Part of you *did* grow up into a grown-up lady and you are not wicked. The grown-up part of you is not wicked or bad either. You know that because you *do* know that part of you, and you need to join up with that part of you again so that you can be all together again.'

'Mavis and I were silly. We was bad.'

'I know what Mavis and Uncle Tom and Aunt Rene did to you. It was very bad, very wicked, but it was *their* fault, not *yours*. You were not bad or wicked, *they* were.'

'You don't know what happened!' (nearly screaming) 'No one must know! I didn't tell you, I didn't! I *didn't* tell anybody, only my rabbit, and they killed her and hung her on the washing line.'

The Filthy Lie

Mrs Collins was walking distractedly about the room, tottering awkwardly, apparently uncomfortable in her shoes. She looked at her feet when at one point she almost fell over, seemed to do a 'double take' at her shoes, removed them and tucked them as far as she could reach under the chair she usually sat on, with every appearance of sudden fear.

I guessed at what was happening: 'They're *your* shoes, you know, not your mother's, they are *your own* shoes.'

'No, not mine, not mine, I didn't take them, no not mine!'

I went on pressing her to recognize that much time had passed since the period she was experiencing, that she had grown up, left home, become independent. I asked her again to look at her arms and legs, her body, her clothing – in order to impress on her that she was no longer the eleven-year-old child she thought herself to be. This aroused nothing more than further distress.

Before long, I began to feel that the adult Mrs Collins was a necessary co-actor in this melodrama, or perhaps 'psychodrama'. There was no response when I asked Mrs Collins to intervene: Little Meggie seemed to be firmly in control and Mrs Collins completely dissociated, 'absent'. I told Little Meggie that it was time she went back to sleep.

'You're like Aunty Rene, she gave me some medicine and it made me tired and go to sleep.'

Wondering if perhaps a sleeping draught had been employed by Rene to facilitate her sexual abuse of the child, I asked: 'What happened then, while you were asleep?'

'I had a sleep.'

'Did anything happen to you while you were asleep?'

'No, I just had a sleep, that's all!' She showed signs of

increasing distress again as she spoke, and then she crawled once more under the table in the corner.

'It's like the shops. Spiders and grasshoppers and it's all dirty. Mum don't like me to get dirty, she'll be cross with me. Why did they kill my rabbit? My rabbit!'

Eventually, when she was curled up tucked into the corner beneath the table, she was persuaded to go to sleep, and Mrs Collins replied when I addressed her. As before, she expressed some surprise at finding herself squeezed under the table, and extricated herself with considerable difficulty. I spoke now about the urgent need for her to recover the split-off child part of herself, emphasizing the distress and tension that both parts of herself experienced as a consequence of their dissociation. She agreed, and went easily into hypnosis when I suggested it.

I asked her to visualize herself at age ten. She was to hold in mind simultaneously the image of the river, at an early stage in its course, and a little whirlpool at one side, and allow this image to develop and change as she gradually united with her child self, until the whirlpool was absorbed into the mainstream. She was to give her child self all the comfort and reassurance she would give a child of her own when in distress until the child, cuddled to her, became absorbed into herself.

She apparently reverted to the child self after a short interval, as she jumped off the chair in which she had been sitting and once again crawled under the table, again showing markedly greater agility than when she had struggled out from under it. She appeared to be struggling where she lay under the table, pushing an invisible other away from herself with both hands, and trying to force herself deeper into the corner. She began to whimper and then said: 'Go away! I don't like you, I don't like you. Go away! You're too close, go away! Man, take her away, I don't like her. No, No!'

I addressed the adult, instructing her to return to the present and to my room but to hold the child firmly and bring her back too. In her usual 'Mrs Collins' voice, she said: 'She won't let me. She's fighting me and I can't hold her.'

The voice changed again to that of the child: 'You sent that lady after me, to get me. I don't like her, I don't want any ladies, they're all nasty.' Then with a sudden grimace of distress and clutching at her lower abdomen: 'I'm going to wet myself!'

I was startled and alarmed. A vision of a pool spreading merged into anxiety about what Mrs Collins's reaction would be on regaining awareness and control if she were to discover such a situation.

I controlled my apprehension and addressed the adult in as firm and commanding a voice as I could muster. Mrs Collins replied after a short space, seeming tired and disappointed. She told me she had been unable to get close enough to the child to hold her firmly as she cowered beneath the wooden platform on which the shops stood, and the child had fought and struggled so that she could not embrace her. She had been shocked by the look of apparent horror on the child's face, and by the violence of her rejection.

Mrs Collins felt, as I did, that some progress had been made in getting in touch with Little Meggie, even though we had not yet achieved enough closeness for her to trust either her adult self or me.

Throughout this session, Little Meggie had, in typical Mrs Collins fashion, dodged from subject to subject whenever cornered: from the rabbit to Mavis, to her shoes, to Rene, and back to the rabbit. I had a strong feeling all this was designed to ensure my belief in the reality of the Little Meggie persona, and at the same time postpone or even avoid altogether dealing with the dissociation.

The telephone calls started early the following morning, well before I arrived at the hospital. I was told that Mrs Collins had asked with intense urgency to speak to me, giving my secretary a clear impression that she did not believe her statement that I had not yet arrived. On my instructions, the first call which came after I had arrived was put through to me. Mrs Collins simply gasped a few times and then put the phone down again. She rang again a few minutes later and told my secretary that she had a knife in her stomach, she did not know how far in, and immediately rang off again. I telephoned her myself when I heard about this. As soon as she heard my voice, she told me dramatically: 'I've lost the use of my arm, I can't control it and it's got a knife in it.'

I broke into the stream of words, saying very firmly that it was her arm and what it did was entirely her responsibility and choice. If she did not choose to control it, that too was her responsibility. I went on to tell her that I simply would not put up with her distressing my secretary in the way that she had done that morning. This must stop immediately, once and for all. Mrs Collins put the phone down without further words, and did not ring again.

As soon as Mrs Collins, in her adult persona, arrived the following day, I tackled her about the highly disturbing way she had talked and behaved towards the secretarial staff on the previous day. I said again that this was totally unacceptable, and explained that they were not trained as social workers or psychotherapists, and while obviously they would and did take messages, they should not be treated as extensions of myself. She was on no account, no matter how great her distress, to make such calls as those she had made yesterday.

This lecture provoked her into telling me she was angry with me. She was convinced that I had been at the hospital when she had first called and that I had not bothered to call her back: I did not care enough about her.

Further reasons for her anger emerged quickly. Heather, together with her colleagues, was 'on strike' and picketing the Social Services offices, and the whole staff had been 'locked out'. Heather had sent her a message explaining that for this reason she would be unable to contact Mrs Collins until the strike was over. This had deeply affected Mrs Collins, not only through the severance of the link with Heather at a particularly touchy time when she was preparing for separation in any case, but also by interrupting the voluntary work she herself did for the Social Services Department – work that was very important to her – since this too was suspended until the end of the strike, whenever that might be.

I dealt with all this rather brusquely. I was conscious of feeling considerable impatience with Mrs Collins on several grounds. I did not believe yesterday's events to have been genuine. I really *was* angry at her abuse of my secretary, a young girl who had been subjected by Mrs Collins to repeated and very distressing dramas which had quite deeply disturbed her.

It was patent that these melodramas represented a growing anxiety in Mrs Collins concerning the rapidly approaching termination of therapy, and my not much more distant departure from the hospital on sabbatical. That they were motivated to ensure the continuation of therapy and postponement of my leaving had to be dealt with if we were not to spend the remaining weeks of our planned time in fruitless acting-out.

I pointed out very briefly and succinctly that her anxiety about ending therapy was getting in the way of our completing what we had to do. It was diverting both her from acknowledging the fact that we had no more than four weeks to go and us from getting on with our work in the sessions. We were now going to deal with the task of resolving or dissolving the split between her and Little Meggie, and we would undertake this today without further discussion, diversions or delay.

I wondered privately whether this more controlling approach should not have been applied much earlier, yet felt uncomfortable with it. Mrs Collins's outwardly submissive and compliant, but subtly manipulative, manner tended to provoke those who tried to help her or work with her into 'managing' her in this way, and so invariably failed to reach the core of her problems. It was clear both from my own observations and from some of the things Mrs Collins had written that it was the fact that I had *listened*, without prejudice, without making the assumption that I knew better, and without judgement, that had enabled her to begin to shift out of the well-established patterns of her behaviour.

Yet at this point we simply did not have time to explore each phenomenon that popped up – or was that part of the same picture? That is to say, was this behaviour, which had led me to take up an authoritarian approach, designed – albeit unconsciously – to ensure that treatment should founder? If I responded by exploring all the strange behaviour that she manifested, and taking yesterday's supposed suicide-murder attempt with the knife as something we must deal with before we could go on, then another week would go by without us tackling the source of her disturbance. On the other hand, if I responded by becoming unsympathetic, not listening – behaving like 'all the other psychiatrists' – then she could justly reject me as not caring, as not interested, and she would abort the work we had planned.

The human mind in therapy is rather like a medieval king's stronghold under siege. As the enemy penetrates the outer defences, he meets increasing opposition. The defenders marshal their better resources the nearer the enemy gets to the central keep, and, as the final wall is about to be breached, launch a desperate and suicidal counter-attack. We were getting near the core of Mrs Collins's psychic pain, and the defences were becoming desperate. It was a *good* sign, I reassured myself.

Mrs Collins now raised the idea that we should go back to a time before the death of the rabbit so that Little Meggie could be spared that distress and also have the rabbit present to comfort and reassure her while the adult made friends with her. This, as I pointed out to her, would be to repeat an earlier error: the rabbit *had* died, and Little Meggie *had* grieved – it could not be undone. Besides, I suspected this was another diversion, and insisted we must tackle Little Meggie in her maximum distress: any other course would leave her with further problems for us still to deal with. I did not add my inner postscript: 'and so *ad infinitum*'.

Briefly, I formulated what we were to do in this session. Little Meggie, in so far as she is a separate person, is terrified, wholly alone, unprotected. She is unaware that she survived the period in which she came into being – or 'split off' – as a separate person, or that it is her separation and isolation that maintain her suffering. Mrs Collins's task now was to handle her as she would handle one of her own children in a state of

241

fear, and provide her with reassurance, protection, and above all comfort, and then go on to tell her about the life experiences she had missed through being 'stuck' at age ten.

Predictably, she replied with a 'Yes, but ...' In this case, it was Little Meggie's deafness: she would not be able to hear what Mrs Collins was saying. I insisted that Mrs Collins could communicate perfectly with Little Meggie: they were, after all, within the same body, parts of each other, and had no need or even use for spoken language. I emphasized that Mrs Collins, the adult, the continuing person of whom Little Meggie was a part, knew more about Little Meggie's experiences than she had allowed *anyone* to know, and that this knowledge allowed her to get close to her and gain her confidence.

At last, the preliminaries were over. Mrs Collins went into hypnosis and set off in search of Little Meggie, determined to reach her and to bring her back into the mainstream of her life.

Ten minutes went by with little apparently happening, and then gradually Mrs Collins's face began to show increasing distress, although not nearly as intense as on the previous occasion. After a few minutes more, her face began to change to the face I recognized as that of 'Little Meggie', and she began to weep. Mrs Collins pressed her fists fiercely into her abdomen, as she had done on previous occasions when Little Meggie had been 'out'.

Another five minutes went by and she began to relax. I repeated the instructions to get really close to the child, embrace her and bring her back to the present as an integral part of herself, no longer separate, no longer an isolated child.

Mrs Collins told me, once she had returned to the present:

I found Little Meggie crouched under the shops, crying and fright-
ened, and so dirty and scruffy. She was so hurt and terrified she
wanted me to go away. She looked like she could do with a good
bath and a hot meal, and clean clothes. Just one look at her made
me feel so sorry for her, I just wanted to get hold of her and hug
her safe, but she backed away from me.

I told her I was here to help her, as I knew how she felt about
losing her best friend, her rabbit, and how much it had meant to
her, that I understood and that she needn't be afraid of me, I was
going to help her. But if looks could kill, I'd have been dead. She
didn't trust me any more than anyone else. There was so much
hate, anger, hurt and distrust – it's unbelievable. She wasn't only
hating and angry at everybody else but also at herself.

I tried talking to her, but didn't have much luck. She wasn't
listening, all she kept saying was they killed her friend who was
good. She was never naughty or bad, and she couldn't talk, but
they killed her 'cause of her. I told her they didn't kill Daisy because
of her – she was good – but she didn't believe me. To her, they'd
killed her friend who never did anything bad or wrong, and
why else would they kill her? You don't hurt and kill someone
good.

Her mind was screaming at me that she wanted to use some
other words: to tell me to drop dead, that she hated me and everyone,
that she just wanted to be left alone, and that she couldn't tell me
anything even if she wanted to, as she was too scared. When she
tells anyone anything they only hurt her. She had told all her
secrets to her rabbit friend, and they had killed her, so now she had
no one to turn to. Her friend hadn't hurt her for talking dirty and
bad, and now they had killed Daisy and made her suffer, all because
of her. Daisy was the only one she could trust. She hated Mum,
her family, everyone, even more now. She was thinking 'It should

243

have been me they killed, not my friend, she was good, I'm the one who's bad.'

Little Meggie was crying, and so was I at the pain in her. I told her I knew all about her, and I didn't think she was bad, that I knew she was good, and I loved her and wanted to help if she'd let me. But that made her panic and start to try to get away. She spoke saying 'Got to get away, don't want no more help.' I told her she needed help and that if she'd let me, I would help her, but her mind went to Rene and she started screaming in her mind she was wishing she had never told Rene, and if she said anything to me, I'd hurt her too.

I told her it hadn't been killed because of her, but that nasty people, her mummy, had done it. I told her she wasn't bad at all but the people who were hurting her was the bad ones. But she wouldn't have it, she went mad when I mentioned Mum. She scuttled away on all fours saying 'Mummy not bad, Mummy not bad, mustn't talk like that,' and she literally shook so much out of fear of my mentioning Mum, I began crying myself at this poor frightened little kid.

I tried to tell her I knew her mummy, and I knew she was bad and didn't listen to her about Daddy. She didn't like that and started running down the embankment towards the lines. I ran after her, she was thinking about what Mum had said years earlier, 'Daddies don't do things like that. It's me, I'm bad, mustn't talk dirty again, me bad, me dirty, killed my budgie, now kill rabbit, soon kill my kitten.'

She was running across the lines in all directions, not knowing which way and where to run. A train was coming, but she didn't know it. It was coming at her, and me behind running too and screaming at her that a train was coming. But there was no response to me, only her mind saying 'my fault, my fault', and crying hysterically.

I was running behind her and the train was getting bigger and nearer, and I was panicking and crying to her to stop. All I could see was the train coming, so close it was terrifying. But somehow I was able to grab her and we both fell to the side out of the way of the train. It went screaming past and I was holding Little Meggie in my arms crying with relief, and she was sobbing too. Then she put her arms round my neck and I carried her to the'embankment and sat there cuddling her and talking softly to her. She wanted to trust me, but she couldn't, she was too scared. In her heart she desperately wanted and needed to, but she daren't.

I was still holding her when I started coming back, but I don't know if she came with me, as I'm sure I felt her let go. I could be wrong, but I don't think so. I'm sure I'd know if she did come too. But I can't say I blame her for not trusting me, knowing all she had gone through.

The account was deeply moving, and perhaps most poignant in the way that Mrs Collins was using this experience to communicate to me indirectly her real current fear. The message I read in this – not at the time, but later, on reflection – was that she was terrified that I too would be destroyed. She had told me all her secrets, and so, like her rabbit, her budgerigar, and her kitten, I would surely die. And die I would, since leaving her and becoming unreachable as I was about to do, was of course a dying to her.

20

November–December, Year Two

A few days later I developed flu and took to bed for several days. I telephoned Mrs Collins myself from home to cancel our appointment. She was very cool and unconcerned in manner, and accepted the appointment I suggested for the following week without comment.

When I returned to work and saw Mrs Collins again, she was able to speak openly – though as always with no feeling and with a disarming smile – about her anger at my absence. She was apologetic, in what sounded a slightly perfunctory way, that she had not expressed more concern and sympathy at my illness when we had spoken on the telephone. I reminded her that our deadline was now three weeks away. Mrs Collins spoke with apparent equanimity of her expectation of ending our sessions at Christmas, but was 'unsure' of when that was. Without pause or emphasis, she went on to tell me that her brother Jack had mentioned in the course of a recent conversation that Rene was dead, and that Mavis had been admitted a long time ago to a psychiatric hospital, and as far as was known had remained there. She expressed some real feeling about these facts: pleasure, gratification, and a – to me – pleasing vengefulness. At the same time, the contiguity of the remark about the therapy ending and mention of the death of Rene was clearly not accidental: to her, I was about to die, and at the same time she felt vengeful towards me.

246

She managed to talk at some length about the anger and conviction of betrayal she had experienced when I had cancelled the previous appointment. While making somewhat unconvincing apologies for her 'selfishness' in not being concerned about my health, she was actually able to speak quite frankly about her disappointment and grief, and also of feeling that I was not really ill, but was simply getting out of having to see her. I probed deeper, exploring to see if we could bring out into the open fantasies comparable with those she had had concerning others in her life who had died: her fantasies of her own responsibility and frightening power, that she had 'made' me ill by her behaviour, her feelings, or indeed simply by coming to see me. She had earlier expressed the conviction that her hostility towards people she knew had been the cause of their illness and death: Tom, her father, her mother, and Bert. Equally, her 'responsibility' in childhood for the death of her rabbit pointed to her deeply embedded belief in the evil and destructive power within her.

Mrs Collins's response to these questions was pretty superficial, but led quite irresistibly back to what was still a major preoccupation: *why* she had permitted Tom to masturbate her, and whether she had enjoyed it. She felt quite confident in her assessment of the total innocence of the little child she had encountered on the last occasion in hypnosis, but still felt that, through accepting what Tom had done, she *must* have been responsible for the 'orgy'.

I recalled something the philosopher R. G. Collingwood had made much of in his *Essay on Metaphysics*: when you question the fundamental presuppositions on which an individual bases his life, he becomes angry and you get nowhere. Her guilt constituted Mrs Collins's most fundamental presupposition about herself. But I was in a position that was quite different from Collingwood's. All he, as a philosopher, had to do was to think and write, but I had to *do* something – *pace* the consultant who gave me my initial training in therapy – something that would enable Mrs Collins to become free from the conviction that to her was an unquestionable and self-evident truth, even though at the same time she could see it was unreasonable. Real people, those whom one meets in everyday life or in the consulting room, are not as logical, consistent, and free from self-contradiction as the philosopher, or as he might believe or wish other people to be.

I led Mrs Collins to talk around this contradiction – that she believed she was unalterably bad and that at the same time this belief was false and had been imposed on her by others – hoping that the contradiction would become more obvious to her. The discomfort that such an awareness would generate should move her towards actively seeking a resolution to the contradiction, instead of ruminatively scratching away at it. She concluded she must seek clarification from or through Little Meggie.

This provided a dual strategy: it offered a metaphor through which a change in this very basic attitude could perhaps be achieved, while at the same time it supplied a face-saving procedure. After all, changing a belief on which one has based one's whole life involves changes in every aspect of one's thinking, feeling, relationships, and behaviour of all kinds – and especially involves admitting that one had been wrong. If the changes and the preservation of self-esteem which she needed could be mediated by the device of 'Little Meggie', then that device would serve. We agreed to undertake this task in two days' time.

During the intervening days, Mrs Collins wrote extensively about her past experiences of psychiatric treatment. Her first admission had been to an Adolescent Unit, where she went at age sixteen. A few years later, following a suicide attempt, she had been compulsorily admitted – as she had described in vivid and horrifying detail quite early in her writing – when she had been locked in a padded cell. For years she had repeatedly made suicide attempts or gestures, and, as she put it, 'lived on so much drugs that I didn't really know what was going on'. Her depressed state had continued unrelieved until she received repeated courses of ECT, which, she wrote, 'at least calmed me down'. This, incidentally, was the first mention of ECT.

The theme throughout was that of her inherent badness and the conflicting feelings she experienced towards her mother. A sub-theme was her conviction that none of the people whom she had seen were actually interested in her or in helping her.

I could tell by one look at a doctor and one sound of his voice as to whether he was going to do me any good. They all seemed to look bored and give the impression they weren't really listening, so my mind would go blank.

At the next interview, I allowed Mrs Collins no time for general conversation or to report how she had been during the previous two days. She accepted the more business-like approach I offered. With minimal preliminaries she entered hypnosis, intent upon making deeper contact with Little Meggie.

We began by spending time in her 'Private Place', where she was to allow herself to become wholly calm, and shed the anxieties she felt concerning the task she was about to undertake. When she told me that she felt ready to begin, and looked fully relaxed and calm, I asked her to find Little Meggie, get close to her, ignoring whatever resistance or flight was offered, and take her to the field by the church. I suggested that if necessary she could appeal to me for help or encouragement.

For a few minutes, Mrs Collins showed no reactions. Then she told me that she had found Little Meggie. She began making small spasmodic movements of her hands. Soon these became more marked, and Mrs Collins spoke in her own voice: 'Please help. There's a train coming,' looking very anxious. I suggested that she should safely avoid the train and get some distance away from the line. In moments, she relaxed again, and then said: 'She's calm now.' I told her to pick her child self up and take her to the meadow by the church. Mrs Collins held up her arms as though holding a child in them.

Mrs Collins unfolded her arms and clenched and re-clenched her fists repeatedly.

'I'm losing her.'

'Hold on to her, comfort her, keep her safe.'

'She doesn't want me, she's struggling to get away.'

'She needs you. She wants you desperately even if she does not know it. Keep hold of her, and take her to your Private Place where she can feel safe, completely safe.'

Mrs Collins's fists relaxed slowly and her arms once more embraced an invisible but patently present small child, and clasped her firmly to herself.

'She doesn't trust me.'

I insisted that she must win the confidence of the child, using all her experience of mothering and her intimate knowledge of what was in Little Meggie's mind. After a few moments, she said Little Meggie was now quiet.

I said she was now to merge all the child's memories with her own adult understanding, so that, on the one side, her child self could re-interpret her experiences in the light of her adult knowledge and understanding, while on the other, her adult self, given now the facts on which the child's reactions had been based, could neutralize the guilt the child had felt through her own lack of understanding.

I continued making suggestions of the need to take away Little Meggie's feelings of guilt, her fear, her sense of badness and dirtiness, and to replace those bad feelings with their opposites: innocence, goodness, purity. Over and again, I told her that her child self need no longer feel fear and guilt, but that instead she could begin to experience good feelings.

'Let all of you, your mind, your thoughts, memories and feelings, join up with the mind of Little Meggie, yourself when you were a little girl ... Let your mind and hers ... and all that both of them contain ... blend together ... so that you know everything she knows ... feel everything she feels ... remember everything she remembers ... and she knows everything you know ... and feels everything you feel ... and remembers everything you remember. Let you and she become one ... merged and blended together to become one whole person.'

Mrs Collins showed fluctuating signs of stress on her face throughout this period. As time passed, and I continued with suggestions on these lines, she gradually became more relaxed, although not fully so. I asked her what was happening.

'She still doesn't trust me completely.'

'Leave her in that place, the field by the church, where she will feel safe. You will always be able to find her there and very soon now she will know that she can trust you and you and she can become one again.'

When Mrs Collins indicated that she felt comfortable about this, we ended the trance. She told me that she now knew and understood just about everything that had been troubling her. She could see everything in the child self's mind and memory.

Despite this apparent success, however, residual guilt and anxiety about her asking for Tom to 'make her better' and permitting him to touch her sexually were still very much in evidence at the next interview. She began immediately with the question of why she had permitted Tom to touch her in the same way that had so distressed her at the hands of her father, Mr Baker and Rene, and was apparently untouched by what she had learned about this from Little Meggie in the previous session. I made hardly any interpretations or suggestions and limited myself to encouraging her to pursue the question herself and find her own solution.

Bit by bit, she became more and more angry. Her feelings about what had been done to her became more and more real, simultaneously losing, for the first time in our sessions, their sanitized and intellectualized quality. Her anger rose, and for the very first time, was real: she was *angry*, and seemed to become nearly oblivious of my presence, speaking with the rage she had occasionally written about.

From time to time she regained control, apologizing for her lack of restraint. I ignored these remarks, responding only by echoing her last angry words, adding some pressure, such as: 'What did they do to you? Your father, Mr Baker, Rene, Tom, your *mother*? What did they do and what d'you think about it? What do you feel about what they did to you?', spoken urgently and emphatically. Each time, she was able to get back into the feeling she had almost side-stepped.

After a little while during which she spoke with increasing vehemence in her voice and gestures, she rose from the chair and began pacing around the room, her fists clenched and waving in the air, looking as though she wanted to smash them into something, or someone. She raged at Rene, Tom, Mr Baker, her father, and, finally – her mother, shouting her fury at what had been done to her so that everyone in the building must have heard her. She stamped around the room, quite oblivious of everything except her violent and completely unrestrained rage.

I almost hugged myself with delight: she was at last, at long last, able to acknowledge her true feelings openly to me and so give them reality and truth, and especially to declare them as hers. She had accepted that I, and all that I represented, acknowledged her right and her rightness to feel what she felt.

Once again I marvelled at the sheer courage and strength of this so grossly abused person. She was simply magnificent as she raged around the room, shouting her defiance of her abusers and torturers, and of the mother who had failed her and who had, with even more appalling abuse, condemned her child to live through a hell that would have destroyed, and indeed has undoubtedly destroyed, so many others. I smiled inwardly at the thought of what would be bothering my colleagues: is Hellmut safe? Is she going to beat him up? How is he going to get *that* outburst under control?

She was marvellous and I needed to do nothing now. She was doing what we had been struggling towards for two years. At length, of course, the episode had to be completed and the rage worked through and not simply discharged. For a long time I was not able to gain her attention, she was too deeply engrossed in the violence of her all-consuming rage, but at last I was able to catch and hold it. I carried out an hypnotic induction very quickly. She stood where she happened to be and went deeply into trance.

I asked her to picture the rage she held inside her and had begun to vent as sharply jagged pieces of stone and rock that were hot, so hot as to be almost glowing. Then I asked her to picture a deep hole in the ground in front of her, a hole so deep that it went down to the very centre of the earth. She was now to throw the lumps of rock, her rage and fury, into the hole until the rage was all gone. Mrs Collins began to make throwing motions with her arms and hands, hurling away from herself rocks I could almost see as they flew away from her and down into the depths of the earth.

It went on for several minutes, then she stopped, looking quite suddenly peaceful, her face and body relaxing into ease, the furious scowling and violent tension fading away completely. I asked her if all the rage had now gone. She nodded, smiling slightly. Then I asked her to walk away from the hole, and as she left it behind, to notice herself feeling a sense of release and relief, all the burdens of the past having now gone, so that she felt light, with a sense of total inner well-being filling her.

Giving her a little time to use these suggestions as fully as possible, I asked her to come back to my room. Slowly she opened her eyes where she was still standing, a smile of pure joy forming on her face.

We talked for a time about how she felt. She said that at first, when she had begun to speak of her anger at her abusers and when she had begun to rage, she had felt an increasing constriction of her chest but had forced herself to stay with the feeling welling up inside her. When she had entered hypnosis, this constriction had faded and she had been able to use the images I had suggested. Fortunately, the 'rocks' had not burned her hands – I had been carried away by the image myself and failed to make sure her hands were protected!

And she was still angry, still aware of the harm her mother had done her, but no longer guilty because of it. She now *owned* the anger. It was now under control, not under inhibition, and although there was indeed pain at her mother's betrayal, it was no longer the destructive force it had been throughout the past. In the terms of another metaphor I had used, quoting one of Aesop's fables, she had, it seemed, let go of the fox cub and it no longer gnawed at her.

She had earned the champagne I had promised. But – and a big 'but' it was – we had not completed therapy. The most important, and perhaps most difficult, part now had to be undertaken: she had to let go of me.

21

The euphoria of the last session had not evaporated during the forty-eight hours before our next meeting. If anything, it seemed to have somehow consolidated. Mrs Collins was poised, cheerful and confident when she arrived. We talked only briefly about what we had achieved in the previous session, as Mrs Collins wished to talk specifically about her new determination to do something about the way that some members of her family were taking advantage of her inability to say 'no' and mean it, and generally battening on her.

She was not yet free of the automatic reaction of fear to anyone who offered a threat. The slightest hint of demand and she reacted much the same as she had done more than three decades ago. Her feelings of guilt towards Lee for having 'deprived him of his own father', and even more, for her negative feelings towards him, were still there.

I found it very difficult to get her to focus on what I knew to be so crucial for this final phase of therapy: the relationship between her and me, and its resolution. Each time I introduced this vital theme, Mrs Collins began to talk about something completely different. Having exhausted Lee and the erotic and abusive aspects of his relationship with her, there was another rehearsal of the time she took her father to court – both topics seeming to me to be indirect references to the erotic qualities of her feelings towards me in the former, and the loss of her 'ideal father' in the latter – she began to talk about her increasing back pain. This too was displaced: the pain she was experiencing lay not only in her back. If anything, the pain in her heart was the more intense, but she *could not* talk about it.

Our final session took place two days before Christmas. Mrs Collins arrived sober and determinedly cheerful. I gave her the champagne I had promised her, refusing to open it then and there for us to share and insisting that it was for her and her family to celebrate. In her turn, she gave me a Christmas present. I spoke at length about the grief, anger, disappointment and even betrayal that she was more than likely to experience over our parting, but without being able to breach the determined composure and self-control she was exerting. She was determined to keep this session light and friendly, and managed to deflect every suggestion I made and every question I asked.

I pinned my hopes on the thought that we might be better able to make that ending successfully when we met in a month's time for the first of the follow-up sessions I planned.

During the following weeks, Mrs Collins wrote extensively, beginning with a passage written immediately after that 'final' therapy interview.

I thought it was funny today because normally when you try to describe something like a ferinstance, you tell me a story or something. But today for the first time you said you couldn't think of a ferinstance. I was amazed and thought it funny – sort of unusual for you, but you managed so's I did understand.

You know, it's hard 'cause I'm different now in a lot of ways. I used to do things not necessarily because I liked doing it, but because I thought I had to, or because it was the right way. For Mum's sake, the children's, or Bert's sake, because I was told to. But a lot of it boiled down to the fact I believed I had no rights, not for myself that is. Everybody else had rights, but not me. I don't believe that any more. I do have rights, rights to live to enjoy myself, to love and be loved. I have rights to do things because I want to and not because I have to or I think it's the right thing or the right way. Do you know something? I've just realized I'm not scared about Christmas coming. I've always worried and been scared of it, it feels and seems strange 'cause I'm not this year. Even though I've always been happy to see my children's faces, them enjoying themselves, it has still always scared me. But this Christmas I don't feel scared, in fact I'm looking forward to it. It feels strange to actually look forward to something I've always dreaded.

I've dreaded Christmas since I was a kid. Could be to do with my doll and pram, or to do with Dad, or both – no, because of Mum and Dad. The party was Christmas Eve, and all the stallholders were coming in for a drink and something to eat. They were popping in and out all afternoon, eating, drinking, laughing, talking. It was fun for a while, I was enjoying it till I ran out of the room all happy and excited. Then Dad called me, and that, as far as I know, started the beginning of my hell.

Still, that's all behind me now. Now I have to start living. I've learnt so much about myself, my family, and so many things this last year or two. I know and understand so much from it, like in a way I'd been asleep all my life and just woke up and came back into the world of living, not dead any more.

And I owe it all to you, for without your help, I'd still be a living dead person. Mind you, maybe I owe some to God, and some to myself as well. God kept me from dying when I tried so many times, and myself I think I've worked hard at it to find out my life. But none of it would have been possible without your help and patience.

I know I praise you a lot, but only because it's the truth, but I also know you're not perfect. As a doctor as far as I'm concerned, you are. As a person I know you must have some faults, as there's no such thing as a perfect person. But whatever faults you have as a person, I'm sure they are not bad ones. You wouldn't be human without some faults, even small ones.

I have a lot of faults and fears, but hopefully in time some of them will go. Some of them already have started to go. I know all this has nothing to do with the book, but I still like to say what I think and feel. I still find it hard to believe some things you say about me, like courage, being a good mother, a good writer you said. The writing was hard and very painful, so was the learning and remembering. I won't say there wasn't times I wanted to stop remembering and learning. And the reliving things were very, very painful indeed and hurt like hell and I felt at times like giving up. But with your help and support, your faith, helped me go on, and I'm awfully glad I did now.

Well, Christmas is over, and a new Year soon to begin. I've just read the writing I did before Christmas, and for some reason I think Big Meggie and Little Meggie had a lot in common – rape, work, fear, abuse. I was never good enough for anyone, at least that was what I felt and thought all my life. The more that happened to me, the worse I felt about myself. I'd shut my mind off to all the very bad things I didn't like. I had to, it was the only way I could live because then even God hadn't wanted me when I tried to go to him. I kept trying, but he wouldn't take me 'cause I wasn't good or right.

I was scared of my Dad even before that day of the party. Mind you, I suppose that would be normal anyway, as he was a violent man. I feared him, but I never feared my Mum till then. Nothing really bothered me till then, not even my deafness. I was even contented being a sort of loner 'cause other kids weren't supposed

259

to play with me and I wasn't supposed to do things either because of my ears. I'd often sit on the steps just watching the others play.

Julie told me she saw Dad with Nora, only Julie said she was too young to know what Dad was doing to her then. It was only when she got older she realized what Dad had been doing to Nora. I've even heard that Mr Baker had been assaulting or interfering with Nora. Maybe he raped her too, I just don't know. Poor Nora must have gone through hell too.

I've often wondered what religion you are. I don't know why 'cause it doesn't make any difference, it's the person you are. It must be the way a person is brought up, but I wasn't brought up, I was dragged along the gutter to the sewers, and it's not something I can feel proud of. It was hell and a disgrace to society, and what's obviously still going on is still a disgrace and inhuman. In a way I'm sorry I brought my kids into this world, the way it is.

The law is all wrong too. They lock up people who steal, sometimes for life, but people who kill and rape and abuse others, they only get a few years, some none 'cause they're not found out or caught. But those who are don't get what they deserve.

I'm confused, totally confused at the moment. I feel I've lost something at the moment, something I'd gained, but it seems to have gone. Who knows, maybe some day I'll get it back. I don't believe that I will now, but I'll just have to wait and see.

One of the hardest things to cope with in psychotherapy is that it is not magic. One goes through the painful process of self-discovery, through the pain of breaking down the barriers one erects in childhood against the intolerable thoughts, feelings, and wishes, or – as in Mrs Collins's case – unendurable experiences, and comes out the other side, aching and bruised. The euphoria of newly discovered freedom from those familiar burdens tends to blind one to the fact that now the *real* work begins: the task of integrating all that one has learned into one's whole life without the old crutches that had enabled one to 'cope' – and without the therapist. The early joy of insight in therapy quickly gives way to what feels like a return to the old problems. And: 'I feel I've lost something.' In losing me, Mrs Collins felt she was losing everything she had gained.

In a very real way, the most important part of therapy is what is done after the therapy is over. Mrs Collins, like most people, could not register that until after it had happened. While the therapist is still there, the feelings cannot be experienced fully: it does not seem true. Then, painfully, you find out that separation and loss are part of the process of growing up.

I'm probably just going through a sorry for myself phase. I feel like giving up. I was a complete fool. You must have had a real good laugh at me asking you to be a true friend. You'd have an even bigger one if you knew what woke me up from hope and trying to believe you were. It was such a small thing, but it meant a lot to me. Still, that's me.

I tried hard to believe the things you said about me, courage, a good mother, brilliant writer, and all that. I didn't believe it, but I wanted to and tried to. I even hoped it was true. I didn't believe anyone could be a true friend but I hoped it could. What a fool I was to believe that anyone could be a true friend to the likes of me. And how you'd laugh if you knew what a stupid small thing made me realize it.

Anger often comes before grief, and is, perhaps, less painful. It is never enough. When you have been starved of everything you need throughout childhood, there is never enough to satisfy you later. The therapist can never be the perfect mother we all need and seek as children, and go on seeking if the mother we had was less than 'good enough' to meet our needs. For a time, the psychotherapist seems like the perfect mother, even though in between he or she also deprives us of what we want, withholds from us what we wish for – is good, bad, and indifferent by turns. But we *want* him or her to be perfect – and as folk-wisdom has had it for millennia, the wish is father to the thought.

As the month between our last appointment in December and the session planned for late January wore on, Mrs Collins had reacted against her idealization of me and begun to feel anger, finding clay feet to discount my 'perfection', and, as she had done all her life, looking to herself for the cause of the rejection she felt.

You know, you really had me trying real hard to believe I was clean, good, and as good as anyone else, and could have hope and a true friendship. You know, you should be an actor, you're pretty convincing. It takes fools like me to be true friends, and you're no fool. But I am, and I'll still be your true friend whether you like it or not.

I knew all along and I even told you, that anyone knowing my background and past wouldn't want to know me, but you said they would. I even tried to believe that. You, nor anyone else, wouldn't be seen dead with me publicly. I know you went to Bermondsey with me. You must have hated it, but you made the sacrifice, which I'm grateful for. I'm just sorry I put you through the embarrassment of being seen with me. Now I know why you didn't want to go in a café for a cup of tea. It must have been very hard and nerve-racking and frightening for you being seen with me.

However, the theme of her own unworthiness and badness

was decidedly less vivid in what she wrote during this period than it had been in the past.

Maybe I felt angry or envious of that little girl I read about in the newspaper, and her courage and her mother helping her. No, that's not the reason, at least not the real reason I'm feeling sorry for myself at the moment. It doesn't matter now anyway. I'm just an old fool, just a sentimental old fool who was hoping that the future was going to be better than the past, was going to make up for all those bad past years. But time can't go back and undo all the bad things.

In a way, it's like a baby learning to walk. Every time the baby tries to get up and walk, someone knocks it down again, and if it keeps getting knocked down, it'll never walk. At least, that's the only way I can describe it. I take a long time to get up, but I fall very quickly and am easily knocked down. But I will walk and run someday, won't I? Like a baby learning to walk, you have to take the first step, then gradually take more steps, until you have the courage and confidence to walk without fear of falling again and getting hurt. I know that babies still fall or stumble at times, and have knocks, but if they don't fall so hard and don't get so hurt, they'll get up again.

Mrs Collins arrived for our first follow-up meeting in good form. Before coming up to my room, she was weighed: her target weight had been set at around sixty kilograms, and she was almost there – at sixty-one kilograms. She had lost altogether forty-nine kilograms – almost eight stone – since we had first met.

She told me that Christmas had gone well and without major disruptions, and she and the children, together with Lee and his girlfriend had had a good time. They had had great fun, she said, with the celebration champagne, which Lee had opened and sprayed around like a motor-race winner. I kept my annoyance at this misuse of her reward to myself.

She said she had missed our regular appointments, and we talked about the difficulties of separation after such a long, intimate and powerful relationship. There were still many unanswered questions which preoccupied her. Many still revolved around those we had already looked at in detail, but the primary one was whether she would be able to attract and respond to a man, should the opportunity offer.

I was aware that it was important that we did not get drawn into beginning a further course of therapy. Saying 'Goodbye' is in itself an important stage in therapy, and I was as unable to do it as she was.

We spoke a little more of the grief and anger that ending therapy brings. I suggested that she must feel that ending therapy was in itself a rejection, since that feeling was one to which she was especially sensitive, and, able at last to put it into words, said that my rejection of her desire to turn our relationship into a continuing personal one felt even more rejecting to her. I spoke also of the feeling that I thought would follow that reaction: that she would find herself believing that all she had experienced with me was fake, untrue, and therefore only confirming her badness. I was of course unaware that she had already expressed a great deal of the feelings I probed for, in the writings she had given me when she arrived for the session.

I spoke of grief, anger, and other feelings. Mrs Collins made no more than the most brief and superficial acknowledgements to what I said, and turned immediately to the themes which

The Filthy Lie

preoccupied her. To be sure, they all had to do with betrayal – a displacement, not a refusal.

I did all, I believe, that I could do to focus on ending, separation, and clarification of our relationship. I was sure that Mrs Collins did hear, and would, in her own time and in her own way, incorporate and use what she could and what she needed, but it was very obvious that all this should have been done months earlier.

265

22

February–April, Year Three

Mrs Collins came as arranged the following month, without any contact during the interim.

So far, she seemed to be coping well without her regular interviews, and with her awareness of my rapidly approaching departure. She arrived for this session in a very positive and cheerful frame of mind, and very self-possessed. She had at last gone with Heather to her old school, and found it just as she remembered it, though the pig, her confidante there, had gone. It had been a happy occasion.

Generally, things seemed to be going well. She still could not respond when I asked her to talk about separation and what it meant to her, but otherwise seemed to be managing well. We were to meet just once more, shortly before my departure.

Mrs Collins was very quiet, controlled and inhibited when we met a month later. This was our very last chance to get the grief and anger she must feel at some level, about my going away and leaving her, into the open, but it was all denied. Where was I going? She knew I was going away in order to write, 'our book' among others I had planned – but where? Why was I being secretive about it? Presumably to keep her away. Still no anger at my refusal to be drawn. Yes, I would keep her in touch with progress on the book, but no, she could not have my address: all correspondence must go through the hospital and would be forwarded to me. Her frustration remained wholly contained and hidden.

At last she began to speak of how she would feel in the time to come: 'alone again', with hints, but no open statement, of loss. However much she might write about now trusting me, she still could not trust me with her feelings except at one remove.

I had prepared a farewell present for her: she had sent me a greeting card a year or so earlier, with a picture of a little girl feeding a group of white rabbits in a meadow. This picture was, so she said, important to her. It seemed to me a material representation of her 'Private Place', a symbol of peace and goodness. I had obtained a large reproduction of the picture and had it framed.

In return she gave me the present she had planned for me: a matching letter opener and pen, although she did not add that the letters she wished me to open and reply to would be from her.

To this day I cannot remember how I found myself being manoeuvred into offering yet another final appointment, like an opera star making a 'positively final appearance' year after year. I was intensely conscious of the huge number of things that I had to do before leaving the country for a year. Every minute of my remaining time was spoken for, but yet I found myself agreeing to another appointment in three weeks' time, during the very last week I would be at the hospital.

This time the break *had* to be acknowledged: therapy, even in the attenuated form in which it had persisted over the last three months and which Mrs Collins had maintained in her inner thoughts at home, was over: there could be no more.

During this session, Mrs Collins was able to express a little of her grief at separation, although still very controlled. The tears were there though not fully shed. The interview was brief and she communicated more direct and mature feeling than in any of our previous meetings. She seemed to be present as a whole person, a full adult, an equal. We were friends saying goodbye, in a controlled way but no less deeply moved for all that. For the very first time in our contact, we shook hands.

Some time later, when I came down to the office and passed the waiting-room, Mrs Collins was still there. She came up to me, her control almost broken, and asked if we could have just a few minutes more, not here in the waiting-room, but in my office. I could not face dealing with this in public and took her to my room ready to be really firm. What she wanted was to embrace me. A final gesture which I allowed, and she went, still hiding her tears.

That evening I went out to dinner. On my return, as I backed the car up the drive, I saw a shadowy bundle in the corner between the garage and the house, and my heart sank. It was Mrs Collins, shivering with cold, and mute. A neighbour happened by at that moment and inquired if all was well. He had found Mrs Collins wandering down a road some distance away and had asked if he could help. She had told him that she was looking for me and he had guided her to my house.

I got her into the house, gave her tea, and telephoned the local psychiatric hospital. Fortunately, they were willing to admit her for the night. She could not have got herself home in the state she was in and I was not going to begin therapy again, at midnight, a week before leaving the country, let alone put her up for the night. I drove her to the hospital. On the way, speaking like a little girl, and to all outward appearances in her child-persona again, she pleaded to be allowed to stay in my home. The desperate need that she had felt since early childhood to be cared for by good parents was in full flood.

A few days later, I telephoned her to satisfy myself all was well. Mrs Collins was glad to hear from me, apologized for having troubled me, and told me that Lee had come down to Eastbourne to collect her the following day, and that he was very angry with me – Lee, not herself, of course – for having taken her to a hospital instead of looking after her myself.

Six months later, I received the first letter from her.

Dear Mr Karle,

I hope this letter finds you well and your books going really well and you wagging both your tails now ... I had part of my roof blown off by the hurricane and a window smashed in my toilet. Now if anyone uses it they either have to wrap up or take an umbrella in there if it's raining, or else get a shower. But the most peculiar thing that happened that night was some legs of my bed going through the floor-boards. Why or what caused it as yet I don't know, but the girl in the Council when I phoned to tell them couldn't stop laughing, she thought it was so funny. I wished it had been the case of what the girl thought, she didn't know I was on my own. It would have been hilarious if it had been Bert and I up to mischief and it had happened ...

I'm writing this in hospital as I had a reticulogram this morning on my back and they keep you in for the day ...

I went to Windsor Safari Park some weeks ago. It was a nice day out, but a little disappointing as I was expecting the lions and tigers to be climbing all over the car roaring away, but it was a hot day and all they did was lie about sleeping, even the alligator was so still I thought it was a statue ...

You don't know the pressure and trouble I've had these past few

months. Well, I'd better close now. Are you nicely tanned yet?
Wishing you all the best,
Yours sincerely,
M. Collins.
PS I took the kids swimming the other day and I swam myself.
That's the first time for years.

That was one of our targets when Mrs Collins first came to see me. And her weight, of course – the reason we had met at all – when last checked, was at her target. How close she had come to our central and primary target – that was not yet to be known.

Now, several years later, we have at last completed The Book. The first draft occupied a major part of my year away, and was far too long. It took a very long time to rewrite, revise, and bring it into the shape it has now. Mrs Collins became very sceptical as time went on: would it really ever see the light of day? She doubted it.

And now we have come to the end of the story which began with: 'My father interfered with me,' but it is not the end of the story of Mrs Collins – she is still a comparatively young woman. Nor is it the end of her relationship with me – that is as yet not wholly resolved.

One could describe what happened during the two years of therapy, as I observed it, rather like watching the development of an image on photographic paper in the developing bath. At first, all is blank, featureless. After a short while, isolated patches appear on the paper, unrelated and isolated, and in consequence not forming any kind of recognizable picture. More patches emerge, while the earliest become more defined and show more detail. As more and more detail becomes visible and the fainter areas begin to show some structure, so the picture begins to take shape and meaning. But it is not until development is complete that the true picture can be seen, and it is then very different in content, mood, feeling, and meaning from what was suggested by the emergent pattern at its various incomplete stages.

This process was experienced even more powerfully by Mrs Collins. Her picture of herself began to develop and change as her history emerged from the largely blank sheet of her memory, piecemeal and without pattern or meaning at first, and then, as meaning and order began to be visible, the very meaning of the picture changed progressively. Mrs Collins began to write after the first year of therapy, by which time she had already begun to perceive order in her memories, and actually to impose order on them. She had begun to re-colonize her own past. By the end of the second year, she was articulating her views and her understanding in an increasingly powerful, purposeful, and directed way.

The change in perspective, the shift in the balance of colour, power, and mood which took place in the latter months of therapy, is made very clear in what she wrote towards the end of therapy.

I've been looking back over my life and seeing what a waste it's been. The filth and shame, the degrading, the plans I used to make but which always went wrong. Everything was a shambles. How many times have I been told life's what you make it, or you only get out of life what you put in it? It's rubbish.

I've planned, I've worked, I've tried to be a good mother and wife, but nothing ever worked. Some people would say it's just bad luck, some might say it's fate. Me, I say it's me. I think my mother must

*have put a curse on me when I was born, it sure as hell seems like
it. Maybe when my half-sister dropped me on my head when I was
a baby, it sent me screwy. But I know it wasn't that.*

*Whether or not it's too late now for me to love and trust someone
and lead a normal life, I don't know. But that's not really important.
What is important is that people realize the horrors a child can go
through when things like this happen. The help, love, comfort, and
understanding they need, the trust they need. They need to be able
to trust you and be trusted back. They need to be handled carefully
with all these things, and the sooner they're helped, the better
chance they have of living or leading a normal life and getting over
it. It's not so much the physical harm that can be done, although
that's important, but the mental harm is much worse and harder
to cure. Maybe it never can be cured completely.*

Maybe, but you, Meggie Collins, have striven and suffered and
won. This is *your* book, which will help, encourage, teach the
rest of the world – perhaps in some small measure repaying
the wrongs you suffered: a tribute to you, Meggie Collins, one
of the bravest people I have ever met.

Appendix

Many important issues are raised by the story that has been told in this book. Here and there in the text, some of these have been touched on but, to preserve the flow of the story, only very briefly. In these final lines, I wish to expand a little on some of the most pertinent topics.

Some of these are very profound – such as the question: what is a person, a personality? Others concern the reality, nature, structure, causation, and dynamics of Multiple Personality Syndrome.

Some are more of technical or professional interest – such as some of the techniques used in the treatment Mrs Collins received: the importance of selection of clients for therapy and of proper evaluation and preparation before entering upon a course of therapy; the need for a clear contract in therapy; the need for the maintenance of 'boundaries'; the vital importance of the professional supervision and support so markedly absent in this story; and the use of hypnosis in analytic psychotherapy.

Another group of questions may be seen as political: is a *psychiatric* service appropriate for people presenting with the kinds of problems, symptoms and condition shown by Mrs Collins? How adequate are the training and skills of doctors – both generalists and psychiatrists – and of clinical psychologists, psychotherapists, social workers, and others working in the field of mental health, for the needs of such clients?

How adequate are current services to protect children who are in danger of abuse or are victims already? How appropriate is available treatment for adults with such a history? These last two questions have become much more of a 'live' topic in the years that have passed since this story took place, but they have by no means as yet been solved.

It would take another volume to do full justice to any one of these themes. Let it therefore suffice, for the moment, to deal, albeit only in summary, just with those that may clarify what may remain obscure in the way this course of therapy was conducted; why what happened, happened; what was going on 'behind the scenes'.

Assessment, Preparation, and Contracts for Psychotherapy

Everyone training for or practising psychotherapy learns very early that one *never* enters on a course of therapy with a client without carrying out a thorough assessment first – and I have taught this for many years. Equally, one must prepare the client with some explanation of what the experience will be like, what it demands, what to expect. It is also normal practice not to embark on a course of therapy without outlining the 'ground rules', mainly relating to 'boundary' issues.

All this I knew, and have practised for years – but not with Mrs Collins. Why was this?

First error: I made no attempt to check Mrs Collins's history, and took the original referral letter as sufficient. I assumed that there was nothing relevant in her past.

Second error: I took Mrs Collins's cheerful, poised, humorous, cooperative, and oh so sensible façade at face value, and 'forgot' what long experience should have kept at the forefront

274

of my mind: no problems, least of all eating problems, occur without a profound and complex aetiology. For example, I am frequently consulted by people seeking help to stop smoking through hypnosis. In nearly every instance, at the second or third session, a quite different reason for seeking help is gradually disclosed – marital disharmony, grief, depression, and so on.

Curiously (and significantly, as it later turned out), I failed to take any of this previous experience into account in the first session with Mrs Collins. There were various pressures on me, to be sure: the treatment of adult patients was not part of my proper or official duties, and I felt some degree of opposition from colleagues to the work I accepted from time to time outside my proper role; I had personal problems preoccupying me to a considerable extent, which perhaps diminished the rigour with which I would normally bring professional principles to bear on my work. In a nutshell, I took Mrs Collins's presenting problem at face value and looked no further.

When Mrs Collins told me of being depressed, just before Christmas, the proper action for me to have taken would have been to refer her on to a colleague working with adults. At that time, I still had not looked carefully enough at the nature and background of Mrs Collins's presenting problem.

I *think* that I would have acted differently later, had it not been for the appeal Mrs Collins presented when I went to see her after her skin grafts: 'When I was a little girl, my father interfered with me.' It was not for several months that I actually examined what had happened on that occasion. In retrospect, it was clear that I had reacted to Mrs Collins's distress at more than one level. Consciously, I was aware of interest in what she had disclosed, an interest which was professional and proper: incestuous sexual experiences in child-hood had been Freud's focus in his early treatment of many neurotic disorders,[1] and despite his later retraction[2] (later demolished by Masson with scholarship, insight and elegance[3]), more, and more irrefutable, evidence had been coming to light in recent years that incest and the sexual abuse of children were far more common than we had been led to believe. Mrs Collins's unexpected and unprompted disclosure of a particularly difficult problem to treat presented me with a tempting challenge.

Much less consciously, however, I had reacted to the implicit appeal for help. I *wanted* to help her, and this desire – better, *need* – inside me had overridden my usual caution and bypassed the normally mandatory diagnostic and preparatory proced-ures. Long after the event, I began to recognize that I was already demonstrating a 'counter-transference': that I was reacting as much on the basis of my own needs, wishes, and fantasies as on a foundation of professional judgement. The flattery implicit in her appeal for help from *me* no doubt also played a part.

What are the motives – or needs – which lead people into working in psychotherapy? Most of us are aware that these motives are complex. First, there is a desire to understand that which we know so intimately and which at the same time is the most puzzling: ourselves. Secondly, there may be a not altogether conscious hope that in treating others we may treat ourselves and so relieve the neurotic difficulties of which we are more or less aware in ourselves, and perhaps a drive to help others to heal the hurts they feel so that our own unacknowledged pain and damage may thereby be magically healed too. Then there is curiosity, which is, of course, a universal human attribute. There is also a desire to help others in distress – another universal human response: the 'Knight in Shining Armour'. So many motives, some known, and some unacknowledged.

Whatever we do, however altruistic, there is always a trace of self-interest in the action – and none the worse for that. Particularly in psychotherapy, however, that self-interest, those personal needs, must be clearly identified, since otherwise they will certainly be confused with the client's interests and needs. Therapists can, and do, project both their conscious and their unconscious needs, feelings, wishes, fantasies, fears, and past experiences on to the client, and the client then becomes the recipient of the therapist's counter-transferences. For example, a therapist whose relationship with his own mother was unsatisfactory, which he has not explored fully, and from which he has not become wholly free, can very easily misread what the client says about her relationship with her own mother, attending only to those aspects which fit with his own experiences, and therefore not *really* hear all of what the client says. This is dangerous and damaging. The client will deeply resent it – and rightly so.

A client may long for a 'Parfit Gentil Knight' of her own to rescue her from the dragons of her inner fears and miseries, and can offer very seductive temptation to perform that role. Once the knight has placed the maiden behind him on his charger and rides towards the sunset, the maiden will discover not only that the dragon is still there after all, but also that the knight, so far short of slaying it, is as powerless in its face as she has always been. Then knight and dragon are equally evil – indeed the dragon may be preferred and the knight seen as the persecutor, the faithless seducer, the abuser.

It gives one a warm feeling to be reflected in the client's eyes as a thoroughly good and properly appreciated carer, but it is a feeling which must be monitored carefully. Psychotherapy is not Hollywood-type knight errantry. It is hard and skilled work that demands more true *self*-knowledge than perhaps any other human activity. It is no accident that Malory emphasized the self-purification, the vigils, the prayer and fasting, and above all the self-denial in the preparation for knighthood. Those rituals were the essential preparations needed to ensure that a knight should not seek his own satisfactions or glorification. Malory's knights were not those of Hollywood – and it is the Hollywood version which is so seductive and dangerous, since it is motivated and fuelled by the desire for recognition.

I had offered my sword and shield and a ride on my charger without real preparation, without surveying the forest and its dragons. The penalties for those failures became evident only much later.

As a result of this 'falling' into therapy, Mrs Collins had no idea of what she was undertaking, and I defined no boundaries, and had no treatment plan. The only rule I did remember concerned any further self-harm: if she injured herself again, then therapy would be ended. In the event, of course, I allowed one major and several trivial slips to pass.

Some may find this rule disconcerting or strange. Clients who are prone to suicide attempts and self-damaging behaviour of all kinds impose a major stress on anyone working with them. The threat of these actions hangs constantly over the therapy. It is quite impossible to try to prevent or protect anyone from injuring or killing themselves if they really want to do so.

To speak of suicide, to make suicidal gestures or attempts, or to damage herself as Mrs Collins had done, is a powerful and aggressive demand upon the therapist. Most people working with such clients become understandably anxious when suicide, or self-damaging behaviour, is a real possibility.

One approach to this is to make it very clear that the therapist will not accept any responsibility for such behaviour, and that any actions of this kind necessarily jeopardize treatment. The client must not be allowed to use the threat of self-damage as a means of pressurizing the therapist into more frequent or longer sessions, to change the way the sessions are conducted, or in any way to take responsibility for the client's life. The client's personal responsibility for herself must be, and must be seen to be, preserved in her own hands.

There are several different sources of anxiety involved in this situation. The thought of a Coroner's questions, such as 'Were you not aware of your patient's suicidal thoughts?', or 'In view of this person's history, did you not think there was a risk?', will hover in the background, together with less obvious and less conscious fears stemming from the therapist's own feelings of responsibility, fantasies of his omnipotence, and the like.

It is all too easy to lose one's nerve in such a situation. The client's transference demand – '*You* must look after me, *you* must love me' – can easily be tacitly accepted by the therapist, who then plays into the role determined by the client's childhood needs for mothering, care, comforting, nurture, protection, and the like, which are by now archaic, out of place, and unreal – however vividly experienced – instead of remaining firmly and clearly rooted in the present, and in the professional requirement of exposing these primitive needs and bringing them into the client's awareness rather than colluding with them. The preservation of the therapist's professional stance and identity is essential if those needs and their expression in 'symptoms' are to be made fully conscious and resolved. At the same time, the client feels genuinely helpless to resist the impulses to self-destruction which erupt violently and which may pervade all thought and feeling.

Another of the components of suicidal behaviour is the violent rage it indicates to be present within the client which she is unable either to recognize or to express directly. A threat of suicide or self-damage in the course of therapy must in part be understood as expressing the client's feelings of rage and frustration at the therapist for not fulfilling the client's felt needs. These murderous feelings originate in profoundly frustrating relationships early in the client's life, and represent responses which were too disturbing to acknowledge at the time, and which have in consequence become deeply repressed. Those needs and the rage which their frustration in infancy aroused are turned on to the therapist: a heavy burden if it is not identified and recognized for what it is. The interpretation of such transference material is ultimately what allows the client to 'see' towards whom these feelings are *actually* directed.

The rule I laid down for Mrs Collins is, in my experience, a fairly effective way of pre-empting such acting-out, although not all therapists take this line. Not only does the client understand clearly where she stands, and where the therapeutic boundaries lie, but she also realizes that the therapist has properly recognized that she may truly feel such impulses to damage herself. The prohibition may then actually be experienced as very reassuring to the client, even though superficially it may raise her anxiety as to whether she will be able to meet its terms, as it implies quite clearly that the therapist has confidence in the client's ability to resist these impulses, and places responsibility where it belongs: with the client.

The therapist should, however, observe an additional safeguard. Exploration of intrapsychic defences may exceed the personal strengths of the client and threaten disintegration. In such circumstances, the client may experience what amount to psychotic impulses towards self-destruction. If this occurs, the client's capacity for regulating her own behaviour is actively reduced and physical protection may be required, and appropriate medication provided.

The condition that I specified prepares the ground for addressing the client's underlying feelings about what is going on in the therapy as the opportunity occurs to talk about them to the therapist, instead of acting those feelings out.

Mrs Collins, despite the force of the guilt feelings which precipitated her self-mutilation, showed no signs of a disintegrative process, and no delusions or hallucinations: there were no signs of any psychotic illness, or of a profound depression. She appeared to me to be under the influence of an extreme and overwhelming neurotic guilt.

I also read in what she had done the well-recognized 'cry for help': I had not 'heard' what she had told me at the end of the last session before our first Christmas about how depressed she felt. Now she had *made* me hear properly.

Hypnosis in Analytic Therapy

Many psychoanalysts and analytically oriented psychotherapists consider that hypnotic techniques have no place in conventional analytic psychotherapy. At the same time, such approaches are increasingly being used in conventional psychiatric circles. For example, techniques of this kind are practised and taught by Graham Burrows, Professor of Psychiatry at the University of Melbourne, and, aside from their specifically hypnotic aspects, are very closely akin to techniques in Gestalt therapy, and indeed to 'free association' in conventional psychoanalysis. They are also increasingly now taught at the hospital where the story of Mrs Collins was revealed.

The differences between hypnotic methods and those of orthodox psychoanalysis are more apparent than real. The differences lie almost entirely in the dramatization employed. In fact, the content and remedial processes are identical. In orthodox analytical approaches, we seek anamnesis – the recovery of repressed material from the unconscious into consciousness – so that the traumatizing memories can be perceived by the adult ego and examined in the light of adult reality, and its wider experience and understanding. In these interviews with Mrs Collins, the purpose is the same – and the method is significantly different only in that it takes a dramatized form. It is, perhaps, a play performed by the client in order to bring the intolerable and unthinkable on to the stage of the client's consciousness where it can be observed, weighed, and thus rendered harmless by the observing adult self of the client.

In the literature on hypnosis,[4] one of the techniques I applied is called ego-state therapy, since it is most readily formulated as a process through which an encapsulated memory of all that the individual consciously experienced at the time of trauma (i.e. her 'ego-state' at that time) is brought into touch with the present-day adult self and thereby sheds not only its functional isolation, but equally and consequently its toxic effects.

Sadly, the myth that Freud abandoned and rejected hypnotic techniques (a myth well-exploded long ago but still adhesively maintained) holds back many psychotherapists from using explicit hypnotic techniques. These techniques do not provide easy short-cuts to psychic health, nor do they necessarily reduce the painful process of psychotherapy, but they do sometimes speed up and enhance the power of orthodox approaches.[5]

Sadly, too, it is sometimes believed that orthodoxy is like virginity: breach it in the least, and it is all gone. It is little remembered now, for instance, that Freud did not avoid physical contact with his patients – he used massage extensively and regarded it as an essential part of therapy in neurosis – and yet such contact between therapist and client is now taboo. The disciples are more rigorous and rigid than their master, whose own departures from the orthodoxy of his time are now regarded as some of the principal fruits of his genius. Freud's ostensible abandonment of hypnosis became Holy Writ.

Among those of my colleagues from whom I sought support and advice in my treatment of Mrs Collins, there were many who regarded my use of hypnosis with the deepest suspicion and disapproval. Many others will feel the same, I am sure, on reading this account, and yet will find it difficult to put a cogent argument together. Others again may wonder if hypnosis may not offer a more effective and efficient form of treatment than the more laborious paths of conventional therapy. The truth, I believe, lies between these two views. The story of Meggie Collins may illuminate this.

I must add at this point that since the end of the story related in this book, training in and use of hypnosis has expanded both at the hospital where I worked and throughout the country. Although many psychiatrists and psychologists remain sceptical, many others have incorporated such techniques in their clinical practice (and thereby returned to the practices of two or three decades earlier), and other professions, such as physiotherapy, show growing interest.

Supervision in Psychotherapy

The term 'supervision' has a somewhat specialized meaning in this context. The supervisor's principal task is to support the therapist, and especially to expose and clarify the therapist's own reactions in the course of the therapy, and so ensure as far as possible that the personal reactions – especially feelings – do not intrude into and distort or block the therapist's understanding of what is going on in the therapy.

The story of Mrs Collins's therapy illustrates vividly how vital such supervision is. Its absence in this story was clearly responsible in large part for the difficulties I experienced in establishing and maintaining proper boundaries; my hesitation to confront her anger at times; the placatory way in which I responded to her on many occasions: a thousand and one 'slips' that may well have prolonged – and could have fatally marred – the course of therapy.

I did spend a great deal of time discussing Mrs Collins with various colleagues, all of whom were well aware of her attendance at the clinic. They tended to interpret what was happening between Mrs Collins and myself as histrionic manipulation by her, and considered that I was at least in part colluding with the maintenance of her condition. Their amused scepticism – or more accurately in some of them disbelief – at my diagnosis of Multiple Personality Syndrome did not help much either.

In addition, I was a member of the *Child* Psychiatry Department. Therapy for an adult in her own right was not the brief of my department: that was the function of the psychiatric and psychological services to *adults*, to which I should, by the nature of the post I held, have referred her at an early stage. I was effectively quite alone in carrying out Mrs Collins's treatment. The vital 'supervision' was lacking for me. There was no one with whom I could discuss my difficulties constructively to arrive at the insights which, in the event, came to me only very much later. I had to find my own way, the more so since I was then the only psychologist in the Health District to take the use of hypnosis seriously for this sort of purpose.

The 'Transference'

The term 'transference' is often loosely used. Classically, and deriving from Freud's original conception, the 'transference' is the central and most potent aspect of any kind of psychological therapy. Its core is the fact that the therapeutic setting, with the therapist's careful attention to maintaining personal neutrality and refusal to develop a normal 'social' relationship, allows and actually prompts clients to react towards the therapist in ways which stem from and portray the early, significant, formative, and emotionally loaded relationships in their personal past. The setting of therapy, with its explicit 'carer' and 'cared-for' roles, re-evokes childhood, with its very similar roles.

In consequence, the client 'projects' her perceptions of the parenting adults from her past on to the therapist. The therapist will be seen by the client as critical, condemnatory, anxious, depressed, angry, uncaring, preoccupied, over-concerned, placatory – and in any number of other ways at different times – quite irrespective of their actual characteristics, attitudes, behaviour, reactions, and moods. These 'perceptions' emerge from the client's gradually developing access to the feelings, expectations, memories, and fantasies of infancy and childhood. In this way, the client's formative experiences of interacting with and responding emotionally to the most significant figures in her early life are brought vividly into the consulting room.

It is not that the *memories* of the events, relationships and feelings are exposed, and then progressively recognized and understood in the therapy sessions. What happens is that the actual feelings, expectations, attitudes, and perceptions of childhood, which have been repressed but which have shaped the client's personality and behaviour, are displayed in front of and in reaction to the therapist in the 'here-and-now' of the actual sessions. Through the interpretation of this as a re-play of past events and especially of past feelings and reactions, the client first becomes aware of such feelings and then becomes able to master and integrate them, thereby being freed from their unconsciously determining effect on behaviour and relationships.

In the first three sessions with Mrs Collins the transference (which is not confined to analytic therapy, but is to be seen to some degree in any therapeutic relationship) was not apparent, or not to me, because I was not looking for it, having been seduced into thinking of her problem as a 'simple' one. What *was* apparent was that Mrs Collins was highly compliant, and that she had begun to feel enough confidence in me and my interest in her to expose more of her neediness. She had begun to ask, carefully and indirectly, but definitely to ask, for more than had been initially offered. It is of course well known in psychological work that many clients will bring out the most important, or perhaps the only important, item in an interview just as they go out of the door, or when the therapist is about to close the interview. It seemed that Mrs Collins was no exception.

Mrs Collins had in fact followed a pattern that I had remarked upon in so many other 'simple' cases: she had presented me with a much more important area of distress than the presenting problem only after she had gained some confidence in me, and begun to form a dependent and trusting attachment: 'transference'.

Throughout most of the two years through which we worked together, Mrs Collins's submissiveness, superficial compliance, and gratitude for the interest and care I was taking overlay a very powerful resistance which seemed to me to defy a direct approach. On those many occasions when I did challenge her openly, and attempted to bring into the open those feelings and thoughts which were expressed by, for example cancelling or failing an appointment, there were always twenty-seven good reasons why she had been unable to come, plus endless apologies for the trouble she knew she was causing me. Nothing I said could break through to what was going on beneath her over-compliant façade.

There was no doubt about the fact that she was 'testing me out'. Would I reject her if she cancelled, failed or changed appointments? Would I become angry, and even punish her? Would I, in a word, re-play the familiar patterns of her childhood?

At the same time as she was compelled to provoke just those reactions she feared on my part by her behaviour, there was also her fear of her own power to damage me. She saw herself as evil, and the fact that I fell ill and even needed medical attention on occasion played right into the fantasy that her hostile or angry feelings had a magical power to inflict harm on the very person she most needed. She had plenty of 'evidence' for that: her first child, which she hated while it was *in utero*, died at birth; and for many years she believed *she* had killed her father, her mother, and, more recently, even her husband.

Despite her protests on one occasion, I 'was' her father – but an ideal father, who she feared could become more like the father she had had. I also 'was' her mother: both an ideal one who would meet all her needs, and the real one who betrayed and abused her.

Then there is another aspect of transference. Among the material Mrs Collins wrote after the interview during which she reached her rage and acknowledged it fully, was this:

You looked so different, and I felt so strange, a peaceful, calm, strangeness. Why you should look so different, I don't know, but to be truthful, you looked like you'd had years taken off you. Mind you, after all the trouble I've been, I'm not surprised. I must have put years on you, but now you looked like you'd had years taken off. Maybe I shouldn't say this, but what I first thought after I became one, I thought you looked so handsome and so good, so wonderful. I think you also looked relieved, and I knew then for certain how I felt about you. Before, I was confused and uncertain, but not any more.

'I knew then for certain how I felt about you' – a declaration of love. She had of course frequently expressed her admiration – of my patience, tolerance and so on – but had not ventured to speak of being in love with me. She had referred previously to the man for whom she felt a special affection, but had emphasized in indirect – and quite unconvincing – ways that it was not *me* for whom she cared. She had now virtually done away with that disguise, while still, of course, not making it completely explicit.

Therapy with depressed clients has something of an element of courtship about it. The therapist has to 'woo' the client into engaging in a relationship before therapy can begin at all, but perhaps an even more pertinent metaphor would be the very beginning of infancy, when the mother and baby begin to build a relationship. This in itself is a form of courtship, and is often – and rightly so – described as mother and baby 'falling in love'. In many ways, the therapist's concern and care reflect a mother's nurture and love, and this creates a core aspect of the transference.

The mother's love and nurturing are the foundations of the capacity to trust. The baby or infant who experiences a severe breach of trust (whether that is objectively real or a subjective experience is irrelevant) becomes depressed, and is highly likely to be especially vulnerable to reactive depression from then on. If a client whose trust has been violated and lost in infancy is to be able to develop the capacity for trust once more, it is vital that the therapist offers a reparative experience.

One aspect of long-term depression of this kind is the lowering or even total destruction of the client's regard for herself, and this too is a central target in therapy. As the therapeutic relationship develops, the client's self-esteem and sense of personal value begin to develop in response to the therapist's regard for her. Simultaneously the client begins to feel a sense of trust for the therapist, and feels increasingly that the relationship is an accepting and 'safe' one. This process is closely parallel to the experience of 'falling in love'. The perception of the therapist's regard, the growth of trust, the development of dependence, and the reaching out to the therapist are, of course, inevitably accompanied by their opposites – but then, mistrust, suspicion, and fear *are* part of 'falling in love' in adult life.

Both the baby 'falling in love' with its mother and the adult falling in love with another idealize the loved one. The object of the attachment is seen as ideal, perfect, omnipotent, and the way to flawless happiness, whether the lover is new-born, or a fully mature adult. To the adult client going through this process, which is a re-play of the earliest phase of infancy, the experience is frequently mistaken for an adult falling in love, and he or she must be helped to recognize it for what it is – a re-play of a much earlier, *failed*, experience.

The task then facing the therapist is ticklish indeed: to help the client recognize the archaic childhood origins and nature of what is happening to them and so discriminate between the feelings aroused by the therapeutic relationship on the one hand, and an adult–adult relationship in the 'real world' outside the consulting room on the other – between therapy, with all its projections on to and idealizations of the therapist, and everyday life. The borderline between accepting what the client feels, and analysing it in the same way as all else has been examined and analysed, and seeming to the client to reject *her* is a fine one, to be followed with care, because the pain of failing to define it can be utterly destructive.

At the same time, the experience can – and should – be powerfully reparative. The adult whose infant falling in love failed or was marred, even destroyed as Mrs Collins's had been, *needs* this transferential experience. Painful though it is for the client to experience the development of the love-relationship and then understand it for what it is, and what it is not, it *is* reparative, and marks clearly the recovery of a sense of self-worth.

And then, I was seduced, not by Mrs Collins, but by my own need to be a helper. None the worse for that, maybe, but seduced first into failing to begin properly, later into all kinds of placatory actions.

I found myself responding to her at times as though she were highly vulnerable, feeling that if I were to press her 'too hard', attempt to go 'too fast', she would break down. That she was indeed somewhat fragile was confirmed by the distress and disturbance she showed towards the end of the first year of therapy, and then by the bizarre events that followed when the secondary personalities emerged. That carefulness too came from *my* feelings, and not solely from her personal state.

It is always difficult to distinguish between resistance: a defence against the threat that therapeutic progress represents to the intrapsychic defences, and a valid signal from the client that the pressure is too great and threatens some degree of disintegration. In retrospect, I believe that I erred in judging Mrs Collins's reactions at times as the latter, when I should have interpreted them as the former.

Her dependence on me was quite explicit and at times felt

really oppressive, so that any interruption in our sessions actually felt welcome to me. I felt considerable relief at those times that she cancelled her appointments, for example, and I was not deceived by finding myself wondering if perhaps a gap might lessen her dependence on me. Mrs Collins made it plain that I was her only hope, that all depended on me, and however much I could recognize her idealization of me, this also constituted an endeavour on her part to evade responsibility for herself by placing it upon me. This, of course, played into my own needs to be a 'good parent' to her, but her dependence on and need for me exerted a pressure that I found uncomfortable. Her mother had been her only source of support and comfort in early childhood, and I was now put into that role. Her mother had failed her and I was now being put under increasing pressure so that I too would finally, and inevitably, fail her.

I was aware of these dynamics. From time to time I tried to spell out to Mrs Collins some of the transferential process involved: her attempt to 're-play' the patterns of her childhood experiences, but I was faced with her apparently total incomprehension. It had nothing to do, she was sure, with her mother or anyone else. Her overt idealization and her covert expectation of betrayal were equally firmly entrenched and untouchable.

Further, without my being fully conscious of the process involved, I was aware that I was in some way intimidated by Mrs Collins: I was concerned and anxious beyond a degree that was appropriate. I found myself trying hard to avoid upsetting her.

It is an inevitable consequence of any therapy which involves facing some of the more unpalatable truths about oneself and one's life that one becomes 'upset'. All therapists are familiar with the task of encouraging clients to experience the inevitable distresses and other even more difficult emotions that they will have to live through before they are free of both their problems and their therapy. I realized, sometimes rather helplessly, that the prospect of Mrs Collins being upset was somehow a more alarming one than the same prospect in scores of other clients.

Sometimes also I acted manipulatively, and at times in the early months of therapy it seemed as though I were surreptitiously punishing her for the threats and dangers I felt, in failing to give her that degree of priority which would ensure regularity in her appointments. Despite the reality that many of my other commitments were beyond my immediate control, I certainly could have exerted greater efforts to maintain the regularity of sessions.

Perhaps there is an additional factor in the need – the vital need – for proper supervision in the therapy of people who experienced abuse in childhood: the characteristic seduction into abuse that often occurs in their response to helpers. In the literature, this is sometimes referred to in connection with a related process: that of 'identifying with the aggressor'. This is a phenomenon which is seen in the apparent inheritance of abuse: the abused child abuses his children or permits her children to be abused. The brilliant pioneering work of Alice Miller is relevant here.

Equally, as I began to recognize much later, Mrs Collins's lifetime experience of abuse was leading her to project dually on to me: I had to be both abuser and abused. I, in turn identifying with the victim, was colluding with the abuse of myself, and had been seduced into abuse of her. This is a highly complex issue, and beyond the bounds of this volume to explore.

Further, Mrs Collins had been denied almost everything a child needs if she is to mature satisfactorily. Now she was demanding that I supply all the things she had missed when she needed them, and simultaneously ensuring that I would be unable to do so, as I was not *actually* her mother – and of course *could* never be. And then, equally inescapably, she was punishing me for failing in this task.

I was also conscious of a marked ambivalence in myself. The 'Freudian slip' involved in giving her a piece of paper with my address and telephone number, out of date though it was, suggested that at some level I wanted to let her know and feel that I *was* totally accessible, although consciously I was only aware of the need to keep some distance and to preserve the privacy of my own life. Perhaps I was trying to placate her in some way for my inadequacy in meeting her needs. I did not *act* effectively to maintain either distance or privacy, which at the same time reduced her feelings of safe boundaries and confidence in my security.

Similarly, her dependence on and need for contact with me were both rewarding and irksome. She made it clear that her well-being and safety were my responsibility, and I could see later that in response, I was trying to be the 'ideal parent' desired both in Mrs Collins's fantasies and needs, and in my own. In addition, it seemed almost as though, despite my satisfaction that she was at last getting in touch with her own anger and becoming more able to express it, I was actually *intimidated* by her anger when it seemed it might be directed towards me, and felt some need to placate and mollify her.

One aspect of the impotence I felt in maintaining proper and inflexible boundaries was, I suppose, the guilt that I could feel from time to time in our sessions simply through being a man: a representative of all those other men who had perpetrated the abuse she had suffered. This is indeed a common experience for male therapists working with abused children and women. These mixed and inconsistent feelings were emphasized then and later by my reluctance to say firmly that she was absolutely not permitted to telephone me at home, and equally to address her demand that contact should not be limited to our sessions.

And yet, and yet – despite all the errors and omission, something was 'good enough'. That phrase comes from Winnicott's work on mothering, of course, work which emphasized that no mother is perfect, that children do not need a perfect mother, and that a 'good enough' mother is indeed good enough. This is as true of therapy as it is of true mothering: no therapist can be perfect, but we *can* be 'good enough'.

Mrs Collins *is* better; she no longer takes antidepressants, tranquillizers and the rest; she has made no further suicide attempts or injured herself; she has a quite different life – and she lost the weight she needed to lose.

Multiple Personality Syndrome

The most widely used standard text in psychiatry is the *Diagnostic and Statistical Manual of Mental Disorders (DSM)* of the American Psychiatric Association. In the Third Edition (1980), then current, the entry for Multiple Personality Syndrome describes the condition as involving the presence within the patient of two or more distinct personalities, one of which is dominant at any particular time. It also indicates that usually the original personality has no knowledge or awareness of the existence of the others. The entry for this condition makes no bones about the reality of the syndrome; the authors of the *Manual* accept it as categorically as any of the other psychiatric disorders listed and defined.

Relatively little literature exists as yet on the topic of Multiple Personality Syndrome, but some writers consider that hypnotic talent, or the ability to go easily and deeply into the hypnotic state, may be a necessary prerequisite for the development of alternate or multiple personalities. One writer, Eugene Bliss,[6] puts forward the hypothesis that the condition results specifically from spontaneous self-induced hypnotic states occurring when a child is stressed beyond endurance. He also suggests that the experience which is effectively removed in this way from the child's consciousness remains intact but out of touch with the individual's continuing psychological development. The child's ego-state, the totality of what was in awareness (conscious and pre-conscious) at the time of the trauma, becomes encapsulated as a complete but separate personality, 'frozen' at the time of the traumatic event. Subsequently, this ego-state may be re-aroused or re-evoked by current circumstances or events which are significantly reminiscent of the original trauma. It then emerges, appearing to take over control from the individual's actual (that is, present-day or primary) personality when the latter is dissociated in some way, such as by going into an hypnotic trance.

This explanatory model seemed to fit Mrs Collins's experience, and especially her description of what had happened on several of the occasions of sexual abuse: she described in detail how, when being abused on various occasions by Mr Baker, she had fixed her eyes on the light bulb or a crack in the linoleum and concentrated so that she became unaware of the pain and horror of what was being inflicted on her. In addition, she showed a marked talent for hypnosis from the very first interview, and was able to apply the routine I taught her successfully in the first two weeks or so.

Her capacity for dissociation was repeatedly illustrated both in what she said and what she wrote. She could consciously make two contradictory and opposite statements about herself in one breath, believe them both and be quite unaware of their logical or existential incompatibility. Note too her unexpected 'forgetting' of the revelation of abuse which set us off on our journey together.

However, from the very first evidence of Mrs Collins's sub-personalities, right up to the end of therapy and beyond, I never ceased to debate the question, internally and with those colleagues who would discuss the topic seriously. Were Little Meggie and Big Meggie real *people*, protective self-delusions, or manipulative developments of incautiously worded interpretations by me? Was I responsible for the emergence of these 'others' through speaking, for example, of the remnants and effects of her childhood experiences as 'the child inside you' or 'Little Meggie'? 'The child inside' is a very commonly used formula in therapy – and its use does not usually have such a result.

Evidence, such as there was, was ambiguous. There was no information at all of any of the sub-personalities having existed before therapy began, although Mrs Collins told me of various occasions of episodes of fugue: periods of time during which she had behaved out of character, and for which she was amnesic, starting long before she met me. Had these actually occurred, or was the report of them stimulated by the therapeutic model?

Using the concept of split-off, isolated but perpetuated ego-states had been highly effective for her several times in achieving anamnesis and even resolution of traumata. If the 'secondary personalities' were only artefacts of the therapeutic strategies I had introduced, they would eventually become unnecessary and so fade away automatically. If, however, they were genuine personalities in themselves, albeit secondary and 'split off', then we should focus on bridging and eliminating the 'split', so that the separated-off memories, thoughts, and feelings once more became reconciled: integrated into Mrs Collins's whole personality.

The scepticism of my colleagues made it difficult for me to find guidance. Those with whom I discussed my uncertainties dismissed the problem: they did not believe that Multiple Personality Syndrome existed. Those books I had read – and now re-read[7] – were of little help. Their authors seemed to meet none of the difficulties Mrs Collins posed. Their clients seemed to have been much more amenable and manageable, and 'cured' with astonishing ease and rapidity!

My own prior experience provided little help either. One client who had been unmistakeably a 'multiple' had been treated rather easily. In this case, during hypnosis, her secondary personality had emerged and spoken with me readily enough, and the 'primary' had listened to the conversation. Her amazement at finding someone else, quite different from herself, occupying her own body had not prevented her from getting to know and then uniting with the 'secondary'. Within a very few sessions, the two had become reconciled, and happily so.

There were many times when I was unconvinced of the reality of Mrs Collins's secondary personalities, although while talking to Little Meggie directly, I was wholly convinced: each time, the experience had been absolutely identical with talking to a little girl in a state of terror. Similarly, 'Big Meggie' was a different person from Mrs Collins: she looked different, she moved with a different gait, held a different posture; her voice and accent were different; the clinic receptionist doubted her own eyes, since the person in front of her on several occasions both was and was not Mrs Collins.

I was aware of a continuing resistance within myself against fully accepting the reality of multiple personality, a resistance which I could justify to some extent intellectually, and which received considerable confirmation and reinforcement from colleagues.

My scepticism stemmed from my own fundamental presuppositions and prejudices about what it is to be a person. The concept of multiple personalities as a metaphor, or as a model for discussing and understanding behaviour – yes, that was perfectly acceptable – but that there should be several whole, entire, integrated personalities within the same body, more or less out of touch both with each other and with external reality – that was more difficult, much more in conflict with my beliefs. All this despite having worked with several unmistakable cases before.

Curiously, I had experienced no such difficulty with them. None of them had shown the elaborate manipulativeness that was so markedly a feature of Mrs Collins's behaviour. It was this characteristic that seemed to be a major source of my doubts about the reality of Mrs Collins's secondary personalities. But I was stuck with it. The question of whether Mrs Collins was a genuine case of Multiple Personality Syndrome, and genuinely had at least three distinct personalities; whether she was faking and the picture she presented was part of an elaborate defence; or whether my own actions and formulations had suggested this idea to a highly suggestible patient, was really irrelevant as far as the course of treatment was concerned. In practical terms I could see no realistic alternative to putting my faith in what I had read, and even more in my previous experience, limited though it was, of treating multiple personalities.

As I wrote earlier: 'A real child, preserved in limbo for thirty-odd years, still suffering the torments which had been inflicted on her, still pleading for the help which had been withheld all those years ago – which to her were a continuous moment of eternity?

'Or an adult woman pleading in what she intuitively felt to be the only acceptable way of pleading her own felt neediness?

'Or an adult "hysterical personality" manipulating her therapist's naïveté to gain the attention and interest she felt she could not get any other way?

'And is there a difference?'

Psychiatry, Clinical Psychology and Psychotherapy

These three terms are often difficult for anyone outside the mental health field to differentiate. Members of these three professions seem, by and large, to do much the same things, and are therefore commonly confused with each other. In fact, however, the training of each, and their professional roles, though they overlap considerably, are very different. Psychiatrists and clinical psychologists usually receive no more than a cursory training in psychotherapy, and in particular do not normally undergo the personal therapy which is a *sine qua non* of psychotherapists. Psychiatrists are medical practitioners who have specialized in mental illness; psychologists and psychotherapists are not medical practitioners. Psychologists are most commonly concerned with behaviour and with technical issues of various kinds, while psychotherapists are the principal providers of psychotherapy, especially analytic or dynamic.

But what about the help available for people like Meggie Collins? She and her story are by no means unique, but the implications of her experiences in the Health Service go far beyond the confines of the treatment of people who suffered in childhood as she did.

The point at issue here is not that she was a sexually abused child (appalling though that is), but that she was an adult, presenting with 'depression', 'immaturity', 'social inadequacy', 'attention-seeking', self-mutilation and multiple 'para-suicide'. Such people throng psychiatric out-patient clinics and casualty departments all over the country; they fill the general practitioners' waiting-rooms; they take up thousands of hours of social workers' time; they consume a massive proportion of the NHS drug bill; they occupy hospital beds.

Looked at from a purely economic point of view, they are a massive drain on the resources of the Health Service and the nation. From a humanitarian viewpoint, their pain and misery demand a better deal from our society than that which they often receive, as Mrs Collins exemplifies.

'Depressed, unhappy, attention-seeking, immature, over-dependent, inadequate.' These terms, ostensibly descriptive, and in that sense not inaccurate, both disguise and mislead. They were applied to Mrs Collins at my own hospital and at the hospital where she was admitted when picked up by the

police on the south coast. Underneath these superficial characteristics there is a real live person.

The differences between the disciplines, the theoretical
models, and the methods of psychiatry, clinical psychology,
and psychotherapy are important here. It is arguable whether
the 'Mrs Collinses' are properly treated by psychiatric services
or whether they are more appropriately the province of clinical
psychology or of psychotherapy services.

Mrs Collins first came to professional attention at the age of
eleven, or soon after that. When she was fished out of the
Thames and taken into care, she must have come within the
purview of a child care officer,[8] and, in all probability, would
have been seen by a child psychiatrist then. In any case,
she would almost certainly have been examined by such a
specialist before she was placed in a special school soon after
coming into care, that being then part of the routine procedure.
There was, therefore, opportunity then for her to be recognized
as needing help.

However, she was at that time severely deaf, although evidently able to communicate. From her own account of her
childhood, she would have seemed somewhat retarded in
development, and her family background was poor. Perhaps
those characteristics – quite apart from what one could be
quite sure was a profound resistance, based on her shame and
terror, to disclosing what had been done to her – ensured that
her distress was not explored and understood.

A few years later, when meeting professional attention after
her next suicide bid, she was still deaf, patently seriously
disturbed, and difficult to manage. Instead of being listened to,
she was regarded and treated as mentally ill, and when she
panicked, was locked into a padded cell. Again, no one seems

to have asked the question: 'What *is* wrong?' and stayed for an answer.

Over the succeeding years, it seems that only the psychiatrist who saw her after yet another suicide attempt during her marriage to Mick took her seriously enough to attempt to reduce her distress.

Even after I had begun to work with her, she was identified as 'attention-seeking, inadequate, unhappy, depressed, or acting-out', whatever these terms really mean: all labels that are pejorative and imply that the patient is to blame – and actually generally also untreatable. Are such labels really anything other than ways of concealing the fact that those who apply them know no way of treating such patients? The terms themselves are *descriptive of behaviour only*, not *diagnostic*, and have no place in medicine.

It is probable that Mrs Collins was not readily accessible to psychotherapeutic intervention at age eleven, sixteen, twenty, or even later, and that it was only at the time when she was referred to me that she was actually ready *in herself* to respond to what I – really by chance – offered her. She herself, however, was in no doubt that it was something quite different in *me* which resulted in her being able to respond to the opportunity I offered her: my manner, my voice – my apparent attitude to her. She felt that I was genuinely concerned. I do not think I am any different from my colleagues, no more concerned or caring. The point is moot, but what remains true is that she was judged both in my own hospital and in the seaside hospital where she was admitted towards the end of therapy to be unsuitable for psychotherapy. Perhaps Mrs Collins is right in a way: I recognized both her need and her capacity for this form of treatment when no one else seemed able to do so.

It is therefore possible that that capacity had been there much earlier in her life. The *need* was certainly there, but no effective response appears to have been made. Had psychotherapy been offered, and had Mrs Collins been ready and willing to engage – at any point from when she had become incontinent at school (probably the first publicly displayed sign of something being wrong) onwards – how much would the course of her life have been different?

However confidently or sceptically one may speculate about an answer to that question, there remains the fact that the course and nature of Mrs Collins's life have been greatly changed since her therapy, despite the judgements made of her in at least two departments of psychiatry during the same period of time as she received treatment from me. I cannot avoid drawing the conclusion that referral to and treatment by *psychiatry* is not the right approach for Mrs Collins and the multitude of others like her. Or, to be more precise, psychiatry as it is currently practised is not the right answer for people like her.

There is a substantial body of thought within both psychology and psychiatry which insists that psychotherapy is not a valid form of treatment. While one case – quite apart from all the other people with whom I have worked in this way – may seem a very small David to confront the Goliath of the academic and medical establishment, I beg to differ.

Thus it seems to me that the story we have related points to an important need to review and revise both the training of the relevant professions and the way in which services are provided. *If* Mrs Collins had been offered psychotherapy at any point in her earlier years, and *if* she had been able to engage in it then, would she have been spared some of her many years of intense suffering, and would the NHS have been spared some of the massive costs her treatment involved? At the most conservative estimate, the various treatments she had received before she met me – from stomach pumps and tranquillizers to hospital admissions and plastic surgery – cost (by present standards) far above £200,000. This does not include the time she consumed in her GP's surgery, and the hundreds of hours of the time of social workers and others.

The time I spent with her – including all the hours I allowed her through my failure to keep the boundaries of therapy firm – cost less than £1,000.

The cost to Mrs Collins, however – that has been immeasurable. To be sure, these comparisons depend upon an 'if': *if* therapy had been possible earlier. Who, having read her own words, could confidently deny that the right treatment was not offered and should have been?

The cost to others has been high too. Her children have paid heavily – and will go on paying – for the betrayal of Little Meggie by her mother, the vice of her father, the unspeakable evil of Mr Baker – and the neglect by us.

The cost to me was high at times. Working with Mrs Collins gave me many a sleepless night. More than most of the many hundreds of people with whom I have worked in this way, she became an ever-present part of my life; she intruded into my personal life more than just by telephoning me at all hours, or even by arriving on my own doorstep at night.

But we have been rewarded. At the time that I write these concluding lines, Mrs Collins continues to write to me about once a month. Her letters are now very different, though occasionally some old themes appear.

The Filthy Lie

Dear Mr Karle

I hope this letter finds you well and I hope all goes well with you.

This week I could only go to work two days as I was in so much pain. I went to throw my rubbish out in the bin at the end of the garden. I didn't realize how heavy the bag was, so as I swung the bag up so it would land in the bin, it went flying alright but took my arm with it and jolted it from its socket. It was agony.

The other day, Sharon and I went out with my niece in her car one evening and Sharon and I took it in turns practising our driving. I wasn't bad. I need to practise more on my reversing into a parking space. Forward parking I'm fine, but hopefully it will improve. I'm trying to earn as much as possible and then get a car, so's we can go out, join clubs, and not worry about being attacked in the streets at night, and if the weather is nice, just hop in the car and go away for a weekend, and visit Scotland, and Wales, Devon and so many places.

Lee hasn't changed much. He's seeing a psychiatrist now, but he hasn't changed his view of me being a rotten mother. My answer to him is he's entitled to his opinion, and if it is that, so be it, but I am entitled to mine too. He asked to come back here to live but I told him no, I'm not prepared to go through all that again. It's about time he stood on his own feet. He has his life and I have mine. I'm happy for him to ring up or to see him now and then as long as he doesn't start any nonsense, otherwise he stays away altogether.

Well, I guess you've had enough of my writing by now. The best time I've enjoyed myself this month was driving my niece's car. It felt great. I must get on with some housework now. Please write soon. How is the book going? Is it nearly finished yet, or when do you expect it to be finished?

Appendix

Take care and look after yourself,
Best wishes,
Yours sincerely,
M. Collins.

NOTES

1 'The Aetiology of Hysteria', Freud, S. (1896).
2 First indicated in various letters and then discussed in detail in *Three Essays on the Theory of Sexuality*, Freud, S. (1905).
3 Masson, J.M. (1984).
4 e.g. Edelstien (1981), Bliss, E.L. (1986), Karle, H.W.A., and Boys, J.H. (1987).
5 See also Karle, H.W.A. (1988) and Karle, H.W.A., and Boys, J.H. (1987).
6 Bliss, E.L. (1986).
7 Bliss, E.L. (1986); Beahrs, J.O. (1982).
8 This occurred before the creation of Social Services Departments, when those social workers responsible for children were employed by the local authorities' Children's Departments, and carried this title.

Bibliography

Berne, E. (1964), *Games People Play*, Penguin, Harmondsworth

Beahrs, J.O. (1982), *Unity and Multiplicity: Multilevel Consciousness of Self in Hypnosis, Psychiatric Disorder and Mental Health*, Brunner/Mazel, New York

Bliss, E.L. (1986), *Multiple Personality, Allied Disorders, and Hypnosis*, Oxford University Press, New York, Oxford

Casement, P. (1985), *On Learning from the Patient*, Tavistock, London

Edelstien, M.G. (1981), *Trauma, Trance, and Transformation*, Brunner/Mazel, New York

Freud, S. (1896), 'The Aetiology of Hysteria', read before the Society for Psychiatry and Neurology, Vienna, reprinted in Masson, J.M. (1984)

(1905), *Three Essays on the Theory of Sexuality*, Standard Edition, Hogarth Press, London (1962)

Karle, H.W.A. (1984), 'Hypnosis as an Adjunct in Analytic Psychotherapy', *Proceedings of First Annual Conference*, British Society of Experimental and Clinical Hypnosis

(1988), 'Hypnosis in Analytic Psychotherapy', in Heap, M. (1988), *Hypnosis: Current Clinical, Experimental and Forensic Practices*, Croom Helm, London

Karle, H.W.A., and Boys, J.H., (1987), *Hypnotherapy: A Practical Handbook*, Free Association Books, London

Masson, J.M. (1984), *The Assault on Truth: Freud's Suppression*

Bibliography

of the Seduction Theory, Penguin Books, Harmondsworth

Matte-Blanco, I. (1975), *The Unconscious as Infinite Sets*, Duckworth, London

Schreiber, F.R. (1975), *Sybil*, Penguin Books, Harmondsworth

'The Troops for Trudy Chase' (1988), *When Rabbit Howls*, Sidgwick & Jackson, London

Thigpen, C.H., and Cleckley, H.M. (1957), *The Three Faces of Eve*, McGraw Hill, New York

Index

Index

Index

READ MORE IN PENGUIN

In every corner of the world, on every subject under the sun, Penguin represents quality and variety – the very best in publishing today.

For complete information about books available from Penguin – including Puffins, Penguin Classics and Arkana – and how to order them, write to us at the appropriate address below. Please note that for copyright reasons the selection of books varies from country to country.

In the United Kingdom: Please write to *Dept. JC, Penguin Books Ltd, FREEPOST, West Drayton, Middlesex UB7 OBR*

If you have any difficulty in obtaining a title, please send your order with the correct money, plus ten per cent for postage and packaging, to *PO Box No. 11, West Drayton, Middlesex UB7 OBR*

In the United States: Please write to *Penguin USA Inc., 375 Hudson Street, New York, NY 10014*

In Canada: Please write to *Penguin Books Canada Ltd, 10 Alcorn Avenue, Suite 300, Toronto, Ontario M4V 3B2*

In Australia: Please write to *Penguin Books Australia Ltd, 487 Maroondah Highway, Ringwood, Victoria 3134*

In New Zealand: Please write to *Penguin Books (NZ) Ltd,182–190 Wairau Road, Private Bag, Takapuna, Auckland 9*

In India: Please write to *Penguin Books India Pvt Ltd, 706 Eros Apartments, 56 Nehru Place, New Delhi 110 019*

In the Netherlands: Please write to *Penguin Books Netherlands B.V., Keizersgracht 231 NL–1016 DV Amsterdam*

In Germany: Please write to *Penguin Books Deutschland GmbH, Friedrichstrasse 10–12, W–6000 Frankfurt/Main 1*

In Spain: Please write to *Penguin Books S. A., C. San Bernardo 117–6° E–28015 Madrid*

In Italy: Please write to *Penguin Italia s.r.l., Via Felice Casati 20, I–20124 Milano*

In France: Please write to *Penguin France S. A., 17 rue Lejeune, F–31000 Toulouse*

In Japan: Please write to *Penguin Books Japan, Ishikiribashi Building, 2–5–4, Suido, Tokyo 112*

In Greece: Please write to *Penguin Hellas Ltd, Dimocritou 3, GR–106 71 Athens*

In South Africa: Please write to *Longman Penguin Southern Africa (Pty) Ltd, Private Bag X08, Bertsham 2013*

READ MORE IN PENGUIN

PSYCHOLOGY

Psychoanalysis and Feminism Juliet Mitchell

'Juliet Mitchell has risked accusations of apostasy from her fellow feminists. Her book not only challenges orthodox feminism, however; it defies the conventions of social thought in the English-speaking countries ... a brave and important book' – *New York Review of Books*

The Divided Self R. D. Laing

'A study that makes all other works I have read on schizophrenia seem fragmentary ... The author brings, through his vision and perception, that particular touch of genius which causes one to say "Yes, I have always known that, why have I never thought of it before?"' – *Journal of Analytical Psychology*

Po: Beyond Yes and No Edward de Bono

No is the basic tool of the logic system. *Yes* is the basic tool of the belief system. Edward de Bono offers *Po* as a device for changing our ways of thinking: a method for approaching problems in a new and more creative way.

The Informed Heart Bruno Bettelheim

Bettelheim draws on his experience in concentration camps to illuminate the dangers inherent in all mass societies in this profound and moving masterpiece.

The Care of the Self Michel Foucault
The History of Sexuality Vol 3

Foucault examines the transformation of sexual discourse from the Hellenistic to the Roman world in an inquiry which 'bristles with provocative insights into the tangled liaison of sex and self' – *The Times Higher Education Supplement*

Mothering Psychoanalysis Janet Sayers

'An important book ... records the immense contribution to psycho-analysis made by its founding mothers' – Julia Neuberger in the *Sunday Times*